HANDBOOK OF DIAGNOSIS AND TREATMENT OF DSM-IV-TR PERSONALITY DISORDERS

SECOND EDITION

HANDBOOK OF DIAGNOSIS AND TREATMENT OF DSM-IV-TR PERSONALITY DISORDERS

SECOND EDITION

by

Len Sperry, M.D., Ph.D.

BRUNNER-ROUTLEDGE

New York and Hove

Published in 2003 by
Brunner-Routledge
29 West 35th Street
New York, NY 10001
www.brunner-routledge.com

Published in Great Britain by
Brunner-Routledge
27 Church Road
Hove, East Sussex
BN3 2FA
www.brunner-routledge.co.uk

Brunner-Routledge is an imprint of the Taylor & Francis Group.
Printed in the United States of America on acid-free paper.

Library of Congress Cataloging-in-Publication Data
Sperry, Len.
   Handbook of diagnosis and treatment of DSM-IV-TR personality disorders /
by Len Sperry.-- 2nd ed.
        p. ; cm.
   Includes bibliographical references and indexes.
   ISBN 0-415-93569-5 (hardback : alk. paper)
   1. Personality disorders--Handbooks, manuals, etc.
   [DNLM: 1. Personality Disorders--diagnosis. 2. Personality Disorders--therapy.
   3. Personality Disorders--classification. WM 190
S751hc 2003] I. Title.

   RC554.S68 2003
   616.89--dc21

                                                                    2003010495

Contents

Foreword

This book is to be read by both clinical professionals and graduate students alike. It is a thoughtful and practical reference text that readers will find useful time and time again as they face the difficult-to-treat patients who meet the criteria for personality disorders. Until two decades ago, the position of these disorders occupied a peripheral, if not a strained place in clinical psychology and psychiatry. The turn of events has been almost startling, with the DSM-III and IV giving these disorders a major position, via Axis II, in their innovative multiaxial model.

Trained as both a psychologist and a psychiatrist, Dr. Sperry is well prepared to be a discerning and organized teacher of clinical diagnosis and treatment. A sound and effective communicator, he presents complex ideas in a clear, and easily understandable, fashion—a talent not especially common among authors in this increasingly central clinical field. His exposition and synthesis is most impressive.

Especially important, Sperry recognizes the significant advances that have taken place in the field of personality disorders in the past decade, hence justifying the updating of his well-received and widely read first edition. Moreover, the increasing need for mental health services has mounted astronomically, as people have become aware that their psychological needs can raise havoc on their health, career, social relationships, personal well-being, and creativity. No longer willing to accept their discontents and the unhappiness that has visited them by unkind circumstances, more people than ever are looking for competent professional help. What has also become strikingly clear is that most patients who seek assistance are suffering from the difficulties of long-standing maladaptive attitudes and coping styles, essentially what have come to be labeled personality disorders. What is needed are efficient diagnostic tools that enable clinicians to quickly recognize problematic character structures and a number of implementable, pragmatic, and short-term modes for treatment. It is in achieving these goals that Dr. Sperry's text will prove most useful.

His approach goes beyond merely describing the simple content of personality disorders. Dr. Sperry helps provide the reader with an understanding of the underlying sources and treatment implications of these disorders. The book will certainly assist those with considerable clinical experience, but it will be especially appreciated by beginners who will soon be introduced to clinical work with these problematic patients. This text assists the novice clinician every step along the way, from initial diagnostic contact to final treatment evaluation.

As Sperry points out, the realm of personality disorders has become increasingly significant in psychotherapeutic practice; it now fills a space that formerly focused solely on schizophrenia and affective psychosis. Whereas these latter illnesses are present in only a small proportion of patients seen by clinicians today, the dysfunctions of personality have become omnipresent, whether one practices marital and family therapy, forensics, behavioral medicine and health psychology, neuropsychology, or any of the other main realms of outpatient work. Not unexpectedly, the literature in this field has grown immensely and shortly will outstrip all other areas of psychological and psychiatric practice in the coming decade. If my own broad-ranging text *Disorders of Personality* has seen some 30 printings in its two editions thus far, then Dr. Sperry's current volume will add further to the impressive growth and acceptance of useful books in the field.

Sperry's text adds meritoriously to the mental health field's decision to assign a key position to this highly prevalent realm of psychotherapeutic practice. It is a noteworthy commendation of this work that his publishers encouraged him to write a revision, a thorough and updated text in a flourishing field of study.

> —Theodore Millon, Ph.D., D.Sc.
> Dean and Scientific Director,
> Institute for Advanced Studies in Personology and Psychology

Preface

When the *Handbook of Diagnosis and Treatment of DSM-IV Personality Disorders* was released in 1995, it was the first personality disorders book based on DSM-IV to appear after the publication of DSM-IV. The *Handbook* was unique in many respects. It was a reader-friendly, single-authored text that offered a comprehensive and integrative approach to the diagnosis and treatment of personality disorders. Rather than focusing on a single treatment approach or modality, it basically covered all the approaches and modalities: individual therapies, group therapy, marital and family therapy, medication management, as well as combined and integrative approaches.

Since the *Handbook*'s publication, a number of exciting and significant developments involving personality disorders have emerged. Most notable has been the increasing number of clinicians who are utilizing effective and successful treatments for what were previously considered untreatable disorders. The paradigm shift in clinicians' attitudes about the treatability of personality disorders was convincingly evident by the late 1990s. This attitude change, reflected in the actual treatment experience of many clinicians, involved a shift from a sense of dread and hopelessness to one of hope and optimism that even the most difficult of these disorders—including borderline personality disorder—are becoming increasingly treatable with the newer, focused treatment strategies and interventions.

In 2000, the American Psychiatric Association published the *Diagnostic and Statistical Manual of Mental Disorders, Fourth Edition Text Revision* (DSM-IV-TR). As the title suggests, the text and background information supporting the DSM diagnostic categories were primarily revised, rather than specific

diagnostic criteria. The main justification for this new DSM was that significant advances in both research and clinical practice had occurred since 1994—
the year DSM-IV was published—and this warranted updating the text.

Because of these significant developments and advances in the diagnosis
and treatment of personality disorders, a revised edition of the *Handbook*
seemed inevitable. As with the first edition, the purpose of this revision would
be to synthesize the many new theories, approaches, and research findings in
a clinician-friendly handbook—that is, a comprehensive yet succinct and practical manual that would also be reader-friendly. I wanted to make this edition
even more clinician-friendly and reader-friendly by summarizing material in
tables and charts and by adding extra section headings to facilitate finding
specific information more quickly.

The first chapter has been completely revised and considerably expanded.
It details several exciting, cutting-edge trends in both diagnosis and treatment. Diagnostic trends include the impact of attachment styles in the etiology of personality disorders, and the influence of temperament, culture,
emotional abuse, and neglect. This chapter also discusses the often unrecog-
nized functional impairment associated with these disorders. Currently, the
DSM-V Personality and Relational Disorders Workgroup is evaluating five
dimensional approaches to supplement or replace the current categorical
models of diagnosis. Accordingly, these dimensional diagnostic models—one
of which is likely to be the diagnostic schema adopted in DSM-IV—are briefly
described. Treatment trends include the brain-behavior perspective, the utilization of newer medications, treatment utilization, and new interventions
such as mindfulness, schema therapy, structured skill intervention and cognitive coping therapy, and developmental therapy.

Chapters 2 through 11 profile each of the personality disorders with regard to its characteristic triggering event, behavioral style, interpersonal style,
cognitive style, emotional style, temperament, attachment styles, parental injunction, self-view, worldview, maladaptive schemas, optimal diagnostic criterion, as well as its DSM-IV-TR description and diagnostic criteria. Similarly,
psychodynamic, biosocial, cognitive-behavioral, interpersonal, and integra-
tive-biopsychosocial clinical formulations and case conceptualization are described. Assessment of personality disorder is discussed in terms of interview
behavior and rapport as well as psychological testing data including MMPI-2,
MCMI-III, TAT, and Rorschach. Finally, treatment considerations for each disorder are described. These include virtually all treatment approaches and
modalities: individual psychotherapy—that is, the various psychodynamic,
cognitive-behavioral, and interpersonal approaches—group therapy; couples
and family therapy; medication strategies; and integrative and combined
therapy interventions.

Several noteworthy additions have been made to Chapter 4. These include an overview and critique of the American Psychiatric Association's recently published *Practice Guidelines for the Treatment of Patients with Borderline Personality Disorder;* a description of recent research on the impact of early child abuse on the treatment process and a discussion of choice of traumatic versus nontraumatic treatment pathways; the value of attachment theory and mindfulness skill training in treatment; updates on dialectical behavior therapy and schema-focused therapy; and the promise of structured skill training interventions and cognitive coping therapy.

Practicing clinicians in psychiatry, clinical psychology, counseling psychology, mental health counseling, marital and family therapy, and psychiatric nursing—as well as those in training—should find specific information and clinically useful tactics and strategies here to aid them in diagnosing, formulating, planning, and implementing treatment with personality-disordered individuals. It is my sincere hope and expectation that this book will enrich your understanding as well as your treatment outcomes.

—Len Sperry, February 2003

CHAPTER 1

Personality Disorders: Trends in Clinical Practice for a New Millennium

The first chapter of the *Handbook of the Diagnosis and Treatment of DSM-IV Personality Disorders* (Sperry, 1995) likened the paradigm shift occurring with personality disorders beginning in the early 1990s to the paradigm shift that already had occurred with depressive disorders. Until the mid-1970s, many clinicians felt relatively ineffective in treating depressive disorders, and until the early 1990s, this same sentiment was shared by many clinicians about treating personality disorders. I insisted that such a paradigm shift involving personality disorders would require a major change in the way clinicians conceptualize, assess, and treat these disorders. I predicted that while such a change in attitude and practice patterns might be resisted by some, most clinicians would respond to the challenge. Such a shift would mean relinquishing the then prevailing view that personality disorders were essentially untreatable conditions. With some trepidation, I ended the chapter with a quote conveying the sentiment that clinicians might even come to consider that personality-disordered patients would "become our most welcome clients in the new century, clients who are deeply troubled, but whom we can help with confidence" (*Clinical Psychiatry News*, 1991, p. 26).

Since then, it appears that much has changed in clinician attitudes and practice patterns. Indeed, the paradigm seems to have shifted. While not all clinicians feel that they can help every personality-disordered individual with confidence, there is, nevertheless, an increasing consensus among clinicians that many patients can be helped with current treatment interventions, even those meeting DSM-IV-TR criteria for borderline personality disorder.

This chapter provides an introduction to the diagnosis and treatment of personality disorders. The main part of this chapter details several exciting, cutting-edge trends in both diagnosis and treatment that are further effecting this paradigm shift. Prior to detailing these trends, the chapter begins by explaining the nature of the paradigm shift underway in the conceptualization, assessment and diagnosis, and treatment of personality disorders, as well as the basic premises underlying effective treatment of these disorders; it also highlights the changes in DSM-IV-TR. Finally, the chapter concludes by providing the reader with an orientation and overview of the structure of Chapters 2 through 11.

THE NEW PARADIGM IN PERSONALITY DISORDERS

What factors have been contributing to the paradigm shift in the diagnosis and treatment of personality disorders within the past 10 years? Primarily these factors include a broader conceptualization, improved assessment methods and diagnostic criteria, and focused, potent treatment methods for personality disorders. More specifically, personality disorders are now being conceptualized to include the neurobiological and temperament dimensions addition to the personality or character dimension. Neurobiological and biosocial formulations of personality disorder have attracted considerable attention and have generated a considerable amount of research. Millon (Millon & Davis, 2000) and Cloninger (1987, 2000; Cloninger, Svrakic, & Przybeck, 1993) hypothesize that temperament and neurotransmitters greatly influence personality development and functioning. Cloninger and colleagues (1993, 2000) describe personality as the influence of character and temperament wherein temperament refers to the innate genetic and constitutional influences on personality, and character refers to the learned psychosocial influences on personality. Cloninger hypothesizes that temperament has formed measurable biological subtracts: novel-seeking, harm avoidance, reward dependence, and persistence; character has three quantifiable factors: self-directedness, cooperativeness, and self-transcendence. He believes that personality style reflects the individual's temperament factors plus positive or high scores on the three character factors. On the other hand, personality disorders reflect negative or low scores on the three character factors.

The Five-Factor Model (FFM) has become the most prominent of the contemporary psychological models of personality disorders. FFM describes personality dimensionally in terms of the factors of agreeableness, conscientiousness, neuroticism, extroversion, and openness (Costa & McCrae, 1990, 1992).

Stone (1993) describes a "grand unified theory" of personality disorders. Basically, this unified theory interdigitates the Five-Factor Model—a psychological model—and Cloninger's Seven-Factor Model—a biosocial model. This unified theory is essentially a biopsychosocial theory of personality disorders. In addition to these research-based theories and models, there are a number of different clinical formulations of personality disorders (Beck, Freeman, & Associates, 1990; Benjamin, 1993; Gabbard, 1990).

In the past, criteria for the assessment of personality disorders were somewhat primitive. DSM-I subdivided personality disorders into five headings: personality pattern disturbance, personality trait disturbance, sociopathic personality disturbance, special symptom reactions, and transient situational personality disorders. DSM-II, which appeared in 1968, eliminated the subheadings and streamlined the number of personality disorders. The descriptions were not based on clinical trials. Although brief descriptions of each disorder were given, diagnostic criteria were not provided. Furthermore, there was no clear distinction made between symptom disorders (Axis I) and personality disorders (Axis II).

This lack of specificity further reinforced some mistaken convictions about personality disorders. A striking example is obsessive-compulsive disorder and obsessive-compulsive personality disorder. Before DSM-III, little or no distinction was made between these disorders for which there is now consensus that there is relatively little overlap (Jenike, 1991). Yet some still fail or hesitate to make this distinction, referring to both as aspects of the "obsessive personality" (Salzman, 1980). Perhaps this harkens back to Freud's case description of the Rat Man in which both obsessive-compulsive disorder and obsessive-compulsive personality disorder were present (Francis, Clarkin, & Perry, 1984). The implication was that both are essentially the same, so treatment should be the same for both disorders. Jenike (1991) notes that the concurrence of obsessive-compulsive disorder in patients with obsessive-compulsive personality disorder is small, probably less than 15 to 18 percent. Currently, the DSM-V Planning Group on Personality and Relational Disorders is considering major changes regarding the diagnosis of the Axis II disorders.

In the past, assessment of personality disorder was by clinical interview and inferred from standardized personality inventories such as the MMPI. Today, there are a number of formal measures of personality disorders. Some are theory and research based, such as Millon's MCMI-III (1994) and

Cloninger's Temperament Character Inventory (TCI; Cloninger et al., 1993). Others are research-based self-report instruments such as the Personality Disorder Inventory (PDI) and the Personality Disorders Questionnaire–Revised (PDQ-R). There are a number of semistructured schedules available, such as the Structured Clinical Interview for DSM-III-R Personality Disorders (SCID-II). Although methodological issues have been raised about these assessment devices, they have served both the clinician and the researcher well (Zimmerman, 1994).

In large part, these assessment measures reflect the increasingly differentiated criteria of DSM-III, DSM-III-R, and DSM-IV. DSM-III subdivided 11 personality disorders into three clusters: odd, dramatic, and anxious. DSM-III-R maintained the essential features of DSM-III but added sadistic and self-defeating personality disorders to Appendix B. DSM-IV further differentiated criteria and dropped self-defeating and sadistic personality disorders. It relegated passive-aggressive personality disorder to the category personality disorder–not otherwise specified (NOS), as well as depressive personality disorder, which joined passive-aggressive personality disorder in Appendix B of DSM-IV.

In the past, the treatment of personality disorders was largely the domain of psychodynamic approaches. Psychoanalysis and long-term psychoanalytically oriented psychotherapy were considered the treatment of choice (Stone, 1993). The goal of treatment was to change character structure. Unfortunately, outcomes were mixed even among patients adjudged amenable to treatment. For the most part, clinicians utilizing a traditional exploratory approach adopted a neutral and passive stance and primarily utilized clarification and interpretation strategies.

Treatment methods were also changing, with interventions becoming more focused and structured, and with clinicians taking a more active role in the treatment. Many of these treatment approaches and intervention strategies are theory based and have been researched in clinical trials in comparison with other treatment approaches or other modalities such as medication, group therapy, and family therapy. The cognitive therapy approach, the interpersonal psychotherapy approach (Benjamin, 1993), and some psychodynamic approaches have been specifically modified for the treatment of personality-disordered individuals.

Furthermore, I emphasized that psychopharmacological research on treatment of selected personality disorders was expanding rapidly. Prior to the paradigm shift, the consensus among clinicians was that medication did not and could not treat personality disorders, per se, but rather concurrent Axis I conditions or target symptoms such as insomnia. This view has changed markedly. Based on investigations of the biological correlates of personality disorders, Siever and Davis (1991) proposed a psychobiological treatment model that has been of inestimable clinical and research value. Essentially, Siever and Davis believe that psychopharmacological treatment can and should be directed to basic dimensions that underlie the personality. The dimensions are cognitive/perceptual organizations, especially for the schizotypal and passive disorders, for which low-dose neuroleptics might be useful; impulsivity and aggression in the borderline and antisocial, for which serotonin blockers can be useful; affective instability for borderline and histrionic personalities, for which cyclic antidepressants or serotonin blockers may be useful; and anxiety/inhibition, particularly in avoidant personalty disorder, for which serotonin blockers and MAOI agents may be useful.

It was also noted that research was increasingly suggestive that effective treatment of personality disorders involved combining treatment modalities and integrating treatment approaches. Stone (1993) suggests combining three approaches. He notes that supportive interventions are particularly useful in fostering a therapeutic alliance and should be augmented by psychoanalytic interventions, which are useful in resolving negative transferences at the outset of treatment, and cognitive behavioral interventions, which are useful in the development of new attitudes and habits. Winer and Pollock (1989) and Stone (1993) also recommend combing medication with individual and group modalities for personality-disordered individuals. This prescription to integrate various approaches, as well as to combine treatment modalities, would have been considered heretical as recently as the late 1990s. Now, integrating and combining treatments is an emerging consensus that reflects the immensity of the paradigm shift.

EFFECTIVE TREATMENT OF PERSONALITY DISORDERS: BASIC PREMISES

The 1995 edition articulated four basic premises that were considered essential to achieving effective treatment outcomes with personality disorders. The passage of time has reinforced their clinical utility. An additional premise on treatment tailoring has been added.

Premise 1: Personality disorders are best conceptualized in integrative and biopsychosocial terms, and the more effective treatment will reflect this biopsychosocial perspective.

Viewing personality disorders simply from a psychosocial or characterological perspective has serious limitations (Stone, 1993). Similarly, viewing personality disorders as basically biological or temperamental is limiting. On the other hand, there is considerable research and clinical support for viewing personality disorders from the perspective of character and temperament. Such a biopsychosocial or integrative clinical formulation should be reflected in a treatment plan that is biopsychosocially focused.

Premise 2: Assessing treatability or amenability to treatment is critical to maximizing treatment planning and outcomes.

Treatability is a function of a patient's readiness and level of functioning. Patient readiness refers to the individual patient's motivation for and expectations for treatment outcomes, as well as past history of treatment compliance and success at efforts to change habits and behavior patterns. Level of functioning can be operationalized in terms of the Global Assessment of Functioning Scale (GAF) of Axis IV. High functioning refers to a score of about 65. Moderate functioning refers to a score of 45 to 65. Low functioning refers to a score below 45.

Stone (1993) suggests that personality disorders lend themselves to a three-category classification with regard to treatability: (1) high amenability: includes dependent, histrionic, obsessive-compulsive, avoidant, and depressive personality disorders; (2) intermediate amenability: includes narcissistic, borderline, and schizotypal personality disorders; (3) low amenability: includes paranoid, passive-aggressive, schizoid, and antisocial personality disorders. Stone adds that since patients show mixtures of various personalty traits, prognosis is largely dependent on the degree to which traits of the disorders in the third category are present. Prognosis also depends in part on the prominence of the psychobiological dimensions described by Siever and Davis (1991): cognitive/perceptual disorganization; impulsivity/aggression; affective inability or anxiety/ inhibition. To the extent that dimensions such as impulsivity or anxiety respond to medication, concurrent psychosocial intervention efforts should be facilitated.

Premise 3: Effective treatment of personality disorders is tailored treatment.

The effectiveness of treatment outcomes is largely a function of how well treatment is tailored to the particular needs, circumstances, expectations, and overall level of functioning of the individual. Tailoring refers to modifying or adapting a particular modality and/or therapeutic approach to the patient's needs, styles, and expectations.

A sartorial analogy might help distinguish between combining, integrating, and tailoring. An adult could go into a clothing store to purchase a gray business suit. The individual could randomly choose a suit from the rack and there would be a small chance of it fitting perfectly, but more likely it would be a poor fit. The individual whose size is usually 38 short could look through the racks and try on 38 short, which might fit quite well but still needs minor fitting work by a tailor—partial tailoring. Of course, the individual could also go to a store for a fitting and have a suit completely custom made—total tailoring. The suit could be pure wool or pure silk, or it could be a blend of wool and silk. This blended fabric would be analogous to integrating treatment. Analogous to combined treatment would be purchasing a blue sports jacket that might be worn with the pants of the gray suit for a more casual look. In short, there can be no one-size-fits-all protocols for successful treatment of personality disorders.

The more treatment can be tailored to specific client factors, the more likely it is to be effective, and tailoring involves much more than simply matching a treatment method to a specific personality disorder. Therefore, it is impossible for any article or book to provide a definitive all-treatment protocol for all personality disorders or even one specific disorder. That being said, it is possible to offer some generalizations about which treatment methods are more likely to be effective with specific personality disorders. Mindful of these generalizations and based on an integrative assessment including treatability and amenability to treatment, the clinician can then tailor treatment to the individual's unique circumstances, needs, and expectations.

Generally speaking, individuals with antisocial, borderline, and histrionic personalities need more confrontation, whereas those with avoidant, dependent, and obsessive-compulsive personalities need more reassurance. For the most part, insight-oriented therapy tends to be more appropriate for individuals with high motivation and fairly high functioning. Furthermore, such therapy appears to achieve better outcomes with less severe forms of narcissistic and obsessive-compulsive personality (Sperry, 1999).

Individuals with certain personality pathology, such as schizoid and schizotypal personality, find it difficult to tolerate emotional probing or a taxing personal relationship with a therapist. Nevertheless, they can respond better to behavioral, coping-oriented, and supportive therapy. Similarly, avoidant personalities tend to be responsive to supportive efforts initially. Only then can they be expected to respond to challenges and new situations (Millon & Davis, 2000). Cognitive therapy can be helpful in analyzing their fears of rejection and humiliation.

Initially, the treatment with obsessive-compulsive personalities should focus on feeling expression over intellectual discussion of their concerns. Often, cognitive therapy is helpful in altering their rigid thinking and obsessional worrying. In addition, relaxation training can aid in reducing tension and compulsive mental strivings. Both psychodynamic and cognitive therapies can be useful in moderating the irrational thinking and excessive emotional reactions common in histrionic personalities. Group and couples therapy may show individuals how their behavior affects others. On the other hand, group therapy usually requires too much self-revelation for paranoid personalities. Furthermore, these individuals often find behavior therapy difficult to tolerate because they are reluctant to take instructions from anyone. The therapist should preserve a cool and respectful relationship with the patient, not challenging or interpreting paranoid ideas but understanding and sympathizing with the underlying feelings (Millon & Davis, 2000).

Individuals with antisocial personalities need to be shown the limitations of the way they respond to the world. They must learn how to weigh the advantages and disadvantages of their actions, partly by being made to understand that there will be clear and consistent consequences (Cloninger, 1999). But they rarely agree to treatment except under coercion, and they may use psychotherapy as another way to exercise their powers of deceit and manipulation.

Finally, individuals with borderline personalities can create complex difficult situations in treatment. For instance, they may provoke crises with suicide attempts and other self-destructive behavior, or they have had multiple treatments with different clinicians and rejected many or all of them. Sometimes these individuals need confrontation and limit setting, whereas other times they need comfort and affection. Group therapy may prove helpful by providing less emotionally intense relationships with those who are not in a position of authority. Yet borderline individuals can resent sharing a therapist—that is, the group therapist—and dislike being exposed to other group members' feelings. Nevertheless, a group component has been shown to be an integral part of some treatment approaches developed specifically for borderline personality–disordered individuals, such as dialectic behavior therapy (Linehan, 1993a).

Premise 4: The lower the level of treatability, the more combining and integrating of treatment modalities and approaches is needed.

Confirming clinical experience, research is now documenting that personality disorders are a significant source of psychiatric morbidity and lead to more functional impairment than major depression (Skodol et al., 2002). Often, low levels of functional impairment are suggestive of low treatability and indicative of the need for combining treatment modalities and approaches. There has been increasing interest in combined therapies and integrative treatment. This follows a long period of time in which clinicians were skeptical or even hostile about combining two modalities such as individual psychotherapy and group therapy, or medication and psychoanalytic psychotherapy. However, research and clinical practice reveal several advantages for combined therapeutic modalities. These include additive and even synergistic treatment effects, diluting unworkably intense transference relationships, and rapid symptom relief (Francis, Clarkin, & Perry, 1984).

In short, combined treatment refers to adding modalities, such as individual, group, couple, or family, either concurrently or sequentially, while integrative treatment refers to the blending of different treatment approaches or orientation, such as psychodynamic, cognitive, behavioral, interpersonal, and so on. Combining treatment modalities is also referred to as multimodal treatment. Finally, tailored treatment refers to specific ways of customizing treatment modalities and/or therapeutic approaches to fit the unique needs, cognitive and emotional styles, and treatment expectations of the patient.

Once considered controversial, psychoanalytically oriented therapy combined with other modalities is now being advocated by dynamically oriented clinicians. Winer and Pollack (1989) indicate that combined treatment—insight-oriented individual sessions with medication, group or family therapy—is particularly valuable in cases of personality disorders.

Treatment delivered in combination can have an additive, and sometimes synergistic, effect. It is becoming more evident that different treatment approaches are differentially effective in resolving different types of symptom clusters. For example, in major depression, medication is more effective in remitting vegetative symptoms, while psychotherapy is better at improving interpersonal relations and cognitive symptoms (Frances, Clarkin, & Perry, 1984). Furthermore, the additive effect of medication and psychotherapy has been established for both major depression (Rush & Hollon, 1991) and agoraphobia (Greist & Jefferson, 1992).

What are the indications and contraindications for these various modalities? A working knowledge of these are probably more necessary for clinicians working with personality disorders than for Axis I disorders. Francis, Perry, and Clarkin (1984) detail the relative indication, relative contraindication, and enabling factors for three treatment modalities: individual, group, and family/marital. The reader is referred to their excellent discussion and summary table.

These authors also discuss a very basic question that needs to be asked every time a clinician considers offering treatment to a personality-disordered individual: Is treatment advisable or would no treatment be the preferred recommendation? The "no treatment option" may be the treatment of choice for individuals who have had negative therapeutic reactions or who have made little or no progress in the course of interminable therapy.

Francis, Perry, and Clarkin (1984) offer specific criteria for making the treatment versus no treatment recommendation. They also note that patients were ten times more likely to initiate "no treatment" decisions than were clinicians to offer this option.

While combined treatment refers to combining different modalities of treatment (i.e., individual, group, marital and family therapy, day treatment, or inpatient) either concurrently or sequentially, integrative or tailoring treatment is different. Integrative treatment refers to blending various treatment approaches (i.e., psychodynamic, cognitive, behavioral, interpersonal, and medication). Several researchers have advocated integrative treatment for treatment of borderline personality disorder (Stone, 1992; Linehan, 1993). Cognitive-behavior therapy represents the integration of two therapeutic approaches: cognitive therapy and behavior therapy. The specific type of cognitive-behavior therapy developed by Linehan, dialectal behavior therapy, is an integration of various cognitive-behavioral intervention strategies and Zen practice (Heard & Linehan, 1994). Stone (1992) prescribes blending psychoanalytic, behavioral, cognitive, and medication intervention or approaches.

The higher the patient's treatability—that is, level of functioning and treatment readiness—the less immediacy there may be to combining and blending most of the modalities and approaches. On the other hand, the lower the functioning, the more modalities and approaches will need to be combined and blended.

This premise may seem quite demanding of the clinician's professional resources. It is. Not every clinician is suited for working with all personality-disordered individuals, particularly those with low amenability to treatment. Specialized training and supervision in the utilization of various approaches is needed in the treatment of personality disorders. It is not being suggested that clinicians should or must also be trained in the various treatment modalities. Obviously, referral to group or family therapy or other treatment modalities beyond the clinician's competence is a reasonable option.

Premise 5: The basic goal of treatment is to facilitate movement from personality-disordered functioning to personality-style functioning.

Treatment goals can be thought of in terms of levels. The first level involves symptoms. The second level involves personality features that are related to environment and are modifiable. The third level involves personality features that are related to character. The fourth level involves personality functions related to temperament. Treatment of levels one and two is relatively straightforward. Medication or behavioral treatments like exposure may quickly remit symptoms of personality. Psychotherapeutic interventions of various approaches and modalities can often be useful at level three. But they may not be, as in the case of rule-breaking behavior of the antisocial individual. Level four is temperament and human nature and is not easily changed.

Stone (1993) uses the analogy of the cabinet maker and carpenter to describe this level of treatment. The clinician working with personality-disordered individuals is not a carpenter who rebuilds a structure, but is rather like a cabinet maker who sands down and takes the rough edges off. The individual's temperament remains, but treatment renders the individual somewhat easier to work or live with. Essentially, then, personality style will be used in the subsequent chapters to refer to high adaptive functioning behavior for a particular personality type, whereas personality disorder refers to functioning that is characterized by specific DSM-IV diagnostic criteria.

Today, I would modify this premise to read: *The basic goal of treatment is to facilitate movement from personality-disordered functioning to adequate personality-style functioning or even to optimal functioning.* From a developmental psychotherapeutic perspective (Sperry, 2002), the continuum of functioning, and subsequently treatment, is broadened to include an optimal level of functioning. (See the section on treatment trends.)

FROM DSM-IV TO DSM-IV-TR

In 2000, the *Diagnostic and Statistical Manual of Mental Disorders, Fourth Edition Text Revision* (DSM-IV-TR) was published (American Psychiatric Association, 2000). As the title suggests, the revision was primarily of the text supporting diagnostic categories and criteria. While there were some changes in diagnostic criteria—that is, paraphilias—this was not the main focus. Significant advances in clinical research since the DSM-IV publication in 1994 warranted updating the text.

There were no changes in diagnostic criteria for any of the personality disorders. Furthermore, passive-aggressive personality disorder (negativisitic personality disorder) and depressive personality disorder remained relegated to Appendix B: "Criteria Sets and Axes Provided for Further Study." Nevertheless, there were changes in the narrative text throughout the personality disorders chapter. These are briefly summarized.

In the introductory section of the personality disorders chapter, there was a further delineation and updating of the categorical versus dimensional issue of diagnosis. Specifically, additional dimensional models under consideration for possible adoption in DSM-V were noted.

In the "Specific Culture, Age and Gender Features" section on dependent personality disorder, the text was changed "to remove the suggestion that reported gender differences is largely artifactual" (p. 842). More specifically, it was noted, "In clinical settings, this disorder has been diagnosed more frequently in females, although some studies report *similar* prevalence rates among males and females (p. 723, italics added).

The "Associated Features and Disorders" section of obsessive-compulsive personality disorder was updated to clarify the relationship between obsessive-compulsive disorders and obsessive-compulsive personality disorders. Presumably, this clarification was necessary because of the prevailing belief that the disorders are often comorbid or that they are essentially variants of the same disorder, as in Freud's famous case of the Rat Man, or in Melvin Udall, the main character in the movie *As Good As It Gets*. The revised text notes, "The majority of individuals with Obsessive-Compulsive Disorders do not have a pattern of behavior that meets criteria for Obsessive-Compulsive Personality Disorders" (p. 727).

Similarly, in the "Associated Features and Disorders" section of antisocial personality disorder, the text was updated to "clarify that features that are part of the traditional conception of psychopathy may be more predictive of recidivism in settings (e.g., prisons) where criminal acts are likely to be non-specific" (p. 842). Specifically, the features referred to are "lack of empathy, inflated self-appraisal and superficial charm" (p. 703).

Finally, text in the "Course" section of borderline personality disorder was added to "emphasize that, contrary to many clinicians' preconceived notions, the prognosis for many individuals with Borderline Personality Disorder is good" (p. 842). The new text reads, "During their 30s and 40s the majority of individuals with this disorder attain stability in their relationships and vocational functioning. Follow up studies of individuals identified through out-patient mental health clinics indicate that after about 10 years, as many as half of the individuals no longer have a pattern that meets full criteria for Borderline Personality Disorder" (p. 709).

TRENDS IN THE DIAGNOSIS OF PERSONALITY DISORDERS

This section describes a number of cutting-edge clinical and research trends that are and will continue to impact the assessment and diagnosis of personality disorders. These include attachment styles, temperament, culture, emotional abuse and neglect, functional impairment, and dimensional vs. categorical models of diagnosis.

Attachment Styles and Personality Disorders

Attachment researchers insist that early life relational deficits lead to both neurophysiological brain deficits as well as psychological deficits (Siegel, 1999). A sensitive and responsive parent helps grow the connections in the orbitofrontal cortex of the infant's brain by communicating—or "collaborating"— with the baby via eye contact, facial expression, gestures, tone of voice, and so on. The gurgling, smiling infant is picked up and "answered" by the parents with a smiling and joyful expression and words. Or, the baby cries in pain or frustration and the parent soothes and consoles it, or calms down the overexcited child at bedtime. These routine and continuous interactions serve to stimulate the growth of synapses in the orbitofrontal cortex of the brain, which enable children to modulate their frustration, rage, and fear, and to respond flexibly to others.

Research indicates that securely attached children develop neural pathways for resilience. Even when their parents are upset or impatient, their brain's wiring "knows" from experience that they will not be abandoned and will reconnect after the storm has passed. Unfortunately, children with insecure attachment styles do not experience such reciprocal parental attention, and consequently they tend to be more vulnerable to emotional assaults—that is, they are less able to modulate rage and aggressive affects, calm and soothe their anxieties and sadness, as well as tolerate high levels of pleasure and excitement (Ainsworth et al., 1978). Needless to say, they are also less likely to correctly interpret others' social cues because of deficits in their orbitofrontal cortex, which further complicates interpersonal relationships.

Types of Attachment Styles in Early Life

Attachment refers to the emotional bond that develops between child and parent or caregiver and subsequently influences the child's capacity to form mature intimate relationships in adulthood. An inborn system of the brain influences and organizes motivational, emotional, and memory processes that involve caregivers. The impact of the process of attachment on development cannot be underestimated, since the "patterning and organization of attachment relationships during infancy is associated with characteristic processes of emotional regulation, social relatedness, access to autobiographical memory, and the development of self-reflection and narrative" (Siegel, 1999, p. 67).

Distinct patterns or styles of attachment in early life can be described. When the style of attachment is characterized by emotional interdependence, trust, and mutual feelings, it is called a *secure* style. As adults, individuals with secure styles exhibit more physical and emotional resilience as compared to those with insecure styles (Erdman & Caffery, 2003). That is to say, they are less vulnerable to stressors and, consequently, are less likely to experience health problems, depression, anxiety, substance abuse, or sexual and other psychiatric disorders. On the other hand, vulnerability is associated with *insecure* styles—that is, attachment styles characterized by inconsistency or emotional unavailability (Ainsworth et al., 1978).

At its core, attachment is based on parental sensitivity and responsivity to the child's needs and signals that foster collaborative parent–child communication. This is referred to as contingent communication, and as such results in secure attachments characterized by collaborative reciprocity of signals and mutual sharing between parent and child. Suboptimal attachments arise from an ongoing pattern of noncontingent communication. A parent's communication and own internal states may be oblivious to the child's needs as in fearful attachment. On the other hand, an ambivalent attached child—dismissing style—experiences the parent's communication as inconsistently contingent, sometimes being intrusive, while at other times being aligned. If the parent is a source of disorientation or terror, the child will develop a disorganized attachment. Here communication is not only noncontingent but the parent's messages create an internal state of chaos and overbearing fear of the parent in the child (Siegel, 1999).

Types of Attachment Styles in Adulthood

Attachment styles tend to persist into adulthood (Main & Solomon, 1990; Bartholomew & Horowitz, 1991; Hazen & Shaver, 1990). Reflecting Bowlby's (1973) concept of working models of self and others, Bartholomew (1990) developed a four-category system of adult attachment that organizes a person's working models along two dimensions: (1) the distinction between self and others and (2) valence—positive vs. negative evaluation. Based on these dimensions, Bartholomew derived four prototypical styles of adult attachment: *secure* (positive view of self and others), *preoccupied* (negative view of self and others), *dismissing* (positive view of self, negative view of others), and *fearful* (negative view of self and others). Subsequently, based on clinical experience, the *disorganized* (fluctuating positive and negative views of self and others) style was added (Main & Solomon, 1990; Main & Goldwyn, 1998).

Accordingly, personality disorders can be viewed as the outcome of insecure working models that have become self-confirmatory. These working models of self and other have become relatively inflexible and closed to new information, and as a result, the individual experiences significant distress in social, occupational, and relational functioning. It is possible to characterize the various personality disorders in terms of this dimensional model of self and others. It should be noted that Bartholomew (1990) does not assume that "all individuals are expected to exhibit a single attachment style" (p. 162).

Instead, these attachment styles are conceptual prototypes, and thus it is more appropriate to view adult attachment multidimensionally, with individuals exhibiting one or more style types as predominant. Accordingly, DSM-IV personality disorders can be categorized in the following adult attachment style designations (Lyddon & Sherry, 2001).

Preoccupied Attachment Style. The preoccupied attachment dimension is characterized by a sense of personal unworthiness and a positive evaluation of others. These individuals tend to be very externally oriented in their self-definitions. Personality disorders that seem to exemplify this adult attachment style include dependent, obsessive-compulsive, and histrionic.

Fearful Attachment Style. Individuals with a fearful attachment style exhibit a sense of personal unworthiness combined with an expectation that other people will be rejecting and untrustworthy. They trust neither their own internal cognitions or feelings nor others' intentions. While they believe themselves to be special and different from others, they guard against threats and unexpected circumstances, since they cannot trust that others will protect them. Paranoid personality disorder is the most characteristic of such a fearful adult attachment style.

Dismissing Attachment Style. Individuals with a dismissing attachment style are characterized by a sense of self that is worthy and positive, as well as a low and negative evaluation of others that typically manifests as mistrust of others. Because they believe they are emotionally self-sufficient while others are emotionally unresponsive, they dismiss the need for friendship and contact with others. Schizoid personality disorder is the most characteristic of such a preoccupied and fearful adult attachment style.

Preoccupied–Fearful Attachment Style. Individuals with a self-view that is negative and an other-view that vacillates between positive and negative exhibit a composite preoccupied and fearful style of attachment. Their avoidance is based on the desire to be liked and accepted by others while fearing rejection and abandonment. Avoidant personality disorder is the most characteristic of such a preoccupied and fearful adult attachment style.

Fearful–Dismissing Attachment Style. Individuals with an other-view that is negative and a self-view that vacillates between positive and negative exhibit a composite fearful–dismissing style of attachment. They tend to view themselves as special and entitled but are also mindful of their need for others who can potentially hurt them. Accordingly, they use others to meet their needs while being wary and dismissive of them. Antisocial, narcissistic, and schizotypal personality disorders are characterized by such a fearful–dismissing adult attachment style.

Disorganized Attachment Style. Individuals with vacillating views of both self and others exhibit disorganized attachment style. "Disorganize attachment develops from repeated experiences in which the caregiver appears frightened or frightening to the child" (Siegel, 1999, p. 117). This style is associated with dissociative symptomatology that increases proneness to posttraumatic stress disorder. Borderline personality disorder is characterized by unstable personality structure that seems to shift among the various insecure attachment styles, creating a disorganized profile.

Temperament and Personality Disorders

Like attachment, temperament is a construct that appears to have both research and clinical utility. Temperament refers to "the characteristic phenomena of an individual's emotional nature, including his susceptibility to emotional stimulation, his customary strengths and speed of response, the quality of his prevailing moods, and the peculiarities and fluctuation and intensity of moods; these phenomenon being regarded as dependent on constitutional makeup and therefore largely hereditary in origin" (Allport, 1937, p. 54). Although proposed many years ago, Allport's definition is remarkably consistent with many contemporary formulations of the construct.

Reflecting the clinician's view that temperament and attachment styles are related, temperament is viewed as "a filter of personality through which information is processed, attachments evolve, and emotions are experienced and expressed" (Graybar & Boutilier, 2002, p. 156). While clinicians seem convinced that temperament influences attachment and vice versa, researchers are still trying to clarify the exact nature of the relationship between the two constructs. This is largely because both constructs represent different origins and different research agendas. Whereas temperament represents a biological determinant of personality (nature), attachment style represents an environmental determinant of personality (nurture). As in other nature-nurture discussions, the relationship is seldom *either-or* but usually *both-and*. Currently, the research consensus seems to be that attachment and temperament are *modestly* related and that "both will influence the formation and expression of personality and self-concept as these are assembled during early childhood" (Vaughn & Bost, 1999, p. 221).

Temperamental traits and patterns are evident from birth. For instance, while some infants are quite sensitive to light and loud sounds, others are not;

while some are calm and placid, others are very active or very fussy. Three main temperament patterns have been observed in infants: *easy* (usually predictable and in a good mood), *slow to warm* (more likely to be resistant to attention and moody), and *difficult* (typically unpredictable and with irritable moods) (Thomas & Chess, 1977). A child's temperament tends to be reflected in adult patterns. For example, optimism and consistency of effort are more common in adults who have easy temperaments, while negativity and suspiciousness are associated with the difficult temperament, and passivity and overdependency with the slow-to-warm-up temperament. Several other temperament traits or descriptors have been identified in adults including impulsivity, irritability, hypersensitivity to stimulation, reactivity, emotional lability, inhibition, reflectivity, mood constriction, hypervigilance, and intensity.

Culture, Temperament, and Personality Disorders

As already indicated, research strongly suggests that insecure attachment influences the development of personality disorders (Brennan & Shaver, 1998). But what about the influence of temperament and culture on the development of personality and personality disorders? Brennan and Shaver (1998) believe that the same environmental conditions that contribute to the development of insecure attachments and subsequently personality disorders also interact with an individual's temperament. "In addition, cultural variations in the extent to which particular traits (e.g., independence, eccentricity) are also likely to result in cross-cultural differences in the expression of personality" (p. 868).

Emotional Abuse and Personality Disorders

A history of childhood verbal, emotional, physical, and/or sexual abuse or neglect can significantly impact functioning in adulthood. Research has confirmed that childhood emotional abuse is associated with development of borderline personality disorder (Zanarini, 1997). This has led to clinician awareness of this traumatic pathway and has also influenced clinical practice of this disorder. Accordingly, potent therapeutic approaches, such as dialectic behavior therapy (Linehan, 1993a), have emphasized this traumatic pathway. Such approaches downplay or discourage the use of exploratory interventions, which can be regressive, in favor of supportive and other nonregressive methods.

Recently, researchers have suggested that a history of early abuse or neglect is common in adults with other personality disorders as well (Herman, Perry, & van der Kolk, 1989; Zanarini et al., 2000). For instance, Bernstein et al. (1998) found that a childhood history of emotional abuse was predictive of the development of personality disorders in all three Axis II clusters: odd, dramatic, and anxious; childhood emotional neglect was predictive of schizoid personality disorder. Bernstein (2002) indicates that childhood histories of *severe* emotional abuse are noted in adults diagnosed with borderline, narcissistic, antisocial, and paranoid personality disorders; *moderate to severe* abuse is present in obsessive-compulsive and histrionic personality disorders; *moderate* levels are noted in avoidant and dependent personality disorders. He also found that a childhood history of *severe* emotional neglect was found among adults with schizoid personality disorders.

Such research is beginning to document the levels of severity of abuse or trauma. But exactly how prevalent is such trauma in clients presenting for treatment? A perusal of the literature on borderline personality leaves the reader with the impression that childhood abuse is a major risk factor or the antecedent cause of borderline personality disorder. However, neither research data nor clinical experience supports this impression. Rather, several research reports, including a meta-analytics study (Fossatti, Madeddu, & Maffei, 1999), indicate that individuals diagnosed with borderline personality disorder report rates of abuse in the range of 60 to 80 percent. Thus, 20 to 40 percent of these individuals do not report such histories. In other words, while there are traumatic pathways in the development of personality disorders, there are also nontraumatic pathways. The implication is that clients who were not traumatized but rather may have been wounded as children in their efforts to meet emotional needs are likely to be responsive to a broader range of therapeutic interventions. This would include exploratory, uncovering, and abreactive interventions, which are less likely to be regressive or iatrogenic than they would be with clients with trauma histories (Graybar & Boutilier, 2002).

Functional Capacity and Impairment

It is a common belief among clinicians that although Axis II disorders can present treatment challenge, they are less impairing than serious Axis I disorders such as major depressive disorder (Skodol et al., 2002). The extent of impairment of individuals with personality disorders as compared to Axis I symptom disorders has been the focus of large-scale research efforts lately. Initial results from the ongoing Collaborative Longitudinal Personality Disorders Study are particularly telling. This is one of the first studies to document and quantify the extent of functional impairment in patients with an Axis II disorder in contrast to patients having an impairing Axis I disorder. It compares psychosocial functioning and impairment among four groups of personality disorders—borderline, schizotypal, avoidant, and obsessive-compulsive—with a group of patients with major depressive disorder and no personality disorder. Patients with borderline and schizotypal personality disorders were found to have significantly more impairment at work, in social relations, and in leisure activities than patients with obsessive-compulsive or major depressive disorder. In contrast, patients with avoidant personality disorders experienced intermediate levels of impaired functioning. Of particular note is that these differences were found across all assessment modalities and remained significant after statistically controlling for demographic differences and comorbid Axis I pathology (Skodol et al., 2002). These results not only underscore clinicians' misconceptions of the extent of psychiatric morbidity attendant to Axis II disorders but also suggest the importance of utilizing integrative treatment interventions that emphasize psychosocial rehabilitation to mitigate the pernicious effects of personality disorders on functioning.

Dimensional Models: Anticipated Changes in DSM-V

The current DSM-IV method for diagnosing and specifying personality disorders is the categorical approach. In the categorical approach, an individual either has or does not have a personality disorder depending on whether the individual meets or exceeds a specified threshold, usually four or five criteria depending on the particular disorder. For example, an individual who meets four of the borderline personality disorder criteria is considered to have borderline traits, whereas if that individual meets five of the criteria, a diagnosis of borderline personality disorder would be given. Unfortunately, the thresholds established in DSM-IV are somewhat arbitrary based on limited empirical research. "Furthermore, there is no documented clinical utility for the DSM-IV categories in terms of guiding treatment decisions" (First, 2002, p. 12).

An alternate method is the dimensional approach. In this method, a personality trait is considered to be a maladaptive variant of general personality functioning. Over the years, several different dimensional approaches have been proposed in place of the categorical approach (First, 2002). These dimensional approaches differ in both how they were developed and the extent to which dimensional items are limited to personality disorder symptoms or reflect a full range of normal and abnormal functioning. Prior to the publication of DSM-IV, the dimensional approach was considered to replace the categorical method of DSM-III and DSM-III-R but was rejected because there was no consensus as to which dimensional approach had sufficient research support and clinical utility. Currently, the DSM-V Personality and Relational Disorders Workgroup is evaluating five such approaches. Presumably, one of these approaches will be incorporated into DSM-V. A brief description of each of these follows.

Pure Dimensional Approach

Although this approach emphasizes the dimensional model, it is closest to the existing Axis II category system. It basically transforms the existing categories into dimensional representations of specified personality disorders in DSM-IV. Dimensional criteria are simply the number of criteria that are met or present in a particular client. The clinician simply checks each of the diagnostic criteria for each of the ten personality disorders. If one to three criteria are met, a *personality trait* is considered present. If four or five criteria are met, a *disorder* can be specified (depending on whether the diagnostic threshold for the disorder is four or five criteria). The dimensional designation is *pervasive* if five to eight criteria are met and *proptypic* if seven to nine are present. In short, the pure dimensional approach allows a client to be mapped in terms of all ten personality disorders—a map similar to the profile configuration of the MMPI-2 and other personality inventories. This approach is advocated by Oldham and Skodol (2000).

Prototype Matching Approach

This approach permits the clinician to diagnose personality pathology on a continuum from less to more severe. Rather than the current DSM-IV system that compares client symptoms or behaviors against specific diagnostic Axis II criteria, the clinician simply rates the overall similarity or resemblance between the client and specific prototypes that describe each personality disorder in its "purest" form. These pure types are based on DSM criteria.

Clinically Derived Personality Prototypes Approach

Developed empirically from descriptions of actual clients provided by more than one thousand experienced clinicians, this system provides a set of personality descriptions or prototypes that reflect what clinicians see in everyday clinical practice. There are three differences in this approach to the current Axis II system: First, the diagnostic criteria are different since they were empirically derived from actual clients in typically clinical settings. Second, personality pathology is diagnosed on a continuum from less to more severe. Third, like the prototype matching approach, the clinician rates the overall similarity or resemblance between the client and specific prototypes. This approach was developed and is advocated by Westin and Shedler (2000).

Five-Factor Model Approach

This approach is based on five broad factors of personality functioning: neuroticism, extroversion, openness to experience, conscientiousness, and agreeableness. Each factor is further differentiated into six specific facets or components, yielding 30 facets. It is believed that this Five-Factor Model provides a comprehensive description of both adaptive and maladaptive personality traits that most individuals find important in describing themselves and others. In this approach the clinician rates a client against each of the 30 facets on a scale of 1 to 7. While these ratings do not translate into specific Axis II diagnostic categories—that is, borderline personality disorder—they provide a rather comprehensive factor map of the client. This approach is advocated by Widiger, Costa, and McCrae (2002).

Two-Step Psychobiological System Approach

This approach conceptualizes personality as a complex interaction between temperament—that is, heritable neurobiological dispositions—and character—that is, social learning and cultural factors. It specifies personality in terms of three character traits—self-directedness, cooperativeness, and self-transcendence—and three temperament traits—harm avoidance, novelty seeking, and reward dependence. The clinician evaluates a client on the three character traits. Low scores on these traits represent a personality disorder. Once such a diagnosis is established, temperament is used for specifying a particular personality disorder. Extreme scores on the temperament traits, individually or as multifactorial combinations, reflect specific personality patterns. Thus, high ratings on novelty seeking and harm avoidance with low ratings on reward dependence are specific for borderline personality disorder. This approach was developed and is advocated by Cloninger (2000).

TRENDS IN THE TREATMENT OF PERSONALITY DISORDERS

This section describes a number of cutting-edge clinical and research trends that are and will continue to impact the treatment of personality disorders. These include treatment utilization, brain-behavior perspective, medication, and various psychotherapeutic interventions such as mindfulness, schema therapy, structured skill intervention and cognitive coping therapy, and developmental therapy.

Treatment Utilization

Clinicians who work with a variety of psychiatric presentations recognize that personality-disordered individuals often have higher rates of treatment utilization than individuals with other diagnoses. Until recently, there was little research on the actual extent and variety of utilization of mental health services by such individuals. A large-scale study of individuals diagnosed with personality disorders, the ongoing Collaborative Longitudinal Personality Disorders Study, has addressed this matter. This major psychiatric epidemiological study indicates that personality-disordered individuals utilized considerably more mental health treatment than individuals diagnosed with clinical depression without a concomitant personality disorder. In addition to the amount of services, the type or variety of utilized services was studied. The treatment histories of four personality disorder groups—borderline, schizotypal, avoidant, and obsessive-compulsive—were compared with a group of individuals diagnosed with major depressive disorder. Compared to the clinical depression group, those with borderline personality disorder were more likely to have received inpatient hospitalization, day treatment, medication, residential care, in addition to outpatient individual and group therapy, whereas those with obsessive-compulsive personality disorder had greater utilization of individual therapy. Of all groups, those with borderline personality disorder utilized not only more treatment but more treatment modalities—except for couples therapy, family therapy, and self-help groups—than other groups (Bender et al., 2001). Unfortunately, the study provides no evidence that these personality-disordered individuals are receiving adequate or even appropriate treatment.

Brain-Behavior View of Treatment Processes

One of the outcomes of recent neuroscience investigations into the brain-behavior correlates is the conceptualization of the treatment of personality disorders as either top-down or bottom-up strategies, particularly regarding efforts to normalize the expression of overmodulated maladaptive personality traits with various psychotropic and behavioral interventions (Fawcett, 2002). *Top-down* refers to treatment efforts that are primarily focused on cortical structures and neural tracts (top), which can also influence subcortical circuits, particularly in the limbic system (down). *Bottom-up* refers to the treatment efforts that are largely focused on limbic circuits, which also can produce changes in cortical circuits.

Of particular promise are recent efforts to normalize the expression of under- and overmodulated maladaptive personality traits with psychotropic and behavioral interventions. For example, top-down treatment strategies typically utilize psychotherapies and behavioral interventions—that is, cognitive behavior therapy—to enhance cortical influences on limbic circuits. The goal is to undo negative learning, particularly maladaptive schemas, and to increase the modulating or normalizing effects of emotional responses. Bottom-up treatment strategies typically involve the use of psychotropic medication in order to modulate harmful personality traits and emotional states by normalizing the activity of limbic structures. Besides medications, it appears that skill training interventions, such as cognitive coping therapy (Sharoff, 2002), function as bottom-up treatments. A subsequent section further describes this intervention.

Medication Strategies

Until recently, medication treatment of personality-disordered individuals has been largely empirical—that is, largely trial and error. That is because, generally speaking, there are not specific drug treatments for specific DSM-IV personality disorders as there are for panic disorder or major depressive disorder. The possible exception is avoidant personality disorder, wherein venlafaxine (Effexor), a selective serotonin-norepinephrine uptake inhibitor, appears to be particularly effective at reducing avoidant personality traits. Since avoidant personality disorder appears to be only quantitatively different from social phobia, it may be that medications effective in treating social phobia are also likely to be effective with this personality disorder (Altamura et al., 1999; Reich, 2000).

Even though there are currently no specific psychotropic agents for specific personality disorders except as noted above, there appears to be increasing confidence that medication treatment can be effective if it focuses on maladaptive personality *traits* associated with various personality disorders. There is mounting clinical research evidence, including some double-blind studies, that specific medications can effectively target such maladaptive personality traits as impulsivity, anger and aggression, inhibition, suspiciousness, and mood lability. Reich (2002) summarizes the efficacy of various classes of psychotropic medications for specific personality traits. He describes three clusters of such traits and provides suggested protocols for treatment.

Each of these three clusters is briefly described in this section. He indicates that such medication trials should last at least 4 to 6 weeks, barring problematic side effects. The question of the duration of medication treatment is complicated, but given that personality-disordered behaviors and concerns are typically long term, ongoing use may be justified if the medication or combination of medications improves symptoms and/or functioning and has an acceptably low level of side effects (Reich, 2002).

Paranoid, Mild Thought Disorder and Dissociation Cluster
Start with an atypical antipsychotic, such as risperidone, at one-fourth to one-half the usual topic range maintenance dose for psychosis. If there is no response, incrementally increase the dosage. If there is no response at the top dose, switch to another atypical. If there is a partial response, consider adding

divalproex. Clozapine should be considered only in refractory individuals. When dissociative symptoms are prominent, naltrexone can be considered.

Depressed, Angry, Labile Mood Cluster

Begin with an SSRI at antidepressant dosages. If that SSRI fails, try another. If there is a partial response, an adjunctive atypical psychotic agent or a mood stabilizer such as valproate or carbamazepine can be considered. For individuals in whom rejection sensitivity is prominent, a trial of an MAOI is reasonable, particularly if the individual has a history of medication compliance. Naltrexone may be a useful adjunctive for individuals with self-harming behavior.

Anxious, Inhibited Behavior Cluster

For personality-disordered individuals with prominent anxiety but without impulsivity, begin with an SSRI. If no response, try another SSRI. If there is a partial response, a long-acting benzodiazepine or clonazepam can be added or even used as the sole medication following multiple SSRI trials. If these also fail, beta blockers and atypical antipsychotics could be the mainstay treatment of such anxiety symptoms. With individuals who have histories or impulsive, dangerous behavior or substance abuse, begin with SSRI trials. If these fail, consider the use of beta blockers or atypical antipsychotics (Reich, 2002).

Psychotherapeutic Strategies

Included here is a discussion of the latest therapeutic interventions and strategies that show considerable promise for optimizing treatment outcomes with personality disorders. These include mindfulness, schema therapy, structured skill interventions and cognitive coping therapy, and developmental therapy.

Mindfulness

Mindfulness is a form of awareness in which an individual can focus on thoughts, feelings, and experiences in the present moment with an attitude of acceptance and without analysis or judgment. The practice of mindfulness can diffuse negativity, aggression, and compulsivity without suppressing emotions or indulging them (Marlatt & Kristeller, 1999). While mindfulness derives from the Buddhist tradition, it has recently been incorporated into medicine and psychotherapy. Since it is associated with developing an awareness of alternative perspectives and reducing habitual response patterns, mindfulness has been proposed as a common factor across various therapeutic systems (Martin, 1997).

Linehan (1994) describes the application of mindfulness techniques as a way of integrating acceptance into psychotherapy, emphasizing its association with intentional rather than automatic information processing as well as the nonjudging, nonevaluative nature of mindfulness attention. Not surprisingly, mindfulness is incorporated into Linehan's dialectical behavior therapy of borderline personality disorder. Recently, mindfulness approaches have been incorporated into several cognitive and cognitive-behavioral treatment interventions including depression (Teasdale et al., 2000; Segal, Williams, & Teasdale, 2002), substance abuse (Marlatt, 1994), borderline personality disorder (Linehan, 1994), panic disorder (Kabat-Zinn et al., 1992), binge eating (Kristeller & Hallet, in press), generalized anxiety disorder (Roemer & Orsillo, 2002), and obsessive-compulsive disorder (Schwartz & Begley, 2002). There is mounting research evidence that mindfulness is effective in these disorders as well as medical conditions such as stroke and Tourette's syndrome (Schwartz & Begley, 2002). The extent to which mindfulness has become the core strategy in Teasdale's approach to depression and other disorders is reflected in the name of his approach: *mindfulness-based cognitive therapy* (Teasdale et al., 2000). It is also interesting to note that Young's schema therapy (2003) has incorporated mindfulness as a key strategy in the treatment of personality disorders.

Schema Therapy

Schema therapy is an elaboration of cognitive therapy that has been developed by Young (1990, 1999, 2003) specifically for personality disorders and other difficult individual and couples problems. It integrates elements of Adlerian psychology, behavior therapy, object relations, and gestalt therapy into a systematic approach to treatment. Recently, it has incorporated mindfulness for clients sensitive to the spiritual dimension.

The most basic concept in schema therapy is an early maladaptive schema. Schemas are defined as broad, pervasive themes regarding one's view of self and others that were developed during childhood and elaborated throughout one's lifetime. They are enduring and self-defeating patterns that typically begin early in life, although they can also form in adulthood, cause negative/dysfunctional thoughts and feelings, and interfere with accomplishing goals and meeting one's needs. These schemas are perpetuated behaviorally through the coping styles of schema maintenance, schema avoidance, and schema compensation (Young, 1999).

Young (1999) has identified 18 schemas. Schemas develop in childhood from an interplay between the child's innate temperament and the child's ongoing damaging experiences with parents, siblings, or peers. Because they begin early in life, schemas become familiar and thus comfortable. We distort our view of the events in our lives in order to maintain the validity of our schemas. Schemas may remain dormant until they are activated by situations relevant to that particular schema.

These schemas are arranged into five broad developmental categories called schema domains. Each of the domains represents an important component of a child's core needs. Schemas interfere with the child's attempts to get the core needs met within each domain. Table 1.1 provides a capsule description of these schemas and domains.

Schema therapy involves identifying maladaptive schemas, deciding on the appropriate level of change, and planning interventions to effect this level or degree of change. Differing levels of schema change are noted: schema reconstruction, schema modification, interpretation, and schema camouflage. Schema reconstruction—that is, maldaptive replacing the schema with a more functional one—is the most extensive level of transformation and often involves long-term treatment, whereas schema camouflage is the least extensive and may be a more appropriate goal in shorter-term treatment (Young, 1999).

Structured Skill Treatment Interventions and Cognitive Coping Therapy

Structured Treatment Interventions. Unlike schemas, which reflect the psychological dimension of personality, temperament—that is, the innate, genetic and constitutional aspect of personality—reflects its biological dimension. Temperament plays an important role in the regulation and dysregulation of an individual's affective, behavioral, and cognitive styles (Sperry, 1999). While research shows that medication can modulate or normalize dysregulated behaviors, a similar modulating effect has also been noted for social skills training (Lieberman, DeRisi, & Mueser, 1989). Thus, it appears that social skills training is a relatively potent bottom-up treatment strategy for normalizing such limbic system–mediated behaviors as impulsivity, aggressivity, and mood lability, to name a few.

Sperry (1999) contends that personality-disordered individuals typically exhibit significant skill deficits, and that structured skill training interventions are useful and necessary in successful treatment of moderate to severe personality disorders. Skill deficits can be reversed by the acquisition of requisite skills in individual and group sessions through practice via modeling, coaching, role-playing, and graded task assignment. Fifteen structured intervention strategies for modifying a personality-disordered individual's affective, behavioral, and cognitive temperament styles have been described (Sperry, 1999). Table 1.2 lists these interventions.

Cognitive Coping Therapy. Cognitive therapies (CT) and cognitive-behavior therapies (CBT) have long been used in the treatment of personality

Table 1.1
Maladaptive Schemas and Schema Domains

Disconnection and Rejection

Abandonment/Instability: The belief that significant others will not or cannot provide reliable and stable support.

Mistrust/Abuse: The belief that others will abuse, humiliate, cheat, lie, manipulate, or take advantage.

Emotional deprivation: The belief that one's desire for emotional support will not be met by others.

Defectiveness/Shame: The belief that one is defective, bad, unwanted, or inferior in important respects.

Social Isolation/Alienation: The belief that one is alienated, different from others, or not part of any group.

Impaired Autonomy and Performance

Dependence/Incompetence: The belief that one is unable to competently meet everyday responsibilities without considerable help from others.

Vulnerability to Harm or Illness: The exaggerated fear that imminent catastrophe will strike at any time and that one will be unable to prevent it.

Enmeshment/Undeveloped Self: The belief that one must be emotionally close with others at the expense of full individuation or normal social development.

Failure: The belief that one will inevitably fail or is fundamentally inadequate in achieving one's goals.

Impaired Limits

Entitlement/Grandiosity: The belief that one is superior to others and not bound by the rules and norms that govern normal social interaction.

Insufficient Self-Control/Self-Discipline: The belief that one is incapable of self-control and frustration tolerance.

Other-Directedness

Subjugation: The belief that one's desires, needs, and feelings must be suppressed in order to meet the needs of others and avoid retaliation or criticism.

Self-Sacrifice: The belief that one must meet the needs of others at the expense of one's own gratification.

Approval Seeking/Recognition Seeking: The belief that one must constantly seek to belong and be accepted at the expense of developing a true sense of self.

Overvigilance and Inhibition

Negativity/Pessimism: A pervasive, lifelong focus on the negative aspects of life while minimizing the positive and optimistic aspects.

Emotional Inhibition: The excessive inhibition of spontaneous action, feeling, or communication usually to avoid disapproval by others, feelings of shame, or losing control of one's impulses.

Unrelenting Standards/Hypercriticalness: The belief that striving to meet unrealistically high standards of performance is essential in order to be accepted and to avoid criticism.

Punitiveness: The belief that others should be harshly punished for making errors.

Table 1.2
Structured Skill Intervention Strategies (Sperry, 1999, p. 36)

1. Anger Management
2. Anxiety Management Training
3. Assertiveness Training
4. Cognitive Awareness Training
5. Distress Tolerance Training
6. Emotional Regulation Training
7. Empathy Training
8. Limit Setting
9. Impulse Control Training
10. Interpersonal Skills Training
11. Problem-Solving Training
12. Self-Management Training
13. Sensitivity Reduction Training
14. Symptom Management Training
15. Thought Stopping

disorders (Beck, Freeman, & Associates, 1990). Cognitive restructuring, wherein maladaptive beliefs or schemas are identified, processed, and challenged, is the most widely known and utilized treatment strategy associated with those approaches. Coping skills methods are commonly an adjunctive to cognitive restructuring. Typically, therapists using CT and CBT "first turn to cognitive restructuring to treat the presenting problem and then pull from coping skills therapy specific skills to fill out the treatment plan" (Sharoff, 2002). But in complex cases, such as those with chronic depression or anxiety symptoms, low motivation for treatment, emotional lability, and histories of chronic relapse—characteristics common to many personality-disordered individuals—cognitive restructuring has limited utility. However, cognitive coping therapy has been developed as an alternative treatment to cognitive restructuring and appears to be a particularly promising and potent treatment strategy with personality disorders.

As described by Sharoff (2002), cognitive coping therapy is an active, directive, didactic, and structured approach for treating clients in a short time frame. It is a complete and self-contained approach to treatment that begins with assessing an individual's coping skills—in terms of skill chains, subskills, and microskills—and then increasing skill competence in targeted areas as needed. Five key skill areas with representative treatment modalities are *cognitive skills*—problem solving, self-instruction training, and self-management; *emotion skills*—emotional containment and compartmentalization; *perceptual skills*—perspective taking, thought stopping, and psychological distance taking; *physiological skills*—meditation and relaxation training; and *behavior skills*—communication and assertiveness training.

Like the structured skill intervention strategies described by Sperry, the cognitive coping therapy approach is also a bottom-up approach. When combined with top-down treatment strategies such as cognitive restructuring, therapeutic confrontation, or interpretation, it can greatly enhance treatment outcomes in personality-disordered individuals.

Developmental Therapy

As increasing numbers of individuals seek or demand that psychotherapy help them to improve personal, relational, or professional performance—in other words, to become more fully functioning—therapists and focused therapies will rise to the occasion. The developmental focus in psychotherapy that began to emerge in the 1960s and 1970s (Blocher, 1974; Shostrum, 1976) and was subsequently eclipsed is now being retrieved (Cortright, 1997; Blocher, 2002; Sperry, 2002). Such a developmentally focused approach conceptualizes an individual's needs and concerns on a continuum ranging from pathological states to growth states.

The developmental perspective is particularly compatible with the treatment of personality disorders, in that it conceptualizes problem-oriented and growth-oriented needs and views in dimensional rather than in categorical terms—that is, on a continuum from the low to high level of functioning: disordered, adequate, and optimal functioning (Sperry, 2002). Such a developmental-dimensional perspective is superior to the current DSM-IV-TR categorical distinction between pathological functioning and normal functioning or optimal functioning. While it is true that third-party payers may not easily be convinced that it is immediately in their best interest to reimburse for therapy that focuses on optimal functioning, such a developmental conceptualization can serve to not only guide therapists' decisions for optimizing treatment but to guide outcomes research on the cost-effectiveness of such treatment. A brief overview of these three levels of functioning for each of the ten personality disorders is presented in Table 1.3.

A protocol for conducting developmental therapy focused on increasing optimal functioning is described by Sperry (2002). Other developmental approaches for fostering optimal functioning have been described by Cortright (1997) and Blocher (2002).

ORGANIZATIONAL STRUCTURE OF SUBSEQUENT CHAPTERS

Each chapter is divided into five major sections: overview, description, clinical formulations, assessment, and treatment. The overview section provides a brief historical sketch of the disorder including its evolution in DSM. It also reports an incidence/prevalence data on the disorder.

Table 1.3
Developmental Levels of Personality

Obsessive

Optimal	Conscientious but spontaneous individuals who balance personal integrity with generosity, hopefulness, and kindness.
Adequate	Less perfectionism and rigidity in tasks and relationships with some degree of emotional involvement.
Disordered	Perfectionism and feeling avoidance that interferes with task completion and relationships; overly rigid thinking and attitudes; pessimistic and stingy.

Histrionic

Optimal	Having found the love they seek within themselves, they are altruistic and giving without expecting reciprocity.
Adequate	While fun-loving and often impulsive, they can delay gratification and be emotionally appropriate much of the time.
Disordered	Uncomfortable in situations in which he or she is not the center of attention.

Narcissistic

Optimal	Energetic and self-assured without expecting special treatment or privilege.
Adequate	Confident, yet emotionally vulnerable, and favor special treatment or privilege.
Disordered	Manifest a grandiose sense of self-importance and demand special privilege.

Avoidant

Optimal	While sensitive to interpersonal cues and possessing a keen intuition about others, they are nonetheless respectful and compassionate toward others.
Adequate	Maintain a reserved demeanor around others, because they are sensitive and concerned about others' opinion of them.
Disordered	Avoid social and work-related activities that involve significant interpersonal contact because of fear of criticism, disapproval, or rejection.

Schizoid

Optimal	Deeply grounded in themselves, they are emotionally connected to the world.
Adequate	Reasonably comfortable being around others, provided there are limited demands for intimacy or emotional connectedness.
Disordered	They neither desire nor enjoy close relationships.

Dependent

Optimal	May seek out the opinions and advice of others when making major decisions, but the decisions they make are ultimately their own.
Adequate	Have the capacity to be responsible and make decisions, but still seek out and rely on others for help and advice.
Disordered	Need others to assume responsibility for most major areas of their life.

Table 1.3
(Continued)

Antisocial	
Optimal	Have the gift of gab and easily befriend others, although they may not offer much depth to these relationships.
Adequate	Earn respect by acting honorably and with compassion, by using power constructively, and by promoting worthwhile causes.
Disordered	Exhibit aggressive, impulsive, self-serving, and irresponsible behavior.
Borderline	
Optimal	Sensitive, introspective, and impressionable individuals who are very comfortable with their feelings and inner impulses.
Adequate	They quickly and easily engage in relationships and are sometimes hurt and rejected in the process.
Disordered	Display frantic efforts to avoid real or imagined rejection and abandonment.
Schizotypal	
Optimal	Possess the unique capacity to view situations and life differently to benefit others.
Adequate	Immersed in the unique and unusual, irrespective of whether it has any socially redeeming value.
Disordered	Exhibit odd, eccentric, or peculiar behavior, thinking, and speech.
Paranoid	
Optimal	Highly observant and discerning, they can defend themselves without losing control or becoming aggressive.
Adequate	Thin-skinned, they are rather sensitive to and hurt by criticism.
Disordered	Suspicious without a sufficient basis that others are exploiting, harming, or deceiving them.

The section on description provides an extensive discussion of the particular personality disorder in biopsychosocial terms. The emphasis is on aspects of temperament such as cognitive style, emotional style, behavioral style, interpersonal style, and attachment style. To assist the clinician in establishing whether the presentation is one of disorder or style, and what the profile of successful treatment of the disorder would look like, criteria and case examples of both the personality style and disorder are provided. Finally, the DSM-IV description and criteria are listed. Psychiatric formulation can be thought of in terms of descriptive, explanatory, and treatment formulations (Sperry, Gudeman, Blackwell, & Faulkner, 1992). This section represents a descriptive formulation of the disorder.

The next section contains five explanatory conceptualizations of the disorder. The five dominant contemporary formulations are psychodynamic; biosocial—represented largely by Millon (1981, 1985, 1990); cognitive—represented largely by Beck and Freeman (1990)—and behavioral—represented by Turkat (1990);

interpersonal—described by Benjamin (1993); and integrative—developed by Sperry (1990) and Sperry and Mosak (1993).

The section on assessment describes typical interview behavior manifested by the personality-disordered patient and the ease or difficulty of establishing rapport. It also describes characteristic response patterns common for this personality disorder on such psychological tests as the MMPI-I, the MCMI-II, which is based on Millon's (1981, 1990) biosocial formulation and research data, and two common projective tests: the Rorschach and the Therapeutic Apperception Test (TAT). Since psychological testing can be particularly useful in clarifying a dimensional characterization of the patient's personality—that is, where more than one personality disorder or clusters of traits are present—this section may be clinically relevant to psychologists and others who utilize psychological assessment.

The last section contains a number of treatment formulations and is perhaps the most clinically useful. Beginning with a list of typical Axis I and Axis II disorders in the differential diagnosis, other treatment considerations such as general treatment goals and strategies are highlighted.

Three general approaches most commonly utilized in the individual treatment of the disorder are detailed. They are the psychodynamic, the cognitive-behavioral, and the interpersonal approaches. Psychodynamic approaches usually include a description of the ways the traditional analytic method has been modified for this disorder in terms of expressive-supportive terms. The cognitive therapy approach of Beck and Freeman (1990) is highlighted and complemented with the research-based behavioral approach of Turkat (1990). Furthermore, Benjamin's (1993) protocol for interpersonal treatment is presented.

Other modalities of treatment relevant to the disorder are explored along with relevant research on theory indications and efficacy. A unique feature of this book is the discussion of group, marital and family, and psychopharmacology modalities for each disorder. The group treatment modality can be either homogeneous or heterogeneous, and structured and time limited, or less structured and ongoing. *Heterogeneous* refers to the composition group being diverse in terms of functioning. *Homogeneous* refers to the group composition being similar in terms of personality types and level of functioning (Francis, Clarkin, & Perry, 1984). Homogeneous groups lend themselves to being structured and time limited. Finally, specific suggestions for combining modalities and integrating or blending treatment approaches round out this section of the book. Because borderline and narcissistic personality disorders have been very widely discussed and studied, those two chapters are the most extensive in terms of treatment protocols.

Table 1.4
Chapter Outline

I. Overview and Background
II. Description
   1. Defining Characteristics
     a. Style vs. Disorder
     b. Triggering Event
     c. Behavioral Style
     d. Interpersonal Style
     e. Cognitive Style
     f. Affective Style
     g. Attachment Style
     h. Optimal DSM-IV-TR Criterion
   2. DSM-IV-TR Description and Criteria
III. Formulations
   1. Psychodynamic
   2. Biosocial
   3. Cognitive-Behavioral
   4. Interpersonal
   5. Integrative
IV. Assessment
   1. Interview Behavior and Rapport
   2. Psychological Testing Data
     a. MMPI-2
     b. MCMI-III
     c. TAT/Rorschach
V. Treatment Approaches and Interventions
   1. Treatment Considerations
   2. Individual Psychotherapy
     a. Psychodynamic Psychotherapy Approach
     b. Cognitive-Behavioral Therapy Approach
     c. Interpersonal Psychotherapy Approach
   4. Group Therapy
   5. Marital and Family Therapy
   6. Medication
   7. Combined and Integrative Treatment Approaches

Defining Characteristics of Personality Disorders

A key to providing effective treatment of the personality disorders is an in-depth understanding of how and why personality disorder pathology develops as well as how it is experienced by both the personality-disordered individual and related others. Although the narrative of each chapter provides a detailed description of a given personality disorder, a table providing a capsule summary of these defining characteristics is included. Its purposes

Table 1.5
Defining Characteristics of a Personality Disorder

Triggering Event(s)
Behavioral Style
Interpersonal Style
Cognitive Style
Emotional Style
Temperament
Attachment Style
Parental Injunction
Self-View
Worldview
Maladaptive Schema
Optimal DSM-IV-TR Criteria

are to facilitate initial learning about the disorder and to serve as a subsequent reference source. Table 1.5 lists these characteristics. This is followed by a brief description of each characteristic.

Triggering Event(s). The characteristic and predictable situations, circumstances, or other stimuli that initiate a characteristic maladaptive response—in family or intimate relations, in social situations, or in work settings (Othmer & Othmer, 2002)—reflected in the individual's behavioral, interpersonal, cognitive, and emotional styles. Triggering events can be intrapersonal, such as failing an exam, or interpersonal—that is, a narcissistic injury.

Behavioral Style. The characteristic way in which an individual reacts personally to a triggering event. Examples include self-centeredness, impatience, defensiveness, and arrogance.

Interpersonal Style. The characteristic way in which an individual relates to others. Examples include exploitive, disdainful, socially facile without empathy, pleasing, clinging, blaming, and condescending.

Cognitive Style. The characteristic way in which an individual perceives and thinks about a problem, and then conceives and implements a solution. Examples include analytic, methodical, global or thematic, cautious, and careless.

Emotional/Feeling Style. The characteristic way in which an individual responds with various types and intensities of affects. Examples include anger, rage, elation, and mood lability.

Temperament. An inborn, characteristic response pattern reflecting an individual's energy level, emotional makeup, intensity, and tempo of response that serves as "a filter of personality through which information is processed, attachments evolve, and emotions are experienced and expressed" (Graybar & Boutilier, 2002, p. 156). Examples include inhibited, impulsive, reflective, and aggressive.

Attachment Style. The pattern of adult relating that reflects the emotional bond between parent and infant, which influences affect regulation, psychological resilience, access to autobiographical memory, and the development of self-reflection and narrative. Styles are either secure or insecure (Ainsworth et al., 1978; Erdman & Caffery, 2003). Examples of insecure styles noted in personality-disordered individuals include preoccupied, fearful, dismissing, and disorganized.

Parental Injunction. An expressed or implied parental expectation for what a child should be or how a child should act. Examples are: "You can't do it by yourself"; "You must be better to be worthwhile"; and "Never make mistakes."

Self-View. An individual's personal conception of self, including a self-evaluation of abilities, personal worth, potential, and goals. Examples include: "I am defective"; "I need the attention of others to feel important and worthwhile"; "I am special and entitled" (Sperry, 1999).

Worldview. An individual's evaluative conception of life, the world, and other people, including beliefs about human nature and finding a sense of belonging and worth. Examples include: "Life is a struggle"; "People can't be trusted"; "Others are here to take care of me" (Sperry, 1999).

Maladaptive Schemas. Schemas are enduring and self-defeating patterns regarding one's view of self and of the world and others developed during childhood and elaborated throughout one's lifetime. They cause negative thoughts and feelings, and interfere with accomplishing goals and meeting one's needs (Young et al., 2003). Examples include defectiveness, social isolation, approval-seeking, and self-sacrifice.

Optimal DSM-IV-TR Criterion. The single criterion—of the seven to nine stated DSM-IV-TR criteria—most useful in diagnosing of that disorder. It is believed that if clinicians could remember one key criterion for each personality disorder, they "could then test for the presence or absence of that criterion and quickly diagnose the personality disorder" (Allnutt & Links, 1996, p. 22). Their "optimal criterion" is based on three characteristics: its protypicality (i.e., having a high correlation with the sum of all criteria for that disorder), an apt behavioral description, and a high positive predictive value (i.e., the probability the individual has the criteria of the target disorder). Data on protypicality and predictive value were derived from research with the *Structured Interview for Diagnosing Personality–Revised* (Allnutt & Links, 1996).

CONCLUDING NOTE

At the outset of this new millennium, clinicians are considerably more confident and effective in working with personality-disordered individuals than any time in the history of psychiatry and the mental health sciences. Whereas 20 years ago many if not most clinicians believed these disorders to be untreatable, now clinicians can point to both clinical experience and research evidence that indicate personality-disordered individuals, including those with borderline personality disorder, can be helped to increase their functioning and well-being. The emerging shift in the treatment paradigm of personality disorders is fully underway and promises to be as exciting and far-ranging as was the earlier paradigm shift in diagnosing and treating depressive disorders.

This chapter has previewed a number of cutting-edge developments involving the conceptualization, assessment and diagnosis, and treatment of DSM-IV-TR personality disorders. Many of these developments in diagnosis and treatment are incorporated in subsequent chapters. My hope is that this revised edition will further foster an attitude of confidence and a measure of competence in clinicians when working with personality-disordered individuals.

CHAPTER 2

Antisocial Personality Disorder

In the past, individuals with antisocial personality disorder have been called psychopaths, sociopaths, or dyssocial personalities. Descriptions of antisocial personality can be traced to early Greek literature. It was the protypal personality disorder, in that the term *psychopath* referred originally to personality disorders in general. The psychopathic personality as described by Cleckley (1941) included superficial charm, unreliability, poor judgment, and a lack of social responsibility, guilt, anxiety, and remorse. The term *psychopath* was replaced by *sociopath* to reflect the social rather than purely psychological origins of the disorder. In DSM-II, the term *antisocial personality* became the preferred designation. DSM-III added detailed diagnostic criteria for this diagnosis, which largely emphasized criminal activity and behavior. Dynamically oriented clinicians criticized the criteria for disregarding psychodynamic qualities such as incapacity for love, failure to learn from experience, and lack of shame or remorse. DSM-III-R responded to such criticism by adding the criterion "lacks remorse." Changes in DSM-IV criteria are notable for their emphasis on psychopathic traits and deemphasis on criminal behaviors (Widiger & Corbitt, 1993; Gabbard, 2000).

In terms of DSM-IV-TR changes to antisocial personality disorder, the "Associated Features and Disorders" section of the text was revised to "clarify that features that are part of the traditional conception of psychopathy may be more predictive of recidivism in settings (e.g., prisons) where criminal acts are likely to be nonspecific" (American Psychiatric Association, 2000, p. 842). Specifically, the features referred to are "lack of empathy, inflated self-appraisal and superficial charm" (p. 703).

Furthermore, a history of conduct disorder in childhood is often present in adults with a diagnosis of antisocial personality disorder. Accordingly, efforts to identify risk factors in children for conduct disorder is an important step in preventing progression of conduct disorder to antisocial personality disorder (Holmes et al., 2001).

Overall prevalence of this disorder is about 3 percent for males and 1 percent for females. In clinical settings, prevalence estimates vary from 3 to 30 percent, with higher rates associated with prisons, forensic settings, and substance abuse treatment programs.

This chapter describes the characteristic features of antisocial personality disorder and its related personality style. Five clinical formulations of the disorder and psychological assessment indicators are highlighted. A variety of treatment approaches, modalities, and intervention strategies are also described.

DESCRIPTION OF THE ANTISOCIAL PERSONALITY DISORDER

Antisocial personality disorder can be recognized by the following descriptors and characteristics: style vs. disorder, triggering event, behavioral style, interpersonal style, cognitive style, affective style, attachment style, and optimal criterion.

Style vs. Disorder. Antisocial personalities can be thought of as spanning a continuum from healthy to pathological, wherein antisocial personality style is on the healthy end and antisocial personality disorder is on the pathological end. Table 2.1 compares and contrasts the antisocial personality style and disorder.

Triggering Event. The typical situation, circumstance, or event that most likely triggers or activates the characteristic maladaptive response of antisocial personality disorder (Othmer & Othmer, 2002), as noted in behavioral, interpersonal, cognitive, and feeling styles, is "social standards and rules."

Table 2.1
A Comparison of Antisocial Personality Style and Disorder

Personality Style	*Personality Disorder*
Prefer free-lancer living, and live well by their talents, skills, ingenuity, and wits	Unable to sustain consistent work behavior
Tend to live by their own internal code of values and are not much influenced by others or society's norms	Fail to conform to social norms with regard to lawful behavior, performing antisocial acts that are grounds for arrest (rule breaking)
As adolescents were usually high-spirited hell-raisers and mischief makers	Irritable and aggressive as indicated by physical fights or assaults
Tend to be generous with money	Repeated failures to honor financial obligation, believing that as money is spent more will turn up somewhere and somehow
Tend to be wonderlusts, but are able to make plans and commitments, albeit for limited time spans	Fail to plan ahead, or impulsive as indicated by moving about without a prearranged job or clear goals
Tend to be silver-tongued, gifted in the art of winning friends	Have no regard for the truth as indicated by repeated lying, use of aliases, or conning others for personal profit or pleasure
Tend to be courageous, physically bold and tough; will stand up to those who take advantage of them	Reckless regarding their own and others' personal safety as indicated by driving while intoxicated or recurrent speeding
Tend not to worry too much about others, expecting others to be responsible for themselves	If a parent or guardian lacks ability to function as a responsible parent
Have strong libido, and although they may desire several partners, they can remain monogamous	Have never sustained a totally monogamous relationship for long periods of time
Tend to live in the present and don't feel much guilt	Lack remorse (feel justified in having hurt, mistreated, or stolen from others)

Behavioral Style. The behavioral style of antisocial personalities is characterized by impulsivity, irritability, and aggressiveness. They are likely to be irresponsible in honoring work commitments and financial obligations. Rule breaking is typical. Antisocial personality–disordered individuals are also noted for their impulsive anger, deceitfulness, and cunning. They tend to be forceful individuals who regularly engage in risk-seeking and thrill-seeking behavior.

Interpersonal Style. Their interpersonal style is characterized by antagonism and reckless disregard of others' needs and safety. They tend to be highly competitive and distrustful of others and often poor losers. Their relationships may at times appear to be "slick" as well as calculating. These behaviors can characterize the successful businessperson, policitican, and professional, as well as the criminal. They tend to develop superficial relationships that involve few, if any, lasting emotional ties or commitments. Furthermore, they tend to be callous toward the pain and suffering of others.

Cognitive Style. The cognitive style of the antisocial personality is described as impulsive and cognitively inflexible as well as externally oriented. They tend to be keenly aware of social cues and may be quite adept at "reading" people and situations. Because they are contemptuous of authority, rules, and social norms, they easily rationalize their own behavior. Impulsivity, irritability, and aggressivity predispose them to argumentation and even assaultive action. Recent research indicates that there tends to be significant neuropsychological impairment in individuals diagnosed with this disorder. In particular, there is likely to be impairment in executive functioning tasks of planning ability and set shifting (Dolan & Park, 2002).

Affective Style. Their emotional or affective style is characterized as shallow and superficial. They avoid "softer" emotions such as warmth and intimacy because they regard these as signs of weakness. Guilt is seldom if ever experienced. They are unable to tolerate boredom, depression, or frustration and subsequently are sensation-seekers. Finally, they may show little guilt, shame, or remorse for their own deviant actions.

Attachment Style. Individuals with a view of others that is negative and a self-view that vacillates between positive and negative exhibit a composite fearful–dismissing style of attachment. They tend to view themselves as special and entitled but are also mindful of their need for others who can potentially hurt them. Accordingly, they use others to meet their needs while being wary and dismissive of them. Fearful–dismissing attachment style is associated with antisocial personality disorder.

Optimal DSM-IV-TR Criterion. Of all the stated DSM-IV-TR criteria for antisocial personality disorder, one criterion has been found to be the most useful in diagnosis. The belief is that by beginning with this criterion, the clinician can test for the presence or absence of the criterion and quickly diagnose the personality disorder (Allnutt & Links, 1996). The optimal criterion for this disorder is "criminal, aggressive, impulsive, irresponsible behavior."

The following two cases further illustrate differences between antisocial personality disorder (Juan G.) and antisocial personality style (Gordon J).

Case Study: Antisocial Personality Disorder

Juan G. is a 28-year-old Cuban male who presented late in the evening to the emergency room at a community hospital complaining of a headache. His description of the pain was vague and contradictory. At one point he said the pain had been present for 3 days, whereas at another point it was "many years." He indicated that the pain led to violent behavior and described how, during a headache episode, he had brutally assaulted a medic while he was in the air force. He gave a long history of arrests for assault, burglary, and drug dealing. Neurological and mental status examinations were within normal limits except for some mild agitation. He insisted that only Darvon—a narcotic—would relieve his headache pain. The patient resisted a plan for further diagnostic tests or a follow-up clinic appointment, saying unless he was treated immediately "something really bad could happen."

Case Study: Antisocial Personality Style

Gordon J. is the 38-year-old president of a rapidly expanding manufacturing company. He has taken over the small business that his uncle had founded after World War II. Gordon has greatly increased production, added new product lines, and formed a marketing and sales group that he has personally supervised in his 9 years of running the company. Prior to taking over the company, Gordon had become the youngest member of the million-dollar club for selling real estate for the firm for which he had worked for just 3 years. His father had died in a freak skiing accident when Gordon was 11, but that didn't seem to stop Gordon from pursuing his fascination with scuba diving and hang glider flying. Gordon was invited to join the Young President's Organization in his region soon after turning his uncle's corporation into a highly profitable enterprise. He was quite popular in the group given his magnetic personality, visionary outlook, and captivating stories of his various exploits.

He had been married for nearly 5 years before divorcing. Since then he has not remarried but has maintained ongoing relationships with two women.

DSM-IV-TR Description and Criteria

Antisocial personality–disordered individuals in and out of therapeutic situations are likely to be impulsive, deceitful, irresponsible, and rule bender and breakers. Table 2.2 provides the DSM-IV-TR clinical description and criteria.

FORMULATIONS OF THE ANTISOCIAL PERSONALITY DISORDER

Psychodynamic Formulation

Psychoanalytic writers describe the antisocial personality as similar to the narcissistic personality. While both form a pathological grandiose self, the antisocial individual's self is based on an aggressive introject, called the "stranger self-object" (Meloy, 1988). This self-object reflects an experience of the parent as a stranger who cannot be trusted and who harbors bad will toward the infant. Not surprisingly, this threatening internalized object derives from experiences of parental neglect or cruelty. Combined with an absence of

Table 2.2
DSM-IV-TR Criteria for Antisocial Personality Disorder (301.70)

A. There is a pervasive pattern of disregard for and violation of the rights of others occurring since age 15, as indicated by at least three of the following:
   (1) failure to conform to social norms with respect to lawful behaviors as indicated by repeatedly performing acts that are grounds for arrest.
   (2) irritability and aggressiveness, as indicated by repeated physical fights or assaults.
   (3) consistent irresponsibility, as indicated by repeated failure to sustain consistent work behavior or honor financial obligations.
   (4) impulsivity or failure to plan ahead.
   (5) deceitfulness, as indicated by repeated lying, use of aliases, or conning others for personal profit or pleasure.
   (6) reckless disregard for safety of self or others.
   (7) lack or remorse, as indicated by being indifferent to or rationalizing having hurt, mistreated, or stolen from another.
B. The individual is at least 18 years old.
C. There is evidence of conduct disorder with onset before age 15.
D. Occurrence of antisocial behavior is not exclusively during the course of schizophrenia or a manic episode.

a loving maternal object is a lack of basic trust and a fixation in the separation-individuation process so that object constancy does not occur. Since the mother is experienced as a stranger or predator, the infant's emotional attachment to her is derailed, leading to a detachment from all relationships and affective experiences as well as sadistic attempts to bond with others through destructive and controlling behaviors.

As a result, antisocial individuals do not perceive others as separate individuals. Hence, they cannot develop the capacity for guilt and depressive anxieties based on how their actions hurt others. A corollary is that they are incapable of true depression. Kernberg (1984) notes that these antisocial individuals are similarly stunned in superego development, except for sadistic superego precursors manifested by cruel and sadistic behaviors. Higher-functioning antisocial individuals are noted to have some development of consciousness with circumscribed areas—called superego lacunae—where the superego does not seem to function. Furthermore, antisocial individuals show little interest in rationalizing or morally justifying their behavior, or adherence to a value system other than the exploitive, aggressive exercise of power (Kernberg, 1984; Meloy, 1988).

Biosocial Formulation

There is mounting evidence that biological factors influence the development of antisocial personality. Low levels of the neurotransmitter serotonin have been noted in individuals prone to aggressive and impulsive behavior. Meloy (1988) suggests that antisocial individuals often have histories of childhood abuse or neglect. They are likely to have had a difficult infant temperament (Thomas & Chess, 1977), meaning they were difficult to soothe and comfort, which may have interfered with the normal attachment process, further increasing the probability of childhood abuse or neglect. Millon and Everly (1985) suggest that low thresholds for limbic system stimulation are likely in antisocial individuals. Meloy (1988) adds that antisocial individuals have been found to be autonomically hyperreactive, possibly because of their inability to learn from experience, and thus manifest less anticipatory anxiety to deter them from ill-advised behavior.

Environmental factors such as parental hostility, deficient parental role modeling, and reinforcement of vindictive behavior appear to interact with these biological predisposing factors. Parental hostility may result from the child's disruptiveness with the parents, from the perception that these children are ill-tempered, or because these children are used as scapegoats for the parents' or family's frustration. Deficient parental modeling, such as when there is little or no parental guidance or there is no authority figure in the home, can also factor into the child's antisocial personality. Without such an authority figure to model and feeling abandoned or rejected, these children often become streetwise and hardened to the world around them. Out of these experiences they learn that "the end justifies the means," "it's a dog-eat-dog world," and "you've got to be strong and crafty to survive." Not surprisingly, this defiant behavior is met with social disapproval, which further reinforces their self-reliance and hardened outlook. As a result, they learn not to trust others, and anticipating that others intend to exploit or humiliate them, they strike out at others with vindictive behaviors.

This personality pattern is self-perpetuated through consistent perceptual distortion, a demeaning attitude toward affection and cooperation, and antagonistic and vindictive behavior that breeds antagonisticism in return. Further, this pattern is perpetuated by their fear of being used and forced into an inferior, dominated position (Millon & Everly, 1985).

Cognitive-Behavioral Formulation

According to Beck and Freeman (1990), the behavior of individuals with antisocial personality disorder is guided by a number of self-serving dysfunctional cognitions. These frequently include justification: the belief that wanting something or wanting to avoid something justifies one's actions; thinking is believing: the belief that one's thoughts and feelings are always accurate; personal inflexibility: the belief that one's choices are invariably right and good; feelings make facts: the belief that one is right because one feels right about one's actions; or the belief that others' views are irrelevant to one's decisions; and low-impact consequences: the belief that undesirable consequences will not occur or will not matter to the individual.

Underlying these dysfunctional cognitions are beliefs about self and the world. Antisocial individuals tend to view themselves as loners, autonomous and strong. They tend to view life as harsh and cruel and others as either exploitive and manipulative or as weak and vulnerable. Accordingly, they believe that they must look out for themselves and adopt the strategy of overtly attacking others, or "con" them by subtly manipulating or exploiting them. Another core belief is that the antisocial individual is always right, which absolves these individuals from questioning their actions. Similarly, because of their mistrust, antisocial individuals are unlikely to seek the advice or guidance of others regarding their past, present, or anticipated actions. Furthermore, they are likely to dismiss unsolicited counsel from others as irrelevant to their purposes. Finally, antisocial individuals are oriented only to the present, eschewing a lack of concern for future outcomes.

Evans and Sullivan (1990) find that several thinking errors or manipulative strategies characterize antisocial individuals. These include mind reading, minimizing, excuse making, blaming, superoptimism, vagueness, power plays, lying, intellectualizing, and excitement seeking. Turkat (1990) describes three subtypes: the clear sociopath—meaning the individuals clearly and obviously meet DSM-III-R criteria; the clever sociopath—these individuals feign psychological symptoms usually to avoid legal responsibility for their actions; and the hurting sociopath—who meet DSM criteria but are sincerely and genuinely distressed. He observes that all three types have deficit regarding the management of impulses and anger, but that only the hurting sociopath is somewhat amenable to treatment.

Interpersonal Formulation

Benjamin (1996) reports that persons with antisocial personality disorders typically have developmental histories of harsh, neglectful parenting. The adult consequence is that the antisocial individual neglects and is insensitive to others' needs, or exploits others. This unpredictable pattern of parenting tends to result in undermodulated parental control and blaming. The result is that as adults, antisocial individuals fiercely protect their autonomy. Furthermore, this pattern of inept parental caring can be internalized by the antisocial individual as substance abuse, criminal behavior, or parental dereliction of duty. The antisocial-to-be is likely to take over parental responsibilities since no one else has. As a consequence of this inappropriate parental role-taking, the antisocial individual is likely to continue controlling others as an end in itself, without emotionally bonding with those being controlled. In short, a sustained pattern of inappropriate and unmodualted desire for control of others is prominent. There is also a strong need for independence and for resisting being controlled by others who are typically held in contempt. Unbridled aggressivity is frequently utilized to sustain control and independence. Finally, antisocial-disordered individuals may present friendly and sociable, albeit in a somewhat detachment, since they have little regard for others.

Integrative Formulation

The following integrative formulation may be helpful in understanding how the antisocial personality developed and is maintained. Biologically, antisocial personalities manifested "difficult child" temperaments (Thomas & Chess, 1977). As such they were unpredictable, tended to withdraw from situations, showed high intensity, and had a fairly low, discontented mood. This ill-tempered infantile pattern has been described by Millon (1996) as resulting in part from a low threshold for limbic stimulation and a decrease in inhibitory centers of the central nervous system. Their body types tend to be endomorphic—thin and frail—or mesomorphic—athletic (Millon, 1981).

Psychologically, their view of themselves, others, the world, and life's purpose can be articulated in terms of the following themes. They tend to view themselves with some variant of the theme: "I am cunning and entitled to get whatever I want." In other words, they see themselves as strong, competitive, energetic, and tough. Their view of life and the world is a variant of the theme: "Life is devious and hostile, and rules keep me from fulfilling my needs." Not surprisingly, their life's goal has a variant of the theme: "Therefore, I'll bend or break these rules because my needs come first, and I'll defend against efforts to be controlled or degraded by others." Acting out and rationalization are common defense mechanisms used by the antisocial personality.

Socially predictable parenting styles and environmental factors can be noted for antisocial personality disorder. Typically, the parenting style is characterized by hostility and deficient parental modeling. Or, the parents might have provided such good modeling that the child could not or refused to live up to the high standards. The parental injunction is, "The end justifies the means." Thus, vindictive behavior is modeled and reinforced. The family structure tends to be disorganized and disengaged. The antisocial pattern is confirmed, reinforced, and perpetuated by the following individual and systems factors: The need to be powerful and the fear of being abused and humiliated leads to a denial of "softer" emotions plus uncooperativeness. This, along with the tendency to provoke others, leads to further reinforcement of antisocial beliefs and behaviors (Sperry & Mosak, 1996).

ASSESSMENT OF ANTISOCIAL PERSONALITY DISORDER

Several sources of information are useful in establishing a diagnosis and treatment plan for personality disorders. Observation, collateral information, and psychological testing are important adjuncts to the patient's self-report in the clinical interview. This section briefly describes some characteristic observations that the clinician makes and the nature of the rapport likely to develop in initial encounters with specific personality-disordered individuals. Characteristic response patterns on various objective (i.e., MMPI-2 and MCMI-III) and projective tests (i.e., Rorschach and TAT) are also described.

Table 2.3
Characteristics of Antisocial Personality Disorder

Triggering Event	Social standards and rules.
Behavioral Style	Impulsively angry, hostile, cunning; forceful, risk-taking, thrill-seeking; temper, verbally or physically abusive.
Interpersonal Style	Antagonistic to belligerent; "slick" and calculating; highly competitive and poor losers; distrustful of others.
Cognitive Style	Impulsive, inflexible, and externally oriented; hard-nosed, realistic, and devious; acting-out defense.
Feeling Style	Glib, shallow, superficial; avoid "softer" emotions (i.e., warmth and intimacy), which connote weakness.
Temperament	Ill-tempered infantile pattern; aggressive, impulsive adult pattern.
Attachment Style	Fearful and dismissing.
Parental Injunction	"The end justifies the means."
Self-View	"I'm cunning and I'm entitled to get what I want." They view themselves as strong, competitive, self-reliant, energetic, and tough.
World View	"Life is devious and hostile, and rules keep me from fulfilling my needs. Therefore, I'll bend or break them because my needs come first, and I'll defend any efforts to be controlled or degraded."
Maladaptive Schemas	Mistrust/abuse; entitlement; insufficient self-control; defectiveness; emotional deprivation; abandonment; social isolation.
Optimal DSM-IV-TR Criteria	Criminal, aggressive, impulsive, irresponsible behavior.

Interview Behavior and Rapport

Interviewing antisocial personality–disordered individuals can be particularly challenging. Although it is easy to communicate with them as long as the clinician plays along, they become angry and critical when the clinician resists their manipulations. It is very difficult to have them focus on their impulsivity, irresponsibility, or the negative consequences of their actions. Such lack of genuineness and sincerity limits rapport. Nevertheless, these individuals crave attention, and the clinician can stimulate discussion by encouraging them to display their accomplishment. By avoiding a judgmental or accusatory tone, the clinician may be able to encourage cooperation and explore the negative consequences of their actions.

When they are unwilling to cooperate, answer questions, or adopt a complaining or hostile posture, the clinician does well to display indifference or initiate termination of the interview. Both of these strategies may quickly reverse their behavior. However, while they are seldom remorseful about their deceit and mistreatment of others, they can be made to realize that things are going poorly for them and they are ruining their lives. The clinician can establish rapport and review their difficulties free of distortions and lies by showing empathy for the consequences of their behavior and failures. Only when they perceive the clinician as a nonpunitive ally who will support their constructive goals and as someone who shows understanding of their inability to follow social forms can they begin to form a therapeutic alliance (Othmer & Othmer, 2002).

Psychological Testing Data

The Minnesota Multiphase Personality Inventory (MMPI-2), the Millon Clinical Multiaxal Inventory (MCMI-II), the Rorschach Psychodiagnostic Test, and the Thematic Apperception Test (TAT) can be useful in diagnosing the antisocial personality style or trait.

On the MMPI-2, the 4-9/9-4 (Psychopathic Deviant–Hypomania) profile is considered the classic profile of antisocial personality disorder. While the 9 represents the activator energizer of acting-out behavior, the 4 represents the cognitive component of the psychopathy (Graham, 2000). Two patterns of antisocial personality or psychopathology have been noted (Megargee & Bohn, 1979). The primary psychopath is easily provoked to violence, and thus a spike on scale 4 (psychopathic deviant) with elevators on 6 (paranoid) and 8 (schizophrenia) are likely. The 4-9/9-4 profile is more suggestive of secondary psychopathy as is the 2-4/4-2 (depression–psychopathic deviant) profile (Meyer, 1995).

On the MCMI-II, elevation on scales 5 (narcissistic) and 6A (antisocial) is most likely. Because alcohol and drug abuse are common in antisocial individuals, elevations in B (alcohol dependence) and/or T (drug dependence) are expected. Since antisocial individuals are usually not highly distressed, elevations on A (anxiety), D (dysthymia), and H (somatoform) are not common (Choca & Denburg, 1997).

Projective techniques can be very helpful in assessing the antisocial patient's object relations and superego development. Although patients are more likely to deceive a clinician during a clinical interview by simulating guilt or remorse, they are less likely to do so with ambiguous stimuli such as Rorschach blots where there are no "correct" answer (Gabbard, 2000).

On the Rorschach, antisocial individuals tend to produce only a low to average number of responses, and they even reject cards that they could clearly handle cognitively. There is often a delayed reaction to the color cards, but then they may respond with C (pure color) responses in a fairly primitive and impulsive manner. They tend to give a high number of A (animal) and P (popular) responses, and a low number of M (human movement) and W (whole) responses. An absence of shading (Y, YF, and FY) and a low number of Form plus (F+%) responses is noted (Wagner & Wagner, 1981).

On the TAT, their stories tend to be juvenile and sophomoric. And, while the protagonist may be caught in a negative act, there is usually no mention of the consequences of the negative act (Bellak, 1997).

TREATMENT APPROACHES AND INTERVENTIONS

Treatment Considerations

This diagnosis is reserved for individuals over age 18 who have a history of symptoms of conduct disorder before age 15. The designation, adult antisocial behavior, is used to describe criminal, aggressive, or other antisocial behavior that does not meet full criteria for antisocial personality disorder.

The differential diagnosis for antisocial personality disorder includes other Axis II personality disorders such as narcissistic personality disorder and paranoid personality disorder. The most common Axis I syndromes associated with antisocial personality disorder are substance abuse and dependence, acute anxiety states, delusional disorders, and factitious disorders.

In terms of treatment goals, there is a consensus that prognosis is guarded with most treatment modalities unless the specific patient attributes are present (i.e., core depressive features). Typically, these individuals are not interested in treatment or are refractory to treatment if it is made compulsory by employees, family members, or the courts (Reid, 1989). What about research support and evidenced-based guidelines for the treatment of this disorder? To date, no controlled treatment outcome studies have been completed for dependent personality disorder (Crits-Christoph & Barber, 2002).

Individual Psychotherapy

This section reviews the psychodynamic, cognitive-behavioral, and interpersonal approaches of individual psychotherapy with antisocial personality–disordered individuals.

Psychodynamic Psychotherapy Approach

There is relatively little literature on successful treatment outcomes of individual dynamic psychotherapy with antisocial personality–disordered individuals. In fact, there is widespread pessimism that dynamic psychotherapy can change the antisocial pattern (Vaillant & Perry, 1985). A number of explanations have been offered for this seeming failure. These explanations involve both patient selection and therapeutic stance and interventions.

Gabbard (1990) indicates that the clinician's task at the outset of treatment is to determine which patients are "worth" the time, energy, and money required by a long-term therapy process with an uncertain outcome. Meloy (1988) has identified five contraindications for psychotherapy with antisocial patients: (1) a history of sadistic, violent behavior toward others; (2) total absence of remorse for such behavior; (3) a longstanding incapacity to develop emotional attachments; (4) high or low intelligence that can thwart the therapeutic process; and (5) clinicians' intense countertransference fear for their personal safety. In short, the more the patient resembles the dynamic profile of the pure psychopath, the less likely he or she is to respond to dynamic psychotherapy.

On the other hand, antisocial patients with narcissistic features may be somewhat more amenable to psychotherapy. They may reveal some dependency in the transferences, and their internal "ideal object" may be somewhat less aggressive than in the pure psychopath (Meloy, 1988). The presence of major depression may reflect amenability to psychotherapy (Woody et al., 1985). Turkat (1990) notes that the "hurting sociopath" who is sincerely and genuinely distressed has potential for profiting from psychotherapy. However, the most important predictor of treatment success is the ability to form a therapeutic alliance. Gertsley et al. (1989) showed a significant association between the ability to form a therapeutic alliance and treatment outcome in their study of 48 methadone-maintained male opiate addicts who meet criteria for antisocial personality disorder.

Parenthetically, a study of sex difference in treatment recommendations for antisocial personality is thought-provoking. A survey was undertaken involving 119 clinical psychologists who responded to case histories depicting either a male or female with antisocial personality disorder and somatization. Results showed that clinicians were less likely to diagnose antisocial personality disorder correctly for female than for male patients. Females were consistently given better prognoses and were more likely to be recommended for insight-oriented psychotherapy than males, who were given poorer prognoses and were more likely to be recommended for group therapy and legal constraints (Fernbach et al., 1989).

Therapeutic stance and intervention strategy and techniques are other important factors in the treatment outcome equation. The traditional dynamic stance of neutrality is contraindicated. Gabbard (2000) contends that neutrality is tantamount to silent endorsement or collusion with the antisocial patient's actions. Instead, the recommended therapeutic stance is active and confrontative. The clinician will need to repeatedly confront the patient's minimization and denial of antisocial behavior. Furthermore, confrontation must focus on here-and-now behavior rather than analyzing unconscious material from the past.

From a dynamic perspective, it is crucial for the clinician to assist the patient in linking actions with internal states. Finally, the clinician's expectation for therapeutic change must be starkly realistic. Gabbard (1994) cautions that antisocial patients take delight in thwarting the clinician's wishes for them to change.

Needless to say, countertransference issues are important in working with antisocial patients. Two common forms are disbelief and collusion (Symington, 1980). Disbelief involves the clinician's rationalization that the patient is not really "that bad." Collusion is perhaps the most problematic type of countertransference. Gabbard insists that the clinician be stable, persistent, and thoroughly incorruptible, as these patients will do whatever is necessary to corrupt the clinician into dishonest or unethical behavior. Through simulated tearfulness, sadness, or remorse, they can manipulate the clinician into empathizing with them.

As noted previously, there are studies of dynamic treatment with antisocial patients. One study of severe personality-disordered individuals, including those with antisocial personality disorder, found that significant split self-representations were present in the 27 patients studied. Relaxation exercises and a merging intervention were utilized to reduce the amnestic barriers that maintained this compartmentalization. Results showed the 24 patients responded with reduced resistance, increased treatment compliance, and improved daily functioning (Glantz & Goisman, 1990).

Cognitive-Behavioral Therapy Approach

Beck, Freeman, and Associates (1990) provide an extended discussion of the cognitive therapy approach to antisocial personality–disordered individuals. They note that it is particularly difficult to develop a collaborative working relationship with these patients. These patients are difficult to work with because they are likely to distrust the therapist, are uncomfortable accepting help, and have little motivation because of the therapist's countertransference. Establishing rapport requires the therapist to avoid, or disengage from, positions of control or power struggles with them, as well as to admit vulnerability to their manipulativeness. Since these individuals are likely to lie, the therapist can avoid entrapment in the role of being arbiter of truth by admitting that it could happen. To avoid premature termination, it is suggested that the therapist work gradually to establish trust, explicitly acknowledge the antisocial individual's strengths and capabilities, and refrain from pressing the individual to acknowledge weaknesses. Premature termination may also occur if the individual's distress (i.e., depression or anxiety symptoms), is quickly alleviated. In such instances, Beck suggests pointing out that continuing in therapy is in the individual's best interest and identifying any remaining distress that the individual may be denying or minimizing.

After treatment goals have been agreed upon, focusing on specific problem situations with problem-solving and behavioral strategies is suggested. For impulse control, acting out, or inappropriate expression of anger, impulse control and anger management strategies are advised. As these individuals become better able to control impulses and anticipate consequences of their actions, shifting the therapeutic focus to automatic thoughts and underlying schemas is possible. This transition from a largely behavioral focus to a more cognitive one gradually allows these individuals to become less vulnerable and more comfortable in disclosing thoughts and feelings. As planned termination of treatment approaches, the focus shifts to the social pressures the individual faces due to continued antisocial behavior. Relapse prevention strategies are useful in sensitizing these patients to people, places, and circumstances that are potential triggers for antisocial thinking and behaviors. Presuming that the individual has learned sufficient social skills to fit in with a prosocial group, the likelihood of effective coping in the face of social pressures is increased. Beck notes that group and family therapy can be a useful adjunct to individual treatment.

Furthermore, Freeman et al. (1990) believe that cognitive therapy can be effective in not only reducing antisocial behavior but in assisting the individual to adopt a more prosocial lifestyle. They caution that these individuals often terminate treatment prematurely unless they experience sufficient distress from an Axis I condition, which provides an incentive for continuing to work in treatment.

Structured Skill Treatment Interventions. While research shows that medication can modulate or normalize dysregulated behaviors, a similar modulating effect has also been noted for social skills training (Lieberman, DeRisi, & Mueser, 1989). Thus, it appears that social skills training is a relatively potent bottom-up treatment strategy for normalizing limbic system–mediated behaviors that reflect specific skill deficits in personality-disordered individuals. When such skill deficits are present, Sperry (1999) contends that structured skill training intervention is a potent and effective strategy in treatment. Several structured intervention strategies for modifying a personality-disordered individual's affective, behavioral, and cognitive temperament styles are relevant for treatment of antisocial personality disorder (Sperry, 1999).

Schema Therapy. Schema therapy is an elaboration of cognitive therapy that has been developed by Young (1999) and Young and associates (2003) specifically for personality disorders and other difficult individual and couples problems. Schema therapy involves identifying maladaptive schemas and planning specific strategies and interventions. Four main strategies are cognitive, experiential, behavioral, and the therapeutic relationship itself. Cognitive restructuring—modification of maladaptive schemas—is an important cognitive strategy, but is combined with imagery exercises, empathic confrontation, homework assignments, and "limited reparenting" (i.e., a form of corrective emotional experience; Young, 1999).

Maladaptive schemas typically associated with antisocial personality disorder are: *mistrust/abuse*—the belief that others will abuse, humiliate, cheat, lie, manipulate, or take advantage; *entitlement*—the belief that one is superior to others and not bound by the rules and norms that govern normal social interaction; *insufficient self-control*—the belief that one is incapable of self-control and frustration tolerance; *defectiveness*—the belief that one is defective, bad, unwanted, or inferior in important respects; *emotional deprivation*—the belief that one's desire for emotional support will not be met by others; *abandonment*—the belief that significant others will not or cannot provide reliable and stable support; and *social isolation*—the belief that one is alienated, different from others, or not part of any group (Bernstein, 2002).

Interpersonal Approach

Benjamin (1996) explains that psychotherapeutic interventions with antisocial personality–disordered individuals can be planned and evaluated in terms of whether they enhance collaboration, facilitate learning about maladaptive patterns and their roots, block these patterns, enhance the will to change, and effectively encourage new patterns.

Benjamin notes that antisocial individuals do not respond well to individual psychotherapy alone. However, when combined with other modalities, such as milieu therapy, positive treatment outcome may be possible. The goal of the collaborative phase of treatment is to establish a bonding and some degree of interdependence. Since collaboration in individual psychotherapy cannot be coerced and is seldom chosen by antisocial individuals, Benjamin suggests joining the individual in his or her initial hostile position, then progressively moving toward collaboration. Other ways of eliciting collaboration are utilizing sports heroes as role models or allowing the antisocial individual to assume a teaching role in supervised, socially acceptable settings. Wilderness survival training is another potential modality. In these instances, nurturance and bonding could be facilitated. Carefully managed group therapy can provide opportunities for bonding and control.

Once bonding and interdependence begin, the preconditions for collaboration have been met. Next, antisocial individuals are helped to recognize and understand the self-destructive features of their exploitive lifestyles and patterns. Benjamin believes that these individuals can then begin to develop needed self-management and social skills such as self-care, delay of gratification, and empathy for others. Unfortunately, Benjamin offers little discussion and few suggestions for facilitating change for individuals with this disorder.

Group Therapy

Structured forms of group therapy may be quite effective with antisocial personality–disordered individuals. Open, exploratory, and nondirective groups (Yalom, 1995) with heterogeneous composition are easily disrupted by antisocial patients; therefore, such groups are not advisable for these patients (Liebowitz et al., 1986).

Three types of group treatment have been utilized with these patients: psychoeducational, psychotherapy, and support groups (Walker, 1992). Psychoeducational groups combine didactic presentation by the clinician, which is then processed by group members. Content and agenda are structured as is patient participation. The group is composed of antisocial patients who meet given criteria for participation and are chosen by the clinician. The groups are time-limited and meet weekly for 90 minutes. Because of the complexity of these patients' interpersonal and other problems, these groups have limited utility for antisocial patients.

Psychotherapy groups have somewhat less structure than psychoeducational groups but make use of cohesive themes relevant to these patients. Group membership is determined by the clinician, who is family in charge of both content and process. These groups tend to be long term, meet weekly for 90 minutes, and are limited to nine or ten patients. Because a group of ten antisocial patients can be quite formidable, two clinician group therapists are recommended.

Two group therapists serve to diminish the group's potential for acting out against the group leaders, as one clinician is an easy target for isolation as well as attack or dismissal by group members. Two group leaders also offer patients more opportunity for constructive identification because of difference in the clinicians' personality and style. Furthermore, this situation allows for a "good guy–bad guy" routine and for "lateral passes" by the leaders, who may find themselves unable to handle a particular issue or patient (Walker, 1992).

Support groups for antisocial patients are useful for individuals who have had intensive inpatient or outpatient group psychotherapy. While they are based on a self-help model, they are led by a clinician. The main focus of these ongoing groups with open membership is relapse prevention and the development of peer support.

Walker (1992) described some useful guidelines for setting up these three different types of groups. He also described a number of rules and specific procedures for doing group work with antisocial patients.

Therapeutic Community. An extension of group treatment in an inpatient or residential setting in which the milieu is a medium of change is the therapeutic community. Recent research indicates that drug-addicted individuals with antisocial personality disorder can benefit significantly from therapeutic community treatment provided they complete the treatment program and continue with aftercare in the community. Treatment completion was found to be the most important factor in reducing recent drug use and postdischarge arrests (Messina et al., 2002).

Marital and Family Therapy

There are a considerable number of studies on the family dynamics and treatment of the antisocial patient mostly involving delinquent youths (Glueck & Glueck, 1950; Minuchin & Moutalva, 1976). A few studies suggest that short-term family therapy can also be effective with delinquent adolescents (Alexander & Parsons, 1973; Parsons & Alexander, 1973). Harbir (1981) notes that antisocial patients are seldom motivated to engage in family therapy, but to the extent that the clinician is able to engage the patient's parents or spouse, the more likely therapeutic change is possible. Since the antisocial patient tends to precipitously leave outpatient treatment when difficult and anxiety-provoking issues are faced, it is incumbent on the clinician to maximize therapeutic leverage. Specifically, this means establishing a consistent therapeutic alliance and involving the family at the outset, usually at the beginning of hospital treatment, as a part of a court stipulation or as a required adjunct to residential treatment.

A major treatment goal is to help family members, or the spouse in couples therapy, set limits on the patient. Typically, family members and spouses have minimized, ignored, or acted inconsistently in the face of the patient's antisocial behavior. As the family or spouse consistently sets and enforces limits, the patient's pathological behavior reduces, and sometimes treatment-amenable symptoms like depression emerge. This suggests the patient is beginning to change and is more motivated to stop destructive behaviors. As family treatment proceeds, changes in destructive communication patterns can be achieved systematically (Parsons & Alexander, 1973).

Nichols (1996) describes the marital interactional patterns and symptomatology of individuals with antisocial personality disorders and histrionic personality disorders in close interpersonal relationships as well as a suggested treatment plan protocol and strategies for dealing with such couples in a therapeutic context.

Medication

Few pharmacological investigations of antisocial personality disorder, per se, have been reported. To date, antisocial personality disorder has not been subject to controlled pharmacological trials (Koenigsberg, Woo-Ming, & Siever, 2002). Nevertheless, Kellner (1978, 1981, 1986) and Reid, Balis, and Sutton (1998) review the use of various classes of psychotropics in the treatment of antisocial personality disorders.

Essentially, clinical research findings indicate that the use of various benzodiazepines and neuroleptics have had limited efficacy or inconsistent results. There was considerable optimism that stimulants, such as methylphenidate (Ritalin) or pemoline, would be effective with antisocial patients with attention deficit disorder symptoms (Satterfield & Contwell, 1975). But there are no controlled studies to support their use. Maintenance therapy with lithium carbonate also held some promise for managing individuals with impulsive, violent, explosive traits or mood swings (Sheard et al., 1976). Unfortunately, many antisocial patients cannot either tolerate its side effects or comply with treatment instructions and regimen. Nevertheless, patients with a positive family history of lithium-responsive illness, recurrent depression or aggression are very good candidates for a lithium trial (Liebowitz et al., 1986). The use of beta blockers such as propanol have also been utilized for their anti-aggressive effect (Yudofsky et al., 1981; Ratey et al., 1989).

There is evidence that serotonergic activity in the brain with selective serotonin receptable inhibitors can reduce impulsive behavior. At least four open trials have reported efficacy of fluoxetine in patients with antisocial personality disorder (Coccaro, 1993). Kavoussi et al. (1994) reported in a open trial study that sertraline (Zoloft) is also effective with aggressivity and impulsivity.

Medication Protocol. For individuals in whom aggressivity and/or impulsivity are of concern, begin with an SSRI at antidepressant dosages. If that SSRI fails, try another. If there is a partial response, an adjunctive atypical psychotic agent or a mood stabilizer, such as valproate or carbamazepine, can be considered (Reich, 2002).

Combined and Integrated Treatment Approaches

Despite widespread pessimism about the treatability of this disorder, there is reason for cautious optimism provided that treatment is combined or multimodal and tailored to the particular needs and circumstances of the individual. There is clear evidence that time itself is the most effective treatment modality. In other words, the intensity of antisocial behaviors tends to dissipate with age (Regier et al., 1988). Purportedly this is due to the cumulative effects of personal, social, legal, and financial repercussions of antisocial behavior. The next most effective step is specialized treatment, therapeutic communities, or wilderness programs that provide firm limits and structure, group work with peers, and a structured work program (Woody et al., 1985). To the extent that sufficient therapeutic leverage is present in outpatient settings, treatment outcomes for antisocial patients can be at least guardedly optimistic.

As with borderline personality disorder, most agree that pharmacotherapy should not be the only treatment for antisocial personality disorder (Gunderson, 1986). Kellner (1986) suggests that treatment often begins with a psychotherapeutic modality, after which a trial of medication may be considered for a specific target symptom such as impulsivity, aggressivity, explosiveness, or violence. In many cases, treatment will be long because of the patient's unwillingness or inability to persevere. It may consist of a few sessions interspersed with long intervals without any therapeutic work, or medication monitoring only. In any case, the clinician must attempt to establish a therapeutic relationship while maintaining firm limits. Psychoeducation, whether in an individual or group format, is usually necessary. Kellner (1986) notes that data support the use of sustained treatment, which invariably involves psychotherapies—individual, group, and family, behavior therapy, and psychoeducation—aimed at teaching self-control and postponement of gratification as well as the use of medication. Though such interventions are exceedingly complex and difficult, Kellner believes they can make a substantial difference in the life and adjustment of these patients.

CHAPTER 3

Avoidant Personality Disorder

Historically, avoidant personality disorder found its way into DSM-III amid considerable controversy. Several individuals contended that there was little distinction between avoidant personality disorder and schizoid and dependent personality disorders (Gunderson, 1983). However, criteria in DSM-IV has been modified to differentiate the three sufficiently. Essentially, avoidant patients long for close interpersonal relations but fear humiliation, rejection, and embarrassment, so they avoid and distance themselves from others. Schizoid patients, on the other hand, have little or no desire for close interpersonal relationships, which accounts for their distancing and avoidance of others. Similarly, while dependent personality–disordered individuals may be timid, submissive, and clinging due to an excessive need for attachment, avoidant personality–disordered individuals are characterized by fear of humiliation and rejection that results in social timidity and withdrawal.

This disorder has a relatively low prevalence in the general population, estimated to be between 0.5 and 1.0 percent. In clinical settings, this disorder has been noted in approximately 10 percent of outpatients.

Like borderline personality disorder, research and clinical interest in avoidant personality disorder is very high. Much of this interest has been fueled because of its similarity to social phobia, an Axis I disorder. Initially, it was believed that avoidant personality disorder was the same as a generalized type of social phobia, but recent research suggests they are separate entities and can be comorbid. While the study of avoidant personality disorder in the context of social phobia has yielded some valuable information, essential research on avoidant personality disorder has been impeded by recommendations that it be treated as a variant of social phobia (Alden et al., 2002). Fortunately, clinical outcome studies involving the comorbidity of social phobia and avoidant personality disorder offer encouragement about treatment response (Brown et al., 1997; Altamura et al., 1999; Osterbaan et al., 2002).

This chapter describes the characteristic features of avoidant personality disorder and its related personality style, five different clinical formulations, interview and psychological assessment indicators, as well as various treatment modalities and intervention strategies and methods.

DESCRIPTION OF THE AVOIDANT PERSONALITY DISORDER

Avoidant personality disorder can be recognized by the following descriptors and characteristics: styles vs. disorder, triggering event, behavioral style, interpersonal style, cognitive style, affective style, attachment style, and optimal criterion.

Style vs. Disorder. Avoidant personality can be thought of as spanning a continuum from healthy to pathological, with avoidant personality style on the healthy end and avoidant personality disorder on the pathological end. Table 3.1 compares and contrasts differences between avoidant style and disorder.

Triggering Event. The typical situation, circumstance, or event that most likely triggers or activates the characteristic maladaptive response of avoidant personality disorder (Othmer & Othmer, 2002), as noted in behavioral, interpersonal, cognitive, and feeling styles, is "demands for close interpersonal relating and/or social and public appearances."

Behavioral Style. The behavioral style of avoidant personalities is characterized by social withdrawal, shyness, distrustfulness, and aloofness. Behavior and speech are controlled, and individuals appear apprehensive and awkward.

Interpersonal Style. Interpersonally, they are rejection sensitive. Even though they desire acceptance by others, they keep distance from others and

Table 3.1
A Comparison of Avoidant Personality Style and Disorder

Personality Style	*Personality Disorder*
Comfortable with habit, repetition, and routine; prefer the known to the unknown	Exaggerates the potential difficulties, physical dangers, or risks involved in doing something ordinary but outside his or her usual routine
Close allegiance with family and/or a few close friends; tend to be homebodies	Has no close friends or confidants—or only one—other than first-degree relatives; avoids activities that involve significant interpersonal contact
Sensitive and concerned about what others think; tend to be self-conscious	Unwilling to get involved with people unless certain of being liked; easily hurt; worriers
Very discrete and deliberate in dealing with others	Fears being embarrassed by blushing, crying, or showing signs of anxiety in front of other people
Tend to maintain a reserved, self-restrained demeanor around others	Reticent in social situations because of a fear of saying something inappropriate or foolish, or of being unable to answer a question
Tend to be curious and can focus considerable attention on hobbies and avocations; however, a few engage in counterphobic coping behaviors	Tend to be underachievers, and find it difficult to focus on job tasks or hobbies

require unconditional approval before being willing to open up. They guardedly test others to determine who can be trusted to like them.

Cognitive Style. The cognitive style of avoidants can be described as perceptually vigilant—that is, they scan the environment looking for clues of potential threat or acceptance. Their thoughts are often distracted by their hypersensitivity. Not surprisingly, they have low self-esteem because of their devaluation of their own achievements and their overemphasis of their own shortcomings.

Affective Style. Their emotional or affective style is marked by a shy and apprehensive quality. Because they are seldom able to attain unconditional approval from others, they routinely experience sadness, loneliness, and tenseness. At times of increased distress, they will describe feelings of emptiness and depersonalization.

Attachment Style. Individuals with a self-view that is negative and an other-view that vacillates between positive and negative exhibit a composite preoccupied and fearful style of attachment. Their avoidance is based on the desire to be liked and accepted by others while fearing rejection and abandonment. The preoccupied–fearful attachment style is common in adults with avoidant personality disorder (Lyddon & Sherry, 2001).

Optimal DSM-IV-TR Criterion. Of all the stated DSM-IV-TR criteria for avoidant personality disorder, one criterion has been found to be the most useful in diagnosing this disorder. The belief is that by beginning with this criterion, the clinician can test for the presence or absence of the criterion and quickly diagnose the personality disorder (Allnutt & Links, 1996). The optimal criterion for this disorder is "avoids occupational activities that involve significant interpersonal contact fearing criticism, disapproval, or rejection."

The following two case examples illustrate the differences between avoidant personality style (Dr. Q. and avoidant personality disorder [Ms. A.]).

Case Study: Avoidant Personality Disorder

Ms. A. is a 27-year-old female student who contacted the University Counseling Center for help with "difficulty concentrating." She indicated that the problem started when Ms. A's roommate of 2 years precipitously moved out to live with her boyfriend. Ms. A. described herself as being "blown away and hurt" by this. She noted that she had no close friends and described herself as being shy and having had only one date since high school. Since then she avoided attempts by men to date her because of being rejected when she was a freshman by a guy who had dated her for a month and never contacted her again. On examination, she had poor eye contact with the admissions counselor and appeared very shy and self-conscious.

Case Study: Avoidant Personality Style

Peter Q. is a 31-year-old eye surgeon who had recently been hired by a large HMO hospital and clinic. He had recently completed residency training, and being new, good-looking, and single, he was quickly noticed by the female staff. His specialty was cataracts and laser surgery, for which he was exquisitely skilled and respected by his patients. Although courteous, he was somewhat emotionally distant and shy. Dr. Q. seldom participated in staff get-togethers, and if he did make an appearance, he would politely excuse himself after his beeper sounded—which seemed all the time—and he wouldn't return. His social life seemed to be a mystery, and he had little contact after hours with his male colleagues, except for one. Dr. S. had run into Peter at a civil war convention in another city and was surprised to learn of Peter's longstanding hobby and collection of civil war books and memorabilia. In time, the two became very good friends, spending considerable time together. Dr. S. recalls Peter saying how he often daydreamed about being a confederate general leading his troops to victory. Although he had his own apartment, Peter spent much of his free time at home with his parents. Dr. S. soon became a regular guest at the Q. home and initially was surprised at how warm, cordial, and comfortable Peter was in this small setting as compared to the hospital.

DSM-IV Description and Criteria

Avoidant personalities are seemingly shy, lonely, hypersensitive individuals with low self-esteem. Although they are desperate for interpersonal involvement, they avoid personal contact with others because of their heightened fear of social disapproval and rejection sensitivity. In this regard, they are quite different than the schizoid personality, who has little if any interest in personal contact. Table 3.2 lists the DSM-IV-TR description and criteria.

Table 3.2
DSM-IV-TR Criteria for Avoidant Personality Disorder (301.82)

A pervasive pattern of social inhibition, feelings of inadequacy, and hypersensitivity to negative evaluation, beginning by early adulthood and present in a variety of contexts, as indicated by at least four of the following:

(1) avoids occupational activities that involve significant interpersonal contact, because of fears of criticism, disapproval, or rejection
(2) is unwilling to get involved with people unless certain of being liked
(3) restraint within intimate relationships due to the fear of being shamed or ridiculed
(4) preoccupation with being criticized or rejected in social situations
(5) inhibited in new interpersonal situations because of feelings of inadequacy
(6) belief that one is socially inept, personally unappealing, or inferior to others
(7) is unusually reluctant to take personal risks or to engage in any new activities because they may prove embarrassing

Reprinted with permission from the *Diagnostic and Statistical Manual of Mental Disorders, Fourth Edition–Text Revision*. Copyright 2000. American Psychiatric Association.

FORMULATIONS OF AVOIDANT PERSONALITY DISORDER

Psychodynamic Formulation

Shyness, shame, and avoidant behaviors are conceptualized as defenses against embarrassment, humiliation, rejection, and failure (Gabbard, 1990). Shame and fear of exposure of the self to others are interconnected. Individuals with avoidant personalities tend to feel ashamed about their self-perceptions as weak, unable to compete, physically or mentally defective or disgusting, and unable to control bodily function (Wurmser, 1981). Shame evolves from many different developmental experiences throughout the early childhood years. These developmental experiences, plus a constitutional predisposition to avoid stressful situations, tend to be reactivated in the avoidant patient upon exposure to individuals who matter a great deal to the patient (Gabbard, 1994).

Biosocial Formulation

Millon (1981), Millon and Everly (1985), and Millon and Davis (1996) believe that the etiology and development of this personality disorder represents an interactive constellation of biogenical environmental factors. They hypothesize that the vigilance characterizing this personality reflects functional dominance of the sympathetic nervous system with a lowered autonomic arousal threshold. This could allow irrelevant impulses to intrude on logical association, and diminish control and direction of thought and memory processes resulting in marked interface with normal cognitive processes. Research cited by Kagan, Reznick, and Saidman (1988) suggests that the trait of shyness is of genetic constitutional origin, which requires specific environmental experiences to develop into a full-blown pattern of timidity and avoidance.

Parental and peer group rejection are two critical and prevalent environmental influences. The amount of parental rejection appears to be particularly intense and/or frequent. When peer group rejection reinforces parental rejection, the child's sense of self-worth and self-competence tends to be severely eroded, resulting in self-critical attitudes. As a result, these individuals restrict their social experiences, are hypersensitive to rejection, and become excessively introspective. By restricting their social environment, they subsequently fail to develop social competence, which tends to evoke the ridicule of others for their asocial behavior. Because of their hypersensitivity and hypervigilence, they are prone to interpret minor rebuffs as principal indicators of rejection where no rejection was intended. Finally, because of their excessive introspectiveness, they are forced to examine the painful condition they have created for themselves. Not surprisingly, they conclude that they do not deserve to be accepted by others.

Cognitive-Behavioral Formulation

According to Beck and Freeman (1990), individuals with avoidant personality are fearful of initiating relationships as well as of responding to others' attempts to relate to them because of their overriding belief that they will be rejected. For them, such rejection is unbearable, so they engage in social avoidance. Furthermore, they engage in cognitive and emotional avoidance by not thinking about things that could cause them to feel dysphoric. Because of their low tolerance for dysphoria, they further distract themselves from their negative cognitions. Underlying these avoidance patterns are maladaptive schemas or longstanding dysfunctional beliefs about self and others. Schemas about self include themes of being different, inadequate, defective, and unlikable. Schemas about others involve themes of uncaring and rejection.

These individuals are likely to predict and interpret the rejection as caused solely by their personal deficiencies. This prediction of rejection results in dysphoria. Finally, avoidant individuals do not have internal criteria to judge themselves in a positive manner. Thus, they must rely on their perception. They tend to misread a neutral or positive reaction as negative, which further compounds their rejection sensitivity and social emotional and cognitive avoidance. In short, they hold negative schemas, which lead them to avoid solutions where they could interact with others. They also avoid tasks that could engender uncomfortable feelings and avoid thinking about matters which produce dysphoria. Because of their low tolerance for discomfort, they utilize distractions, excuse making, and rationalizations when they begin to feel sad or anxious.

Turkat (1990) describes this disorder as primarily anxiety based and characterized by timidity and anxiety concerning evaluation, rejection, and/or humiliation. He notes that the disorder is very responsive to behavioral interventions, particularly anxiety management desensitization methods where the hierarchy is based on fear of rejection, criticism, and/or evaluation.

Interpersonal Formulation

According to Benjamin (1996), persons diagnosed with avoidant personality disorder tended to begin their development sequence with appropriate nurturance and social bonding. As a result, they continued to desire social contact and nurturance. Unfortunately, these individuals were subject to relentless parental control with regard to creating an impressive social image. Visible flaws were cause for great embarrassment and humiliation, particularly for the family. Besides exhortations to be admirable, they experienced degrading mockery for failures, personal imperfections, or shortcomings. The adult consequence is that avoidant individuals are socialized to perform adequately and manage an appropriate impression while avoiding occasions for embarrassment or humiliation. Typically, this humiliation was associated with exclusion, banishment, or rejection. As a result, they anticipate rejection and thus socially isolate themselves. Because they are well bonded, they crave relationships and social contact but only when they are absolutely convinced there is little or no risk of rejection or dejection.

Furthermore, although they experienced rejection and ridicule from their families, they also internalized the belief that family is their source of support. Thus, they have intense family loyalty while harboring equally intense fears of outsiders. In short, avoidant individuals exhibit intense fear of humiliation and rejection. To avoid this, they socially withdraw and restrain themselves, while prying for love and acceptance. They can become very intimate with a select few who pass their highly stringent safety test. Occasionally, they can lose control and explode with rageful indignation.

Integrative Formulation

The following integrative formulation may be helpful in understanding how avoidant personality disorder is likely to have developed. Biologically, avoidant personality was likely to have been a hyperirritable and fearful infant. In Thomas and Chess's classification (1977), the avoidant would likely exhibit the "slow-to-warm-up" infant temperament. Millon and Everly (1985) suggested that avoidant personalities often experience maturational irregularities as children. This, as well as a hyperirritable pattern, is due in part to a low arousal threshold of the autonomic nervous system.

Psychologically, avoidants view themselves, others, the world, and life's purpose in terms of the following themes. They tend to view themselves by some variant of the theme: "I'm inadequate and frightened of rejection." They see themselves as chronically tense, fatigued, and self-conscious, and they devalue their achievements by their self-critical attitude. They tend to see the world as some variant of the theme: "Life is unfair—people reject and criticize me—but I still want someone to like me." As such, they are likely to conclude, "Therefore, be vigilant, demand reassurance, and if all else fails, fantasize and daydream about the way life could be." The most common defense mechanism of the avoidant personality is that of fantasy.

Socially, predictable patterns of parenting and environmental factors can be noted for avoidant personality disorder. The avoidant personality is likely to have experienced parental rejection and/or ridicule. Later, siblings and peers will likely continue this pattern of rejection and ridicule. The parental injunction is likely to have been, "We don't accept you and probably no one else will either." Individuals may have had parents with high standards and worried that they might not have or would not meet these standards and therefore would not be accepted.

This avoidant pattern is confirmed, reinforced, and perpetuated by the following individual and systems factors: A sense of personal inadequacy and a fear of rejection lead to hypervigilance, which leads to restricted social experiences. These experiences, plus catastrophic thinking, lead to increased hypervigilance and hypersensitivity, leading to self-pity, anxiety, and depression, which lead to further confirmation of avoidant beliefs and styles.

ASSESSMENT OF AVOIDANT PERSONALITY DISORDER

Several sources of information are useful in establishing a diagnosis and treatment plan for personality disorders. Observation, collateral information, and psychological testing are important adjuncts to the patient's self-report in the clinical interview. This section briefly describes some characteristic observations that the clinician makes and the nature of the rapport likely to develop in initial encounters with specific personality-disordered individuals. Characteristic response patterns on various objective (i.e., MMPI-II and MCMI-III) and projective tests (i.e., Rorschach and TAT) are also described.

Interview Behavior and Rapport

In the initial interview, avoidant personality–disordered individuals tend to be monosyllabic, circumstantial, and guarded. Some may even appear suspicious or quite anxious, but all are hypersensitive to rejection and criticism. Reluctance and guardedness should be approached with empathy and reassurance. The clinician does well to avoid confrontation, which likely will be interpreted as criticism. Instead, use empathic responses that encourage sharing of past pain and anticipatory fears. When these individuals feel that the clinician understands their hypersensitivity and will be protective of them, they are willing to trust and cooperate with treatment. After feeling safe and accepted, the character of the interview can change dramatically. Rapport has been achieved, so they feel relieved when they can describe their fears of being embarrassed and criticized and their sensitivity to being misunderstood.

Table 3.3
Characteristics of Avoidant Personality Disorder

Triggering Event	Demands for close interpersonal relating and/or social and public appearances.
Behavioral Style	Shy, mistrustful, aloof; apprehensive; socially awkward; controlled, underactive behavior; feelings of emptiness and depersonalization.
Interpersonal Style	Guardedly tests others; rejection sensitive as self-protectant; desires acceptance but maintains distance; has basic interpersonal skills, but fears using them.
Cognitive Style	Perpetual vigilance; thoughts easily distracted by hypersensitivity.
Feeling Style	Shy and apprehensive.
Temperament	Irritable.
Attachment Style	Preoccupied and fearful.
Parental Injunction	"We don't accept you and probably nobody else will either."
Self-View	"I'm inadequate and frightened of rejection." Chronically tense, fatigued, self-conscious; devalue their achievement, self-critical.
Worldview	"Life is unfair. People reject and criticize me, but I want someone to like me. Therefore, be vigilant, demand reassurance, and, if all else fails, fantasize and daydream."
Optimal DSM-IV-TR Criteria	Avoids occupational activities that involve significant interpersonal contact, fearing criticism, disapproval, or rejection.

They may experience these fears of being embarrassed as silly and express it. If the clinician identifies with position, they are likely to feel ridiculed and withdraw again (Othmer & Othmer, 2002).

Psychological Testing Data

The Minnesota Multiphase Personality Inventory (MMPI-2), the Millon Clinical Multiaxial Inventory (MCMI-II), the Rorschach Psychodiagnostic Test, and the Thematic Apperception Test (TAT) can be useful in diagnosing avoidant personality disorder as well as the avoidant personality style or trait.

On the MMPI-2, a 2-7/7-2 (depression-psychasthenia) profile is typical. This profile reflects depression about assumed rejection, as well as apprehension and self-doubt about relating to others (Graham, 2000). When social withdrawal is also present, a high score on O (social introversion) is likely, as well as a lowered 9 (hypomania) scale. When social withdrawal and self-rejection lead to decreased functioning, an elevation on scale 8 (schizophrenia) may occur (Meyer, 1995).

On the MMCI-III, an elevation of 85 or above on scale 2 (avoidant), along with low scores on 4 (histrionic) and 7 (obsessive-compulsive), are likely. Moderate elevators on scales 8B (self-defeating) and C (borderline) may also be present. The higher S (schizotypal) is elevated, the more likely decompensation has occurred (Choca & Denburg, 1997).

On the Rorschach, blocked or relatively inactive M (human movement) responses are likely. A high number of P (popular) responses occurs, and C (contrast) often involves passive animals such as deer and rabbits—sometimes being maimed or killed—or passive interactions in M responses (Meyer, 1995).

TREATMENT APPROACHES AND INTERVENTIONS

Treatment Considerations

Included in a differential diagnosis of avoidant personality disorder are other Axis II personality disorders: schizoid personality disorder, schizotypal personality disorder, borderline personality disorder, and dependent personality disorder. The most common Axis I syndromes associated with avoidant personality disorder are agoraphobia, social phobia, generalized anxiety disorder, dysthymia, major depressive episode, hypochondriasis, conversion disorder, dissociative disorder, and schizophrenia. Recent investigations indicate that there are two subtypes of social phobia: circumscribed and generalized (Liebowitz et al., 1989). The traditional description of social phobia is the circumscribed subtype. The generalized type, however, involves fear and avoidance of a wide range of social and performance situations. For instance, patients may be unable to attend social functions, return goods to a store, and the like. Considerable overlap exists between generalized social phobia and avoidant personality disorder. The treatment implications, particularly regarding pharmacotherapy, are described later in this chapter. It has been said that next to borderline personality disorder, avoidant personality disorder is the most liable and likely to decompensate (Reid, 1989).

In terms of treatment goals and strategies, there are relatively few clinical case reports and almost no controlled research on treating avoidant personality. Nevertheless, Francis and Clarkin (1981) believe that avoidant personality—

disordered individuals are excellent candidates for various psychotherapeutic approaches, the choice depending on the patient's goals, preferences, and psychological mindedness, and the clinician's expertise. Generally, the goal of therapy should be to increase the individual's self-esteem and confidence in relationship to others and to desensitize the individual to the criticism of others. Finally, irrespective of the type of treatment approach, it is useful to note that avoidant personalities tend to evoke two types of countertransference. These patients invite therapeutic protectiveness or excessive overambitiousness in clinicians. In the first instance, the clinician insulates patients from risk, thus reaffirming their self-view of insecurity and weakness. In the second instance, patients are forced to face new situations prematurely without adequate preparation and are then criticized for failing to be braver.

Individual Psychotherapy

Psychodynamic Psychotherapy Approach

Both expressive and supportive aspects of psychodynamic psychotherapy can be most effective in the treatment of the avoidant personality–disordered individual (Gabbard, 1994). The supportive aspect involves an empathic appreciation of the humiliation and embarrassment associated with exposure to fearful interpersonal circumstances and the pain connected with rejection. The supportive aspect also involves the clinician's prescription of exposure to the feared situation. Needless to say, firm encouragement must accompany this prescription. More of their fantasies and anxieties will be activated in the actual situation of exposure rather than in their defensive posture of withdrawal. Explaining this fact will further encourage avoidant patients to seek out fearful situations.

The expressive aspect of therapy focuses on exploring the underlying causes of shame as related to past developmental experiences. To the extent the patient is willing to risk confronting the feared circumstance, the expressive aspect of therapy is greatly enhanced. Initial exploratory efforts can be frustrating in that avoidant individuals may be somewhat uncertain about who it is they fear. They tend to provide vague and global explanations such as rejection and shyness rather than specific fantasies. Thus, the clinician does well to explore specific fantasies within the context of the transference.

These individuals tend to have a considerable degree of anxiety about the psychotherapeutic requirement to openly share thoughts and feelings. Accordingly, when they nonverbally react (i.e., blush), about something that has been verbalized, the clinician might ask them to share their embarrassment and what they imagine the clinician could be thinking and feeling. By pursuing the details of specific situations, these patients can develop a greater awareness of the correlates of the shame affect (Gabbard, 1994).

Interpretive techniques are also useful as either the primary intervention or adjunctive to behavioral and interpersonal approaches. The basic strategy involves interpretive unconscious fantasies that their fear or impulses will become uncontrollable and harmful to self and others. Not surprisingly, their avoidant behavior maintains a denial of unconscious wishes or impulses (Mackinnon & Michels, 1971). Furthermore, these patients tend to have harsh superegos and subsequently project their own unrealistic expectations of themselves onto others. In so doing, they evade expected criticism and embarrassment by avoiding relationships with others. A complete interpretation identifies the unconscious impulse and the fear, and traces the resulting avoidant defensive pattern in early life experiences, in outside relationships, and in the transference (Fenichel, 1945).

Cognitive-Behavioral Therapy Approach

Beck, Freeman, and Associates (1990) provide an in-depth discussion of the cognitive therapy approach with avoidant personality–disordered individuals. Avoidant individuals are often difficult to engage in treatment given their basic strategy of avoidance and their hypersensitivity to perceived criticism. The therapist must work diligently and carefully at building trust. Trust tests are common in the early stage of treatment and can include a pattern of canceling appointments or having difficulty scheduling regular appointments. It is important not to prematurely challenge automatic thoughts, as such challenges can be viewed as personal criticism. Only after these individuals are solidly engaged in treatment should the therapist use cognitive interactions to test their expectancies in social situations. To the extent that the therapist utilizes collaboration rather than confrontation, and guided discovery rather than direct disputation, these individuals are more likely to view therapy as constructive and are likely to remain in treatment.

Since these individuals often experience high levels of interpersonal anxiety, it is useful to employ anxiety management interventions early in the course of treatment. Because these individuals work at avoiding not only unpleasant affects but thinking about matters that elicit unpleasant feelings, it is useful to work at increasing emotional tolerance with desensitization methods and reframing. Furthermore, since these individuals may not have learned the basics of social interaction, structured social skills training may need to be incorporated.

Later in therapy, when these individuals have achieved some of their short-term treatment goals and developed sufficient trust in the therapist, efforts to challenge automatic thoughts and restructure maladaptive schemas are appropriate. Issues involving risk of developing close relationships and intimacy are central. Typically, it is necessary to decatastrophize disapproval and rejection. To the extent that these individuals have developed sufficient self-efficacy and have experienced enough success on a variety of levels of relationships, they are more receptive to entertaining the notion that disapproval in a close relationship does not equal rejection or devastation. Adding group therapy has a place in the treatment of this disorder so that they can learn new attitudes and practice new skills in a socially benign and accepting environment. In summary, the cognitive therapy approach to this disorder recognizes the significant challenge of engaging the avoidant individual in treatment and utilizing efforts to build trust, reduce social anxiety, and reduce cognitive and emotional avoidance. It then proceeds to correcting social skills deficits with behavioral methods before turning to cognitive analysis and disputation of automatic thoughts and schemas, and provides a safe environment to try out socially proactive behavior.

From a behavioral perspective, management of the avoidant pattern is relatively straightforward (Turkat, 1990). Anxiety management procedures, assertiveness and social skills training through role-playing, direct instruction, and modeling are effective in developing confident social behavior. However, graded exposure is the single most effective behavioral intervention strategy for extinguishing avoidant behavior and anxiety intolerance (Greist & Jefferson, 1992).

Paradoxical intention may also prove useful, particularly with avoidant patients who are also oppositional. With this strategy, the patient seeks rejection in a way that is both predictable and under the patient's control. For instance, a single male with a fear of dating agrees to an experiment requiring that he be rejected for dates by two women in the coming week. If one of the women accepts his offer, he can go out with her on the condition that he asks out an additional woman who rejects him. In other words, being rejected becomes a treatment goal. This intervention reduces rejection sensitivity. Use of such a paradoxical intervention may work with the oppositionally avoidant patient by accentuating the patient's need to defeat the clinician by doing the opposite of what is suggested or prescribed (Weeks & L'Abate, 1982; Haley, 1978).

Regarding treatment involving comorbid avoidant personality disorder and social phobia, Brown et al. (1997) found that individuals with both generalized and nongeneralized social phobia treated with cognitive-behavior therapy improved similarly to those with the more generalized form of social phobia but remained more impaired after treatment. Curiously, the presence of avoidant personality disorder was not predictive of treatment outcome; however, several individuals who met criteria for this diagnosis before treatment no longer met criteria after treatment. Similarly, Osterbaan et al. (2002) found that individuals with social phobia and comorbid avoidant personality disorder had a poorer response to treatment and remained more impaired in the short term compared to those with the comorbidity. Nevertheless, after 15 months, those with comorbid avoidant personality disorder showed similar progress in the long term.

Structured Skill Treatment Interventions. While research shows that medication can modulate or normalize dysregulated behaviors, a similar modulating effect has also been noted for social skills training (Lieberman, DeRisi, & Mueser, 1989). Thus, it appears that social skills training is a relatively potent bottom-up treatment strategy for normalizing limbic system–mediated behaviors that reflect specific skill deficits in personality-disordered individuals. When such skill deficits are present, Sperry (1999) contends that structured skill training intervention is a potent and effective strategy in treatment. Several structured intervention strategies for modifying a personality-disordered individual's affective, behavioral, and cognitive temperament styles are described and illustrated for avoidant personality disorder (Sperry, 1999).

Schema Therapy. Schema therapy is an elaboration of cognitive therapy that has been developed by Young (1999, 2003) specifically for personality disorders and other difficult individual and couples problems. Schema therapy involves identifying maladaptive schemas and planning specific strategies and interventions. Four main strategies are cognitive, experiential, behavioral, and the therapeutic relationship itself. Cognitive restructuring—modification of maladaptive schemas—is an important cognitive strategy but is combined with imagery exercises, empathic confrontation, homework assignments, and "limited reparenting"—that is, a form of corrective emotional experience (Young, 1999).

Maladaptive schemas typically associated with avoidant personality disorder include *defectiveness*—the belief that one is defective, bad, unwanted, or inferior in important respects; *social isolation*—the belief that one is alienated, different from others, or not part of any group; *self-sacrifice*—the belief that one must meet the needs of others at the expense of one's own gratification; and *approval-seeking*—the belief that one must constantly seek to belong and be accepted at the expense of developing a true sense of self (Bernstein, 2002).

Interpersonal Approach

Benjamin (1996) explains that psychotherapeutic interventions with avoidant personality–disordered individuals can be planned and evaluated in terms of whether they enhance collaboration, facilitate learning about maladaptive patterns and their roots, block these patterns, enhance the will to change, and effectively encourage new patterns.

Fortunately, avoidant individuals already know how to relate to a select few individuals, and thus a supportive therapist can easily provide a safe haven for them. Avoidant individuals respond favorably to accurate empathy and warm support. Gradually, as they share intimacies and feelings of inadequacy, guilt, or shame, they begin to increase self-acceptance. Only then can they realistically begin exploring maladaptive patterns. Since they are exquisitely sensitive to criticism, premature confrontation must be avoided.

General reconstructive changes will occur only if these individuals understand and appreciate the impact of their maladaptive patterns in a way that helps them decide to change. Benjamin advocates couples therapy for avoidant individuals in long-term relationships. Typically, these relationships are characterized by intimacy that assures interpersonal distance and safety for the avoidant partner. Such a pattern of hiding on the margins of relationships is often rooted in unconscious loyalty to the family mandate that the avoidant individual remain isolated and safe. In couples therapy, the clinician blocks attempts of partners to humiliate or thrash each other, which previously justified the avoidant individual's withdrawal. The most difficult therapeutic task for avoidant individuals is deciding to sacrifice the benefits of their maladaptive patterns and accept the risk of developing new ones. Insight into their humiliation and loyalty to abusive parents or siblings is insufficient. However, Benjamin believes that steady reassurance in a context of competent, protective instruction fosters this change. She advocates safe group therapy, wherein clinicians block "trashing" and critical appraisals, for helping avoidant individuals accept themselves and learn the basic relational skills they missed earlier in life. This is not to say that training and other social skills cannot occur in individual therapy but rather that they are greatly facilitated in a safe group context.

Group Therapy

Avoidant personality–disordered patients typically fear group therapy in the same way they fear other new and socially demanding situations. It is for this very reason that group therapy may be specifically and especially effective for the avoidant patients who can be persuaded and role induced to undertake the exposure (Yalom, 1995). Empathetic group therapy can assist these individuals in overcoming social anxieties and developing interpersonal trust and rapport.

A combination of cognitive therapy and social skills training appears effective. Alden (1989) included aspects of cognitive therapy in the group process: (1) identifying underlying fears, (2) increasing awareness of the anxiety related to fears, and (3) shifting attentional focus from fear-related thinking to behavioral action. Didactic information, modeling, and the practice of role-playing were basic techniques incorporated into the sessions. Stravynski, Grey, and Elie (1987) found that a briefer course of group therapy centered on social skills training can be highly effective in ameliorating social skills deficits that exacerbate anxiety about social relatedness.

These individuals tend to avoid activities that involve significant interpersonal contact for fear of being exposed or ridiculed. Therefore, it takes them longer to adapt to a group setting and begin to actively participate in treatment. The group therapist's role in pacing the avoidant patient's disclosure and engagement within the group can be very important (Cramer, 1983). Rennenberg et al. (1990) found clients with this disorder so extremely anxious and avoidant that processing directly to social skills training and behavioral rehearsal was unproductive. Stravynski et al. (1987) suggest beginning with progressive relaxation training and systematic desensitization. Behavioral reversal was used in the group for exposure, itself an effective treatment for social phobia (Stravynski, Marks, & Yule, 1982). Turner et al. (1986) used communication and social skills training during behavioral rehearsal as well.

Structured activities help avoidant individuals organize how they think and act so that they are more efficient in therapy. Alden (1989) established specific goals for patients to accomplish between sessions in order to enhance generalization from treatment sessions to daily life. The patients selected several social tasks to try, beginning with easier situations and progressing to more difficult ones. In the group setting, she also introduced interpersonal skills training. The process of friendship formation was presented and clients were encouraged to incorporate these skills into their weekly social tasks. Four sets of behavioral skills that facilitate relating to others were described, modeled by therapists, and discussed and practiced by group members: listening/attending skills, empathic sensitivity, appropriate self-disclosure, and respectful assertiveness.

Rennenberg et al. (1990) found that treatment gains through group intervention were stable over 1 year; however, most patients continued with individual therapy after completing group treatment. It is quite possible that the continued therapy served to reinforce and maintain gains made during the group treatment program. Clinically important changes were reported by patients themselves or their individual therapists. Treated subjects reported decreases in their social reticence, less interference due to social anxiety at work and in social situations, fewer symptoms of social anxiety, and greater satisfaction with social activities (Alden, 1989).

Marital and Family Therapy

Although avoidant individuals need to recognize how their current dysfunctional patterns were developed, they need to focus on their current interpersonal experiences with significant others in their life. While they generally provide clinicians with vague descriptions of their interpersonal experiences, others may be helpful in filling in the important gaps of information. Couple and family treatments may be indicated in order to establish a family structure that allows more room for interpersonal exploration outside the tightly closed family circle (Gurman & Kniskern, 1991). Benjamin (1996) advocates couples therapy for avoidant individuals in long-term relationships, since typically these are characterized by intimacy that assures interpersonal distance and safety for the avoidant partner.

Medication

Until recently, the majority of publications on the treatment of the avoidant personality were focused on psychotherapeutic interventions, while only a few studies of pharmacological treatment were reported. The reluctance to view personality disorders as amenable to pharmacological treatment seems to account for the paucity of studies on the biological treatment of avoidant personality disorder (Deltito & Stam, 1989). Many patients fear medication and its side effects just as they do any other new experience. Nevertheless, evidence is accumulating that some aspects of extreme social anxiety may be highly drug responsive. Recent data suggest that avoidant personality disorder significantly overlaps with the global subtype of social phobia, also called generalized social phobia. Therefore, the use of MAOIs or fluoxetine may prove quite useful for avoidant patients (Deltito & Stam, 1989).

Liebowitz et al. (1991) indicate that social phobia, in its generalized form, often overlaps with avoidant personality disorder and is quite responsive to MAOIs. Deltito and Perugi (1989) have documented a case of social phobia and avoidant personality disorder successfully treated with phenelzine. The patient showed improvement in specific fears of eating and speaking in public, as well as global improvements in terms of comfort, confidence, and assertiveness in social situations. Studies by Liebowitz et al. (1986) administered phenelzine to a pure sample of patients with social phobias, with marked or moderate improvement on all subjects. The results demonstrated the disappearance of the physical manifestations of social anxiety, as well as increased comfort and initiative in work and social settings. A more recent study by Liebowitz et al. (1991) has postulated that patients with discrete social pho-

bias respond preferentially to beta blockers while those with generalized social phobias respond best to MAOIs.

To date, clinically useful and carefully controlled research on the clinical
efficacy of medication for personality disorders is still in its infancy. Nevertheless, Koenigsberg et al. (2002) reports two double-blind studies suggesting
that SSRIs may be helpful for avoidant personality disorder.

Medication Protocol. The studies discussed above and other recent studies suggest that for such personality-disordered individuals with prominent
anxiety, but without impulsivity, the clinician might begin with an SSRI. If
there is no response, the recommendation is to try another SSRI. If there is a
partial response, a long-acting benzodiazepine or clonazepam can be added,
or even used as the sole medication following multiple SSRI trials. If these
also fail, beta blockers and atypical antipsychotics could be the mainstay treatment of such anxiety symptoms. With individuals who have histories or impulsive, dangerous behavior or substance abuse, begin with SSRI trials. Finally,
if these fail, the clinician might consider the use of beta blockers or atypical
antipsychotics (Reich, 2002).

Combined and Integrated Treatment Approaches

Clinical experience reveals that many avoidant personality–disordered individuals are often unable to focus on the patient–clinician relationship to the
extent necessary to work with a purely dynamic therapy. Similarly, many have
difficulty fully utilizing cognitive-behavioral interventions in the interpersonal
context of therapy. Thus, an integrative treatment strategy may be required.
Alden (1992) describes an integration of cognitive and psychodynamic-interpersonal approaches. The cognitive is, of course, based on Beck and Freeman
(1990), and the psychodynamic-interpersonal is based on the time-limited
dynamic psychotherapy approach developed by Strupp and Binder (1984).

The cognitive-interpersonal patterns that characterize avoidant personality are dysfunctional beliefs of being different or biologically defective as
well as beliefs that these defects and feelings are visible to others who will
react with disgust, disapproval, or dismissal. These individuals tend to protect
themselves by looking to the clinician to provide direction and by understat-
ing or even withholding feelings and reactions if they fear the clinician will
disapprove. Thus, the clinician's primary task is to work collaboratively with
the patient to modify his or her cognitive-interpersonal style. Alden (1992)
describes four steps in the integrative approach. The first step is recognition
of treatment process issues. The clinician must quickly recognize that these
patients tend to withhold or understate information that is clinically relevant.

Clinicians should expect these patients to respond to direct questions with "I'm not sure" or "I don't know." Such evasive and avoidant responses characterize the thought process and prevent these patients from encoding details about social encounters.

Unfortunately, clinicians may find themselves interpreting resistance or focusing on global and vague interpersonal beliefs and behavior as treatment targets. In either instance, both clinician and patient will experience discouragement and treatment outcomes will be limited. Furthermore, clinicians must recognize the avoidant patient's infectious hopelessness and depression largely due to inability to process positive information, lack of attentiveness, and firmly established negative beliefs and schemas.

The second step is increased awareness of cognitive-interpersonal patterns. Patients need to be encouraged to observe their interpersonal encounters outside sessions by means of self-monitoring and diary keeping. Alden notes four components of the interpersonal pattern: their beliefs and expectancy of the other person; the behavior that arises from these beliefs; the other's reaction to them; and the conclusion they draw from the experience. As this process of self-observation and analysis proceeds, these patients come to realize their mutual understanding of their interpersonal problem is incomplete and a common pattern emerges. The clinician's role is to draw attention to the beliefs that underlie self-perception that leads to self-protective behaviors.

Step three focuses on alternative strategies. As patients recognize and understand these cognitive-interpersonal patterns and styles, the clinician can increase their motivation to try new behavior by helping them recognize that old and new views of self are in conflict, and that this conflict can be reconciled. Working with patients to integrate their current beliefs with their earlier interpersonal experiences helps them understand that their social fears and expectations resulted in part from their temperament and parenting. As patients continue to identify and understand their cognitive-interpersonal patterns they begin to try new strategies either on their own or at the clinician's prompting.

Step four involves behavioral experimentation and cognitive evaluation. These therapeutic strategies are discussed in detail by Beck and Freeman (1990). Friendship formation and assertive communication are the two basic interpersonal skills that avoidant patients must increase. Role-playing and directed assignments are particularly useful in this regard. I have found that the section of Zimbardo's (1977) social skills has been extremely useful as a handout for avoidant patients. Patients are gently guided through exercises to develop assertive communication skills. As a matter of fact, the entire book is an invaluable adjunct in the treatment of the avoidant personality.

The basic premise of this book is that a single treatment modality like psychotherapy may well be effective for the highest-functioning personality-disordered individual, but less effective for moderate functioning, and largely ineffective for more severely dysfunctional individuals. These lower-functioning patients tend to be more responsive to combined treatment modalities. Combined modalities include integrative psychotherapeutic intervention with medication and/or group treatment such as group therapy or support groups. As noted in the section on group treatments, avoidant patients have considerable difficulty with any kind of group. Ideally, lower-functioning avoidant patients should be involved in both individual and group therapy concurrently. When this is not possible, time-limited skill-oriented group training sessions or a support group may be sufficient. Aware that their pattern of avoidance and social inhibition makes entry into and continuation with therapeutic groups distressing, individual sessions should be focused on transitioning the patient into the group.

Medication is often necessary in the early stages of treatment and can be particularly useful in reducing distress and self-protective behavior during the transition into concurrent group treatment.

CHAPTER 4

Borderline Personality
Disorder

Borderline personality disorder is, without a doubt, the personality disorder that is most researched, written about, and a major source of concern for clinicians. Despite its notoriety, not everyone agrees that it should be an Axis II diagnostic category, contending instead that it is really a variant of depression, bipolar disorder, or another Axis I disorder (Silk, 2002).

Historically, the borderline personality was known as psuedoneurotic schizophrenia, schizophrenic characters, ambulatory schizophrenia, or latent schizophrenia. Efforts to understand this condition that seemed to be between or on the border of neurosis and psychosis have occupied many psychoanalytic theorists and researchers, and more recently, descriptive and phenomenological researchers. Largely because of the increasing interest and literature about this disorder, borderline personality disorder was added to DSM-III. Prior to that, borderline patients often were diagnosed with the DSM-II category of schizophrenia, latent type. Dissatisfaction with the failure of DSM-III and DSM-III-R to account for brief psychotic episodes prompted the inclusion of transient, stress-related paranoid ideation of severe dissociative symptoms as a criterion in DSM-IV. Still, there remained concern about the borderline designation: Is it a specific personality disorder, or is it a dimension of personality or a personality organization (Kernberg, 1984) or spectrum disorder (Meissner, 1988)? If the borderline designation refers to a continuum, then all the personality disorders in Clusters A and B could be considered borderline conditions.

Despite this debate, this disorder, with a prevalence rate of 2 percent in the general population and 10 and 20 percent among those in outpatient and inpatient treatment, respectively, remains a DSM-IV-TR Axis II disorder. The Collaborative Longitudinal Personality Disorders Study (Sanislow et al., 2002) tested the factor structure of borderline personality disorder. This important longitudinal study supported the viability of borderline personality disorder as a statistically coherent construct and internally consistent diagnostic category. This research concluded that all nine DSM-IV (and DSM-IV-TR) diagnostic criteria are subsumed under three factors: affect dysregulation, behavior dysregulation, and disturbed relatedness. In short, this study lends considerable conceptual clarity to this disorder as a separate and unique Axis II diagnosis. Another important study supported the distinct character of borderline personality disorder with regard to individuals with other personality disorders and with a nonclinical population. With regard to sensitivity and specificity, results indicated that borderline personality disorder can be characterized by a dimensional profile that is distinct from other personality-disordered individuals and healthy controls (Pukrop, 2002).

In terms of DSM-IV-TR changes to borderline personality disorder, the text in the "Course" section was updated to "emphasize that, contrary to many clinicians' preconceived notions, the prognosis for many individuals with Borderline Personality Disorder is good" (p. 842). The new text reads: "During their 30s and 40s the majority of individuals with this disorder attain stability in their relationships and vocational functioning. Follow up studies of individuals identified through outpatient mental health clinics indicate that after about 10 years, as many as half of the individuals no longer have a pattern that meets full criteria for Borderline Personality Disorder" (p. 709).

This chapter describes the characteristic features of this disorder and its related personality style. Five different clinical formulations and psychological assessment indicators are highlighted. Also described are a variety of treatment approaches, modalities, and intervention strategies.

DESCRIPTION OF BORDERLINE PERSONALITY DISORDER

Borderline personality disorder can be recognized by the following descriptors and characteristics: style vs. disorder, triggering event, behavioral styles, interpersonal style, cognitive style, affective style, attachment style, and optimal criterion.

Table 4.1
Comparison of Borderline Personality Style and Disorder

Personality Style	Personalty Disorder
Tend to experience passionate, focused attachments in all relationships. Nothing in the relationship is taken lightly	Pattern of unstable and intense relationships noted by alternating between extremes of overidealization and devaluation
Emotionally active and reactive, they show their feelings and put their hearts into everything	Impulsive in at least two areas that are potentially self-damaging, e.g., spending, sex, substance abuse, shoplifting, reckless driving, binge eating, suicidal threats, gestures, or behavior
Tend to be uninhibited, spontaneous, fun-loving, and undaunted by risk	Affective instability marked by shifts from baseline mood to depression, irritability or anxiety usually lasting a few hours and only rarely more than a few days
Tend to be creative, lively, busy, and engaging individuals. They show initiative and can stir others to activity	Inappropriate, intense anger or lack of control of anger, e.g., frequent displays of temper, constant anger, recurrent physical fights; chronic feelings of emptiness or boredom
Imaginative and curious, they are willing to experience and experiment with other cultures and value systems	Marked and persistent identity disturbance characterized by uncertainty about at least two of the following: self-image, sexual orientation, long-term goals or career choice, type of friends desired, preferred values
Regularly tend to be deeply involved in a romantic relationship with one person	Frantic efforts to avoid real or imagined abandonment

Style vs. Disorder. The borderline personality can be thought of as spanning a continuum from healthy to pathological, wherein borderline personality style is on the healthy end, and borderline personality disorder is on the pathological end. Table 4.1 compares and contrasts the antisocial personality style and disorder.

Triggering Event. The typical situation, circumstance, or event that most likely triggers or activates the characteristic maladaptive response of borderline personality disorder (Othmer & Othmer, 2002), as noted in behavioral, interpersonal, cognitive, and feeling styles, is "frantic efforts to avoid real or imagined abandonment."

Behavioral Style. Behaviorally, borderlines are characterized by physically self-damaging acts such as suicide gestures, self-mutilation, or the provocation of fights. Their social and occupational accomplishments are often less than their intelligence and ability warrant. Of all the personality disorders, they are more likely to have irregularities of circadian rhythms, especially of the sleep-wake cycle. Thus, chronic insomnia is a common complaint.

Interpersonal Style. Interpersonally, borderlines are characterized by their paradoxical instability. That is, they fluctuate quickly from idealizing and clinging to another individual to devaluing and opposing that individual. They are extremely rejection sensitive and experience abandonment depression following the slightest of stressors. Millon and Davis (1996) consider separation anxiety as a primary motivator of this personality disorder. Interpersonal relationships develop rather quickly and intensely, yet their social adaptiveness is rather superficial. They are extraordinarily intolerant of being alone and they go to great lengths to seek out the company of others whether in indiscriminate sexual affairs, late-night phone calls to relatives and recent acquaintances, or late-night visits to hospital emergency rooms with a host of vague medical and/or psychiatric complaints.

Cognitive Style. Their cognitive style is described as inflexible and impulsive (Millon, 1981). Inflexibility of their style is characterized by rigid abstractions that easily lead to grandiose, idealized perceptions of others not as real people but as personifications of "all good" or "all bad" individuals. They reason by analogy from past experience and thus have difficulty reasoning logically and learning from past experiences and relationships. Because they have an external locus of control, borderlines usually blame others when things go wrong. By accepting responsibility for their own incompetence, borderlines believe they are powerless to change circumstances. Accordingly, their emotions fluctuate between hope and despair because they believe that external circumstances are well beyond their control (Shulman, 1982).

Their cognitive style is also marked by impulsivity, and just as they vacillate between idealization and devaluation of others, their thoughts shift from one extreme to another: "I like people. No, I don't like them"; "Having goals is good. No, it's not"; "I need to get my life together. No, I can't. It's hopeless." This inflexibility and impulsivity complicate the process of identity formation. Their uncertainty about self-image, gender identity, goals, values, and career choice reflects this impulsive and flexible stance.

Adler (1985) suggested that borderlines have an underdeveloped evocative memory, so they have difficulty recalling images and feeling states that could structure and soothe them in times of turmoil. Their inflexibility and impulsivity are further noted in their tendency toward "splitting," which is the inability to synthesize contradictory qualities, so the individual views others as all good or all bad and utilizes "projective identification," attributing his or her own negative or dangerous feelings to others. Their cognitive style is further characterized by an inability to tolerate frustration.

Finally, micropsychotic episodes can be noted when these individuals are under a great deal of stress. These are ill-defined, strange thought processes especially noted in response to unstructured rather than structured situations and may take the form of derealization, depersonalization, intense rage reactions, unusual reactions to drugs, and intense brief paranoid episodes. Because of difficulty in focusing attention and subsequent loss of relevant data, borderlines also have a diminished capacity to process information.

Affective Style. The emotional style of individuals with this disorder is characterized by marked mood shifts from a normal or euthymic mood to a dysphoric mood. In addition, inappropriate and intense anger and rage may easily be triggered. On the other extreme are feelings of emptiness, a deep void, or boredom.

Attachment Style. Individuals with a vacillating view of both self and others exhibit the disorganized attachment style. "Disorganized attachment develops from repeated experiences in which the caregiver appears frightened or frightening to the child" (Siegel, 1999, p. 117). This style is associated with dissociative symptomatology, which increases proneness to posttraumatic stress disorder. Borderline personality disorder is characterized by unstable personality structure that seems to shift among the various insecure attachment styles, creating a disorganized profile called disorganized attachment style (Lyddon & Sherry, 2001).

Childhood Abuse and Etiology. There is increasing research evidence that a history of early abuse or neglect is common in adults with personality disorders, particularly borderline personality disorder (Herman, Perry, & van der Kolk, 1989; Zanarini et al., 2000). Bernstein (2002) indicates that childhood histories of *severe* emotional abuse are noted in adults diagnosed with borderline personality disorders. Data on sexual abuse among individuals with this disorder are troubling, in that the odds of such an individual attempting suicide in adulthood are over ten times that of those who were never sexually abused (Soloff, Lynch, & Kelly, 2002).

Many clinicians have come to assume that this disorder is caused by childhood abuse. Research largely supports this presumption. Nevertheless, it does not suggest that abuse is the primary cause of all cases of borderline personality disorder. But exactly how prevalent is such trauma in those presenting for treatment? A meta-analytics study (Fossatti, Madeddu, & Maffei, 1999), indicates that in individuals diagnosed with borderline personality disorder the prevalence rates of abuse are in the range of 60 to 80 percent, which means that 20 to 40 percent of these individuals do *not* report such histories. Presumably, such individuals are more likely to be so-called higher-functioning borderlines. In other words, while there are traumatic pathways in the development of personality disorders, there are also nontraumatic pathways. An important treatment implication is that clients who were not traumatized but rather may have been otherwise wounded as children in their efforts to meet emotional needs may be responsive to a broader range of therapeutic interventions than very focused approaches such as dialectical behavior therapy. These other interventions might include exploratory, uncovering, and abreactive interventions, which are less likely to be regressive or iatrogenic than they would be with clients with trauma histories (Graybar & Boutilier, 2002).

Optimal DSM-IV-TR Criterion. Of all the stated DSM-IV-TR criteria for borderline personality disorder, one criterion has been found to be the most useful in diagnosis. The belief is that by beginning with this criterion, the clinician can test for the presence or absence of the criterion and quickly diagnose the personality disorder (Allnutt & Links, 1996). The optimal criterion for this disorder is "expectation of meeting personal goals and/or maintaining close relations." The following case examples further illustrate the differences between borderline personality disorder (Mr. J.) and borderline personality style (Ms. B.).

Case Study: Borderline Personality Disorder

Mr. J. is a 31-year-old unemployed male who was referred to the hospital emergency room by his therapist at a community mental health center after 2 days of sustained suicidal gestures. He appeared to function adequately until his senior year in high school, when he became preoccupied with transcendental meditation. He had considerable difficulty concentrating during his first semester of college and seemed to focus most of his energies on finding a spiritual guru. At times, massive anxiety and feelings of emptiness swept over him, which he found would suddenly vanish if he lightly cut his wrist enough to draw blood. He had been in treatment with his current therapist for 18 months and became increasingly hostile and demanding as a patient, whereas earlier he had been quite captivated with his therapist's empathy and intuitive sense. Lately, his life seemed to center on these twice-weekly therapy sessions. Mr. J.'s most recent suicidal thoughts followed the therapist's disclosure that he was moving out of the area.

Case Study: Borderline Personality Style

Ms. B. is a 29-year-old graduate student in Oriental literature. She had completed her undergraduate degree at the university in business and management with honors and had planned on starting her MBA that fall. A summer tour of Japan and China dramatically changed her life. She fell in love with the Orient: the people, the food, the customs, the ambiance, but especially a literature professor at a Tokyo university. She fell madly in love with him the first time she met him and spent the next 2 weeks before her flight back to the States totally engrossed with his poetry, his stories, and his life. Although he was married, his wife was on a holiday alone. Ms. B. was conflicted about returning home even though he broke off the relationship. Ms. B. was crushed that he would not leave his wife. Nevertheless, she returned to the university with an ardent desire to immerse herself in the study of Oriental literature. She had fantasies of returning to Tokyo as a visiting professor and working alongside the love of her life, with the goal of eventually having him all to herself. Yet, even though she was doing well in her classes, she occasionally got in touch with the anger and hurt she had experienced that summer. Midway into her first semester in grad school, she met a stunning Asian graduate student with whom she instantly fell in love.

DSM-IV-TR Description and Criteria

Table 4.2 provides the DSM-IV-TR description and criteria for this disorder.

FORMULATIONS OF BORDERLINE PERSONALITY DISORDER

Psychodynamic Formulation

Kernberg (1975) targets the rapprochement subphase of Mahler's separation-individuation developmental theory as the point of fixation for borderline pathology. At that phase, children lack object constancy and thus cannot integrate the good and bad and aspects of themselves or their mothers. Neither can they separate from the mother, since they have yet to internalize a whole, soothing internalized usage of her that sustains them during her physical absence. Kernberg points to a disturbance in the mother's emotional availability during the rapprochement subphase that is attributable to the constitutional excess of aggression in the child, to maternal problems with parenting, or to both.

Table 4.2
DSM-IV-TR Criteria for Borderline Personality Disorder (301.83)

A pervasive pattern of instability of interpersonal relationships, self-image, affects, and control over impulses beginning by early adulthood and present in a variety of contexts, as indicated by at least five of the following:

(1) frantic efforts to avoid real or imagined abandonment. Note: Do not include suicidal or self-mutilating behavior covered in criterion (5).
(2) a pattern of unstable and intense interpersonal relationships characterized by alternating between extremes of idealization and devaluation
(3) identity disturbance: persistent and markedly disturbed, distorted, or unstable self-image or sense of self
(4) impulsivity in at least two areas that are potentially self-damaging (e.g., spending, sex, substance abuse, reckless driving, binge eating). Note: Do not include suicidal or self-mutilating behavior covered in criterion (5).
(5) recurrent suicidal behavior, gestures, or threats, or self-mutilating behavior
(6) affective instability due to a marked reactivity of mood (e.g., intense episodic dysphoria, irritability, or anxiety usually lasting a few hours and only rarely more than a few days)
(7) chronic feelings of emptiness
(8) inappropriate, intense anger or lack of control of anger (e.g., frequent displays of temper, constant anger, recurrent physical fights)
(9) transient, stress-related paranoid ideation or severe dissociative symptoms

Reprinted with permission from the *Diagnostic and Statistical Manual of Mental Disorders, Fourth Edition–Text Revision.* Copyright 2000. American Psychiatric Association.

Masterson (1976) and Masterson and Klein (1990) implicate the rapprochement subphase but emphasize the mother's behavior rather than the child's aggression. Typically a borderline herself, the mother is deeply conflicted about her children growing up and becoming their own person. Thus, these children receive the message that if they grow up, something awful will happen to them and/or to their mothers, and that remaining dependent is the only way of maintaining the maternal bond. This prospect of separation and individuation thus provokes abandonment depression in borderlines. No integration between a rewarding object unit and a withdrawing object unit is possible at this subphase, which accounts for the symptom of borderline syndrome.

Adler's (1985) understanding of borderline pathology is influenced by Kohut (1971, 1977) and Fraiberg (1969) and is based on a deficit rather than a conflict model as with Kernberg. Inconsistency in maternal behavior and availability results in the borderline's failure to develop a "holding-nothing" internalized object. This accounts for feelings of emptiness, depressive tendencies, and oral rage. Furthermore, the borderline individual has difficulty summoning up internal images of the natural nurturing figure in stressful situations. This cognitive deficit of evocative memory suggests a regression to developmental age between 8 and 18 months. These inadequate resources leave the borderline prone to fragmentation of the self, which is accompanied by profound emptiness called annihilation panic.

Biosocial Formulation

Millon and Davis (1996) view the borderline's lack of a clear, coherent sense of identity as central to the pathogenesis of this disorder. They believe that identity confusion and/or diffusion is the result of biopsychosocial factors that combine to impair a coherent sense of identity. Because of this central deficit, poor coordinated actions, overmodulated affects, poorly controlled impulses, and a failure of consistent effort result. Thus, the borderline individual depends on others for protection and reassurance, and is hypersensitive to loss or separation of these supports. Based on this research, Millon (1981) and Millon and Everly (1985) contend that borderline syndrome is essentially a more severe and regressed variant of the dependent, histrionic, or passive aggressive personalty disorders. Biologically and temperamentally, borderline-dependent individuals tend to exhibit a passive infantile pattern and possess family histories of low energy levels. This pattern evokes parental warmth and overprotection, and they subsequently form strong attachments and dependency to a single caregiver, which ultimately restricts their opportunity to learn the necessary skills of social independence and self-efficacy. This sets the stage for rejection by those on whom they have come to rely.

Borderline histrionic individuals more often possess family histories characterized by high autonomic reactivity, and they exhibit hyperresponsiveness as a result of exposure to high levels of stimulation. Parental control tends to be exercised by contingent reinforcement patterns for which these children feel competent and accepted only if their behavior is explicitly approved by others, and thus they "perform" to secure support, attention, and nurturance.

Borderline passive-aggressive individuals tend to have exhibited "difficult child" (Thomas & Chess, 1977) temperaments. As irritable, difficult-to-soothe infants, they likely received inconsistent responses from their caregivers: caring at times, harried and frustrated at others, and even withdrawal. They might have been products of broken homes and likely had a parent who modeled the erratic, vacillating, passive-aggressive behavior they display as adults.

Cognitive-Behavioral Formulation

According to Beck et al. (1990), three basic assumptions are noted in borderlines: "I am powerless and vulnerable"; "I am inherently unacceptable"; "The world is dangerous and malevolent." Because of their inherent belief that they are helpless in a hostile world without a source of security, they vacillate between autonomy and dependence without being able to rely on either. In addition, borderlines tend to display dichotomous thinking: the tendency to evaluate experiences in mutually exclusive categories, all good or all bad, success or failure, trustworthy or deceitful. The combination of dichotomous thinking and basic assumptions is the basis of borderline emotion and behavior, including acting-out, self-destructive behaviors.

Young (1990) believes that early maladaptive schemas develop during childhood and result in maladaptive behavior patterns that reinforce these schemas. Schemas such as abandonment/loss: "I'll be alone forever. No one would live with me or want to be close to me if they really got to know me"; and emotional deprivation: "No one is ever there to meet my needs, to be strong for me, to care for me" are believed to be common early maladaptive schemas in borderlines.

Linehan (1987) describes a behavioral formulation of borderline pathology. She claims that a dysfunction in emotional regulation is the core feature of borderline pathology, resulting in dramatic overreaction and impulsivity. This dysfunction is believed to be physiologically based and reinforced by experiences with significant others who discount the individual's emotional experiences. Subsequently, borderline individuals develop little or no skill in emotion regulation. The combination of intense emotional responses, inadequate emotional regulation skills, impulsive behavior, and a disparaging self-attitude presages unrelenting crisis for which they are unable to effectively cope, and they overrely on others. From a different behavioral perspective, Turkat (1990) believes that problem-solving deficits are the basis for borderline pathology.

Interpersonal Formulation

Benjamin (1996) documents that persons with borderline personality disorder typically grew up in a family marked by a chaotic, soap-opera lifestyle. Without these dilemmas, life was experienced as hollow, boring, and empty. Whether these chaotic dramas were blatant or sequestered from public view, the borderline-to-be played a central role, resulting in the impulsivity, mood instability, and unpredictability characteristic of life without constancy. The developmental histories of these individuals often included traumatic abandonment experiences, the isolation of which was typically marked by physical and/or sexual abuse. This abuse-laden aloneness became inexorably linked with the notion that the borderline-to-be was a bad person. These abuse experiences "taught" the individual to shift from idealization to devaluation. And to the extent that sexual abuse experiences were painful, they set the stage for self-mutilation, as pleasure became confused with pain during such episodes.

Family norms dictated that autonomy was bad while dependency and sympathetic misery with the family were good. Movement toward independence, competence, or happiness elicited self-sabotage. Furthermore, young borderline individuals learned from their families that misery, sickness, and debilitation draw forth love and concern from others. The adult consequence is that borderline-disordered individuals believe that caregivers and lovers secretly love misery. In short, there is a morbid fear of abandonment and a wish for protective nurturance particularly from a lover or caregiver. Initially, friendly dependency on the nurturer gives way to hostile control when the caregiver or lover fails to deliver enough. Borderline individuals believe that significant others secretly like dependency and neediness, and a vicious introject attacks the self in the face of any signs of success or happiness.

Integrative Formulation

The following integrative formulation may be helpful in understanding how the borderline personality pattern is likely to be developed and maintained. Biologically, borderlines can be understood in terms of the three main subtypes: borderline dependent, borderline histrionic, and borderline passive-aggressive. The temperamental style of the borderline-dependent type is that of the passive infantile pattern (Millon, 1981). Millon hypothesized that low autonomic nervous system reactivity plus an overprotective parenting style facilitates restrictive interpersonal skills and a clinging relational style. On the other hand, the histrionic subtype was more likely to have a hyper-responsive infantile pattern. Thus, because of high autonomic nervous system reactivity and increased parental stimulation and expectations for performance, the borderline histrionic pattern was likely to result. Finally, the temperamental style of the passive-aggressive borderline was likely to have been the "difficult child" type noted by Thomas and Chess (1977). This pattern plus parental inconsistency marks the affective irritability of the borderline passive-aggressive personality.

Psychologically, borderlines tend to view themselves, others, the world, and life's purpose in terms of the following themes. They view themselves by some variant of the theme: "I don't know who I am or where I'm going." In short, their identity problems involve gender, career, loyalties, and values while their self-esteem fluctuates with each thought or feeling about their self-identity. Borderlines tend to view their world with some variant of the themes: "People are great. No, they are not"; "Having goals is good. No, it's not"; "If life doesn't go my way, I can't tolerate it." As such they are likely to conclude "Therefore, keep all options open. Don't commit to anything. Reverse roles and vacillate thinking and feelings when under attack." The six defensive operations utilized by borderline personality–disordered individuals are denial, splitting, primitive idealization, projective identification, ominpotence, and devaluation (Shulman, 1982).

Socially, predictable patterns of parenting and environmental factors can be noted for borderline personality disorder. Parenting style differs depending on the subtype. For example, in the dependent subtype overprotectiveness characterizes parenting, in the histrionic subtype a demanding parenting style is more evident, and in the passive-aggressive subtype an inconsistent parenting style is more noted. But because borderline personality is a syndromal elaboration and deterioration of the less severe dependent, histrionic, and passive-aggressive personality disorders, the family of origin in borderline subtypes of these disorders is likely to be much more dysfunctional, increasing the likelihood that the child will have learned various self-defeating coping strategies. The parental injunction is likely to have been, "If you grow up and leave me, bad things will happen to me (parent)."

This borderline pattern is confirmed, reinforced, and perpetuated by the following individual and systems factors: Diffuse identity, impulsive vacillation, and self-defeating coping strategies lead to aggressive acting out, which leads to more chaos, which leads to the experience of depersonalization, increased dysphoria, and/or self-mutilation to achieve some relief. This leads to further reconfirmation of their beliefs about self and the world as well as reinforcement of the behavioral and interpersonal patterns (Sperry & Mosak, 1993).

ASSESSMENT OF BORDERLINE PERSONALITY DISORDER

Several sources of information are useful in establishing a diagnosis and treatment plan for personality disorders. Observation, collateral information, and psychological testing are important adjuncts to the patient's self-report in the clinical interview. This section briefly describes some characteristic observations that the clinician makes and the nature of the rapport likely to develop in initial encounters with specific personality-disordered individuals. Characteristic response patterns on various objective (i.e., MMPI-2 and MCMI-II) and projective tests (i.e., Rorschach and TAT) are also described.

Interview Behavior and Rapport

Interviewing borderline personality–disordered individuals presents a special challenge because of their instability and ambivalence. Instability or labil-

Table 4.3
Characteristics of Borderline Personality Disorder

Triggering Event	Expectation of meeting personal goals and/or maintaining close relations.
Behavioral Style	"Hemophiliacs" of emotion; resentful, impulsiveness, acting out; helpless, dysphoric, empty void; irregular circadian rhythms (sleep-wake, etc.).
Interpersonal Style	Paradoxical—idealizing and clinging vs. devaluing and oppositional; rejection sensitivity—abandonment and depression; separation anxiety as prime motivator; role reversal.
Cognitive Style	Inflexible, rigid; abstraction—grandiosity and idealization, splitting; reasons by analogy: doesn't learn from experience; external loss of control—blaming; poorly developed evocative memory.
Feeling Style	Extreme lability of mood and affect.
Temperament	*Dependent type*: passive infantile pattern—low autonomic nervous system reactivity. *Passive-aggressive type*: "difficult" infantile pattern—affect irritability.
Attachment Style	Disorganized.
Parental Injunction	"If you grow up, bad things will happen to me (parent)." Overprotective or demanding or inconsistent parenting.
Self-View	"I don't know who I am or where I'm going." Identity problems involving gender, career, loyalties, and values. Self-esteem fluctuates with current emotion.
Worldview	"People are great. No, they're not. Having goals is good. No, it's not. If life doesn't go my way, I can't tolerate it. Don't commit to anything."
Maladaptive Schemas	Abandonment; defectiveness; abuse/mistrust; emotional deprivation; social isolation; insufficient self-control.
Optimal DSM-IV-TR Criteria	Frantic efforts to avoid real or imagined abandonment.

ity is noted in their moods, goals, and rapport with the clinician. Instability regarding rapport is handled by empathically focusing on it. This is done by directing the discussion, keeping the discussion on track, and curbing diversions and outbursts. Asking open-ended questions is preferable to seeking precise answers to closed-ended pointed questions. Instability is also processed by separating it as a pathological part that needs to be explored. Since it also affects rapport, the clinician must continually acknowledge its presence and effect. The result is that these patients become less defensive and more willing to disclose, thus furthering rapport.

Dealing with ambivalence requires confronting their contradictions while exhibiting and understanding their ambivalent feelings. Therapeutic confrontation illustrates their splitting and projective identification and moderates overidealization or devaluation. It further helps these individuals to realize that their ambivalence results from a perceived lack of support and understanding of their mother, which they allow to profoundly influence their sense of well-being (Othmer & Othmer, 2002).

Psychological Testing Data

The Minnesota Multiphasic Personality Inventory (MMPI-2), the Millon Clinical Multiaxial Inventory (MCMI-III), the Rorschach Psychodiagnostic Test, and the Thematic Apperception Test (TAT) can be useful in diagnosing borderline personality disorder as well as the borderline personality style or trait.

On the MMPI-2, elevations on scales 2 (depression), 4 (psychothemia), and 8 (schizophrenia) are common (Groth-Marnat, 1999). Scales O (social introversion) and K (correction) tend to be high; F (frequency) is typically low. If emotional dysregulation—particularly of anger—is prominent, scale 6 (paranoia) will be high (Graham, 2000). Although relatively rare, a 2–6 (depression-paranoia) profile is associated with borderline pathology (Meyer, 1995).

On the MCMI-III, an elevation on scale C (borderline) is most likely and a concurrent elevation on scale 8A (passive-aggressive) is also likely. Elevations on such clinical scales as A (anxiety), H (somatoform), N (bipolar-manic), and/or D (dysthymia) can be expected (Choca & Denburg, 1997).

On the Rorschach, illogical and fabulized combinations (e.g., "a horse's head with two sea horses growing out of his ears" for card 10) are common (Meyer, 1995; Swiercinsky, 1985). Such responses are most likely on cards 10.9 and 2.

On the TAT, "primitive splitting" may be noted in characters judged as all bad, (e.g., devils), in characters wherein only one side of the personality is admitted to or portrayed, or when good-bad characteristics are juxtaposed incongruously. Separation anxiety themes, extreme portrayals of affect, and acting out rather than delayed gratification themes are not uncommon (Bellak, 1997).

TREATMENT APPROACHES AND INTERVENTIONS

Treatment Considerations

Included in the differential diagnosis of borderline personality disorder are these other Axis II personality disorders: passive-aggressive personality disorder, histrionic personality disorder, dependent personality disorder, and schizotypal personality disorder. The most common Axis I syndromes associated with the personality disorder are generalized anxiety disorder, panic disorder, and dysthymia. In addition, other syndromes may be brief reactive psychoses, schizoaffective disorder, hypochondriasis, and dissociative disorders, especially psychogenic fugue.

Borderline personality disorder may be the most common Axis II presentations seen in both the public sector and in private practice. It can be among the most difficult and frustrating conditions to treat. Clinical experience suggests that it is important to assess the individual for overall level of functioning and treatment readiness in making decisions about treatment approaches, modalities, and strategies. Borderline personality disorder is the most researched of all the personality disorders. To date, several randomized controlled treatment studies have been published including two involving psychosocial interventions (Crits-Christoph & Barber, 2002). These studies have led to the development of a series of treatment protocols and guidelines that are described throughout this section.

APA Treatment Guidelines

In 2001, the American Psychiatric Association published *Practice Guidelines for the Treatment of Patients with Borderline Personality Disorder* (Oldham et al., 2001). This represents a significant milestone in the emergence of personality disorders as an important domain of psychopathology and psychiatric treatment. This is the first time that APA clinical practice guidelines have addressed the management of Axis II conditions. Much like the highly touted guidelines for the treatment of major depression, these recently released guidelines will inevitably exert considerable influence on clinical practice. These evidence-based guidelines are notable for (1) identifying the multidimensional nature of borderline psychopathology, (2) recommending a treatment approach that is both flexible and tailored to individual need and expectation; (3) highlighting the value of a combined approach—that is, medication and therapy; and (4) providing guidelines for inpatient admission and care.

Unlike the guidelines for the treatment of depression, which reflect a very large research literature, "the empirical data base for the treatment of BPD is painfully limited" (Paris, 2002, p. 131), leading some to question the quality of the evidence base for these guidelines. In instances where cogent clinical questions have yet to be addressed in randomized controlled trials, the APA guidelines offer a clinical consensus based on uncontrolled trials and case studies, which, although better than no research support, will not be particularly satisfying to some clinicians.

Three areas of the borderline personality disorder guidelines that have been criticized are specific recommendations for psychotherapy, psycho-pharmacology, and inpatient treatment based on clinical consensus. In terms of *psychotherapy*, these include suggestions for working with issues ranging from dissociative symptoms to transference. And, while randomized clinical trial data support certain treatments such as dialectic behavior therapy (Linehan, 1993a), the guidelines raise questions as to the applicability of this approach to a broader range of patients seen in clinical practice, particularly those who are higher functioning. In terms of *psychopharmacology*, concern is mainly about the use of algorithms to guide treatment of targeted borderline pathology without succumbing to polypharmacy. Unfortunately, the guidelines are not clear about addressing targets beyond impulsivity. In terms of *inpatient treatment*, specific guidelines for admitting patients for acute suicide risk appear to be overly broad (Paris, 2002). Like in other areas, future data from large-scale studies should help sharpen these guidelines, which should increase both clinician competence and confidence.

Individual Psychotherapy

Many consider individual psychotherapy to be the cornerstone of treatment for borderline personality disorder. Although there are widely divergent opinions on the appropriateness or efficacy of the various individual psychotherapeutic approaches, there is consensus on some general principles. Waldinger (1986) describes five points of consensus on treating the borderline personality. First, the therapist must be active in identifying, confronting, and directing the patient's behaviors during sessions. Second, a stable treatment environment must be afforded in terms of setting and maintaining limits and boundaries, scheduling, payment of fees, and role expectations of patient and clinician. Third, connection between the patient's actions and feelings on the present need to be established. Fourth, self-destructive behavior must be made ungratifying. Fifth, careful attention must be paid to countertransference feelings.

Regardless of the specific psychotherapeutic approach utilized, the literature indicates that treatment of the borderline patient is difficult, countertransference problems are common, and the results are uneven (Gunderson, 1989). Some borderline patients experience negative therapeutic reaction and other untoward effects of individual psychotherapy. In some instances, these patients should not be afforded individual treatment. Francis, Clarkin, and Perry (1984) offer the "no treatment option" and offer specific criteria for its use. Nevertheless, when treatment is indicated, attention to the patient's needs and expectations for treatment and efforts to match and tailor treatment are essential in maximizing treatment outcomes. This section describes various psychodynamic, cognitive-behavioral, and interpersonal approaches.

Psychodynamic Psychotherapy Approach

Here is a brief outline of various psychodynamic approaches to the borderline personality: psychoanalytic psychotherapy, supportive psychotherapy, and short-term dynamic psychotherapy.

Psychoanalytic Psychotherapy. There are basically two psychoanalytic opinions regarding the treatment of borderline patients based on the role of early interpretation and the management of negative transference. One view is that confrontation must occur early in the course of treatment and that interpretation of primitive transference must be made in here-and-now situations. The other view is that the early interpretations of aggressive themes are ineffective and possibly disruptive. Kernberg (1984) and Masterson (1976), among others, espouse the first view, while Chessick (1982) and Buie and Adler (1982) and others advocate the second. Nevertheless, both views agree that personality reconstruction is the goal of treatment, requiring three or more sessions a week for a minimum of 4 years.

Masterson (1976) and Masterson and Klein (1990) have elegantly described the psychotherapeutic process with borderline patients. Supportive psychotherapy is differentiated from reconstructive psychotherapy. The goal of reconstructive psychotherapy is to work through the abandonment depression—feelings of depression, anger and rage, fear, guilt, passivity and helplessness, emptiness and void that follow a recent experience of separation and loss—associated with the original separation-individuation phase. This leads to the achievement of ego autonomy and the transformation of split object relations into whole object relations and the split ego into a whole ego. Three stages of psychotherapy are noted by Masterson. The testing phase in which the clinician utilizes confrontation and communicative matching to support the patient's emerging individuation as the principal technique; the working-through phase; and the separation phase.

The expected outcome of such treatment is not only a reduction in impulsive behavior and other regressive reactions to stressors but improved stability in interpersonal relationships. Such personality reconstruction allows the individual to function normally or on a neurotic level (Gunderson, 1989).

Supportive Psychotherapy. From a dynamic perspective, supportive psychotherapy is less intensive and regressive than psychoanalytic psychotherapy or psychoanalysis. The goals of supportive therapy with borderline individuals are principally to improve their adaptation to daily life and reduce their self-destructive responses to interpersonal stressors (Kernberg, 1984).

The basic techniques of supportive psychotherapy consist of exploring the patients' primitive defenses in the here-and-now for the purpose of helping them achieve control by nonanalytic means, and fostering a better adaptation to reality by helping them become more aware of the disorganizing affect of their defensive operations. Manifest and suppressed transferences—rather than unconscious and repressed transferences—are explored and utilized for classification of related interpersonal problems faced by the patient (Kernberg, 1984).

Such supportive psychotherapy is utilized commonly with moderate and lower-functioning borderline outpatients. Typically, sessions are scheduled weekly and may continue for several years. The results of the Menninger Outcome Study suggest that supportive treatment is able to bring about the basic personality changes that were expected only from reconstructive dynamic psychotherapy (Wallerstein, 1986). So, despite Kernberg's (1984) characteristic of supportive psychotherapy as "a treatment of last resort," supportive psychotherapy is a potent intervention.

Klein (1989a) describes two types of supportive treatment for lower-functioning borderlines. In the first, confrontive psychotherapy, the treatment process involves confronting resistances that maintain maladaptive behaviors until they become ego dystonic. A therapeutic alliance takes the place of transference acting out. Treatment also involves the implementation of adaptive modes of dealing with underlying affects, such as new patterns replacing previous self-destructive behaviors and defenses. Unlike reconstructive psychotherapy, this approach does not facilitate the patient working through abandonment depression. The goals of this therapy are limited to increasing the patient's capacity to work to achieve some consistency in interpersonal relationships.

Klein (1989a) also describes an approach to "counseling" with very low-functioning borderline patients. This approach is the treatment of choice for patients with a history of repeatedly early abuse, neglect or separation trauma, or repeatedly severe psychiatric regressive episodes; or a history of repeating life-threatening suicidal or homicidal actions. The goal of this treatment is to reduce anger, anxiety, and depressive affects that persistently interfere with the patient's capacity to function adaptively. The counselor serves as an auxiliary ego for the patient and utilizes a combination of such techniques as reality testing, encouragement, direction, problem solving, and medication.

Short-Term Psychotherapy. Although it was previously assumed that borderline patients were unfit for short-term dynamic psychotherapy, it now appears that short-term and time-limited approaches have some utility with selective patients. In as few as 10 to 20 sessions, treatment can be focused on specific relational or situational problems. And, because of such a specific focus the likelihood of a regressive transference developing is limited. This approach may be suitable for borderline patients who present with concerns about being engulfed, overwhelmed, or too dependent. It may also be useful for those who have a history of terminating more regressive treatment. Furthermore, it may serve as a springboard for moving into long-term therapy.

Klein (1989b) describes a short-term treatment protocol for borderline patients. The goals are containment—that is, they come to recognize, control, and contain their propensity to act out; learning—that is, emerging affects that covered their defenses can and must be verbalized rather than acted out; and adaptation—that is, they channel their energies associated with these affects into adaptive and sublimated behavior and expressions. This short-term approach follows Masterson's model except that the frequency of sessions is limited and confrontation is the principal technique utilized, although clarification, interpretation, and communicative matching are sometimes needed. Sessions are scheduled only once or twice a week for a year or less, and day-to-day problems of adaptation and healthy defenses are the focus of treatment.

Research Support for Psychodynamic Interventions. There are now some empirical studies supporting the clinical value and utility of dynamically oriented therapy with borderline personality disorder. In one study, individuals treated with an approach based on self-psychology who remained in treatment for 2 years appeared to have profited from therapy (Stevenson & Meares, 1992; Meares, Stevenson, & Comerford, 1999). Because it was a post-hoc, naturalistic study with a waiting list control group for comparison, it is not certain that the results can be attributed to this dynamic approach.

A random controlled study of a psychoanalytically oriented approach to treatment in a partial hospitalization study has also been reported (Bateman & Fonagy, 1999, 2001). The treatment was intensive and extensive and consisted of weekly psychoanalytic psychotherapy, thrice-weekly group analytic psychotherapy, weekly psychodrama and expressive therapy, and a weekly community meeting, along with mediation management. Whether positive treatment outcomes could be attributed to the specific structure and milieu of the partial hospitalization program itself or to the psychodynamic approach utilized by therapists in the program is unclear.

Finally, a structured, manualized approach, specifically designed for treating borderline personality disorder and called transference-focused psychotherapy, appears promising. This approach focuses on affect-laden themes in the current patient–therapist relationship. These include containment of self-destructive and suicidal behaviors, various ways of sabotaging treatment, and the identification and recapitulation of significant object relations patterns. This uncontrolled trial showed markedly decreased hospitalizations, day hospital treatment, and very low dropout rate (Clarkin et al., 2001).

Cognitive-Behavioral Therapy Approach

According to Beck, Freeman, and Associates (1990) the cognitive therapy approach has significant advantages over other approaches in the treatment of borderline personality–disordered individuals. Basically, completion of cognitive therapy is possible in 1½ to 2½ years (Freeman et al., 1990) as compared to psychoanalytically oriented therapies, which typically require 5 to 7 years (Masterson, 1981).

Establishing a collaborative working relationship is the very challenging first step in the treatment process. Since trust and intimacy are major issues for these individuals, taking a collaborative, strategic approach based on guided discovery is suggested. Explicitly acknowledging and accepting the individual's difficulty in trusting the therapist, communicating clearly, assertively, and honestly, following through on agreements, and behaving in a consistently trustworthy manner provide the individual with evidence on which trust can be based. Furthermore, setting limits including specifying a treatment contract is advised.

An initial focus on concrete behavioral goals is useful in reducing the impact of the borderline individual's difficulty with intimacy and trust. Many of these individuals find it less threatening to work on issues for which little introspection is required, and where the focus is on behavior rather than feelings or thoughts. Not surprisingly, a major focus in cognitive therapy is changing maladaptive schema. Borderline individuals believe that the world is a dangerous place, that they are helpless, and that they are inherently flawed in a way that inevitably leads to rejection and abandonment by others. It is suggested that these beliefs must be gradually challenged by chipping away at them, by testing expectancies against previous experience, developing behavioral experiences to test expectancies, and developing new competencies and coping skills. These individuals must learn to challenge dichotomous thinking both during and between sessions, as decreased dichotomous thinking often results in decreased mood lability and impulsivity. Behavioral interventions such as self-instructional training (Meichenbaum, 1977) may be useful in further reducing self-destructive impulsive behaviors.

Noncompliance with treatment is not an uncommon problem with borderline individuals, and often the reason is fear of change. Since they assume the world is dangerous and they have a low tolerance for ambiguity, they find change, including growth in the course of treatment, threatening. Addressing change openly, examining risks and benefits, planning changes as a series of small steps, and not pressing for change too quickly are recommended. Fears about termination of treatment evoke abandonment and rejection issues that must be carefully addressed. In summary, cognitive therapy of borderline personality–disordered individuals begins with development of a collaborative working relationship of trust, then focuses on modulating moods, impulses, and behavior with cognitive-behavioral methods, setting the stage so that basic schemas such as abandonment, defectiveness, incompetence, and mistrust can be modified and changed.

In line with Turkat's (1990) formulation that the basic issue for borderlines is problem-solving deficiencies, Turkat proposes a treatment methodology involving several strategies. They are basic problem-solving training, concept formation training, categorization management, and processing speed management.

Dialectical Behavior Therapy. Dialectical behavior therapy was originally developed by Linehan (1983, 1987, 1993a, 1993b, 1994) for the treatment of parasuicidal borderline personality–disordered females. More recently, this approach has found broader applicability with a wider range of individuals meeting criteria for borderline personality disorder. There are four primary modes of treatment in DBT: individual therapy, group skills training, telephone contact, and therapist consultation. Skills training is carried out in a group context, with a focus on four groups of skills: mindfulness, interpersonal effectiveness, emotion modulation, and distress tolerance skills. Between sessions the patients are offered phone contact with their therapist. Clear limits on such contact is defined. The core mindfulness skills enable the patient to become more clearly aware of the contents of experience and to develop the ability to stay with that experience in the present moment. The focus of the interpersonal effectiveness skills that are taught is on effective ways of achieving one's objectives with other people: to ask for what one wants effectively, to say no and have it taken seriously, to maintain relationships, and to maintain self-esteem in interactions with others. Emotion modulation skills provide ways of changing distressing emotional states, and distress tolerance skills include strategies for coping with difficult emotional states if they cannot be changed easily (Linehan, 1993b). Medication can also be included to reduce certain target symptoms.

Early studies reported the efficacy of this approach. When compared to patients receiving treatment as usual, those in DBT had a significant reduction in suicidal behavior and hospitalizations and remained in therapy longer—that is, attrition rates were only 16.7 percent for those receiving DBT while over 50 percent for the others (Linehan et al., 1991; Linehan, Heard, & Armstrong, 1993). Evidence for the efficacy of dialectical behavior therapy continues to mount. This approach has now been supported by several randomly controlled studies (Koerner & Linehan, 2000). Furthermore, dialectical behavior therapy has been adjudged superior to the typical supportive, intermittent treatment that many borderline individuals receive in their community (Oldham et al., 2001). Is dialectical behavior therapy for everybody diagnosed with this disorder? The answer is a qualified no. Although it was developed for lower-functioning, chronically suicidal females, there are features of this approach, such as mindfulness, that would be useful for even those with much higher functioning.

Structured Skill Treatment Interventions. While research shows that medication can modulate or normalize dysregulated behaviors, a similar modulating effect has also been noted for social skills training (Lieberman, DeRisi, & Mueser, 1989). Thus, it appears that social skills training is a relatively potent bottom-up treatment strategy for normalizing such limbic system–mediated behaviors as impulsivity, aggressivity, and mood lability, which reflect specific skill deficits in individuals with borderline personality disorder. When such skill deficits are present, Sperry (1999) contends that structured skill training intervention is necessary in successful treatment. Various structured intervention strategies for modifying a personality-disordered individual's affective, behavioral, and cognitive temperament styles are described and illustrated for borderline personality disorder (Sperry, 1999).

Cognitive Coping Therapy. This therapy is an active, directive, didactic, and structured approach for treating personality-disordered individuals (Sharoff, 2002). It is a complete and self-contained approach to treatment that begins with assessing an individual's coping skills—in terms of skill chains, subskills, and microskills—and then increasing skill competence in targeted areas as needed. Five key skill areas with representative treatment modalities are *cognitive skills*—problem solving, self-instruction training, and self-management; *emotion skills*—emotional containment and compartmentalization; *perceptual skills*—perspective taking, thought stopping, and psychological distance taking; *physiological skills*—meditation and relaxation training; and *behavior skills*—communication and assertiveness training. Sharoff (2002) describes a detailed protocol and case example for using this structured approach with borderline personality disorder.

Schema Therapy. Schema therapy is an elaboration of cognitive therapy that has been developed by Young (1999, 2003) specifically for personality disorders and other difficult individual and couples problems. Schema therapy involves identifying maladaptive schemas and planning specific strategies and interventions. Four main strategies are cognitive, experiential, behavioral, and the therapeutic relationship itself. Cognitive restructuring—modification of maladaptive schemas—is an important cognitive strategy but is combined with imagery exercises, empathic confrontation, homework assignments, and "limited reparenting" (i.e., a form of corrective emotional experience; Young, 1999).

Maladaptive schemas typically associated with borderline personality disorder are: *abandonment*—that is, the belief that significant others will not or cannot provide reliable and stable support; *defectiveness*—that is, the belief that one is defective, bad, unwanted, or inferior in important respects; *mistrust/ abuse*—that is, the belief that others will abuse, humiliate, cheat, lie, manipulate, or take advantage; *emotional deprivation*—that is, the belief that one's desire for emotional support will not be met by others; *social isolation*—that is, the belief that one is alienated, different from others, or not part of any group; and *insufficient self-control*—that is, the belief that one is incapable of self-control and frustration tolerance (Bernstein, 2002). Young et al. (2003) provides a detailed treatment protocol for utilizing the schema-focused approach with borderline personality disorder.

Other Cognitive-Behavioral Interventions. Smucker (1999) describes a cognitive-behavioral approach that incorporates guided imagery to focus directly on images and affects associated with early childhood abuse in borderline individuals. This approach developed out of Smucker's experience in working with severe traumatized borderline individuals who often met criteria for posttraumatic stress disorder and had failed in previous treatments.

Interpersonal Approach

Benjamin (1996) says that psychotherapeutic interventions with borderline personality–disordered individuals can be planned and evaluated in terms of whether they enhance collaboration, facilitate learning about maladaptive patterns and their roots, block these patterns, enhance the will to change, and effectively encourage new patterns.

Benjamin offers a number of observations on facilitating collaboration. She insists that therapists offer these individuals a contract for strength building rather than in enabling regression. A collaboration based on strength building must be emphasized in sessions as well as in phone calls and even in the clinic lobby that the mutual goal is to build on strengths so that these individuals can pull themselves back together. The collaboration must be against "it"—their destructive pattern(s). Healthy collaboration further requires that transference and countertransference disasters be avoided through firm physical and verbal boundaries. Benjamin cautions that the treatment approach she advocates is not appropriate for individuals who are unable to agree to a contract in strength building.

Borderline individuals need to learn to recognize that perceived abandonment sets off a chain of self-destructive patterns. These individuals are likely to relinquish self-mutilation, self-sabotage, and homicidal or suicidal acting out if they can divorce their internalized abusive attachment figures. Essentially, they must give up the desire to be affirmed by these internalized representations. This occurs by developing a dislike of those figures, or by developing a superseding attachment to someone more constructive, such as the clinician. Once these tasks are achieved, the focus of treatment shifts to facilitating new learning. The basic goal is learning how to give and take autonomy while remaining friendly. Benjamin recommends standard treatments of facilitating personal growth.

Group Therapy

Data on the efficacy of group therapy for the treatment of personality disorders is rather soft. There are many case reports and even a few controlled studies but no randomized clinical trials, except for borderline personality disorder. There are numerous case reports and clinical trials, and even one randomized clinical trial, reported on group treatment with borderline personality–disordered individuals. Also, there is general consensus that group therapy under specified conditions has enormous therapeutic efficacy. This section will review both dynamic and behavioral group approaches as well as highlight some representative research studies.

The psychodynamic group literature on borderline personality begins in the 1950s. There is general consensus that group dynamic therapy can be a useful adjunct to individual dynamic therapy, but it cannot be the only treatment (Hulse, 1958; Slavson, 1964; Day & Semrad, 1971; Horowitz, 1980). Horowitz (1980) cautions that borderline patients require individual psychotherapy to support them throughout group-engendered stress and to integrate the affects that the group provokes in them. Furthermore, without individual psychotherapy, premature termination from group therapy is likely. On the other hand, Pines (1975) contends that concurrent dynamic individual psychotherapy is not necessary because the group process itself is a potent holding environment capable of containing primitive impulses and projections. Horowitz (1977) also contends that the individual psychotherapist not function as the group therapist in order to reduce the possibility of jealousy and fantasies of favoritism among other group members.

Most writing on dynamic group therapy for borderline personality disorder prefers heterogeneous to homogeneous groups. Researchers insist that borderline patients are more effectively treated in groups consisting of higher-functioning individuals with neuroses and other personality disorders (Day & Semrad, 1971; Horowitz, 1977; Stone & Weissman, 1984). There is, however, outcome research that supports the use of homogeneous groups wherein all patients have borderline personality disorder diagnoses (O'Leary et al., 1991; Finn & Shakir, 1990; Linehan et al., 1991).

The advantages of dynamic group therapy include "dilution of intense transference" (Horowitz, 1980), which results from the presence of multiple transferential objects, instead of the single all-encompassing individual clinician. Rage is diluted and directed toward other group members. Borderline patients also find it easier to accept feedback and confrontation from group peers than from a therapist. In addition, groups provide many opportunities to understand and master such borderline defenses as splitting and projective identification.

There are some disadvantages and difficulties with group treatment of borderline patients. First, these patients may be easily scapegoated because of their primitive manner of expression. Second, they may feel deprived amidst the competition of other group members for the group leader's nurturance. Third, they may maintain a certain distance in the group because of their privacy attachment to their individual psychotherapist (Gabbard, 1994). Dynamically oriented groups with borderlines tend to span the continuum from ego psychology (O'Leary et al., 1991; Finn & Shakir, 1990) to self psychology (Harwood, 1992).

Behavioral group therapies for borderline patients focus less on underlying explanations for the symptomatic behavior and more on helping these patients acquire the specific skills necessary to control their affects, reduce their cognitive distortions and projective identifications, and find alternatives to self-destructive behaviors. Linehan (1983, 1987, 1993a) provides a manual-guided strategy for the treatment of self-destructive behavior and impulsivity called dialectical behavior therapy. Although geared primarily to chronically parasuicidal borderline females, the treatment strategies and interventions have applicability to higher-functioning individuals. The group session employs didactic, shell training, and behavioral rehearsal techniques directed at dependency and other interpersonal patterns, as well as improvement of affect tolerance. These twice-weekly sessions for 1 year are complemented with weekly individual counseling.

There is some noteworthy research with borderlines in group treatment. Nehls (1991) and Nehls and Diamond (1993) report process and outcome data on group therapy of borderline patients in a homogeneous treatment format. The group format was highly structured, although group members defined their own treatment goals. Patient outcomes included decreased depression and hostility, which was associated largely with two interventions: providing and seeking information. Dick and Wooff (1986) reported data on time-limited dynamic group therapy with heterogeneous groups containing a number of borderline patients. The groups met daily for 12 weeks. One year later, group follow-up showed an 82 percent reduction in the use of psychiatric services compared to a control group of untreated patients. Three-year follow-up showed the gains had been maintained. Similarly, Linehan et al. (1991) reported on a randomized clinical trial of group-focused treatment. Parasuicidal female borderline patients were randomly assigned to dialectical behavior therapy groups or to traditional community treatment for 1 year. Those in behavioral groups had fewer incidents of parasuicide, were more likely to remain in individual therapy, and had fewer inpatient psychiatric days as compared to those in traditional treatment. Finally, a structured, time-limited group approach called relationship management psychotherapy was compared with open-ended individual dynamic psychotherapy in a randomized clinical trial. The study found that while both approaches showed significant improvements on all major outcomes, the structured group approach was a briefer, less expensive treatment that can be offered by a wide range of clinicians (Munroe-Blum, 1992).

Marital and Family Therapy

Families of borderline patients often exhibit severe pathology, which may be of etiological significance. Parents of borderline patients have a high incidence of affective disorders, alcoholism, antisocial personality disorder, and borderline personality disorder or traits. The parental relationship is usually characterized by neglect and overprotectiveness. Family therapy can be useful, and in some instances necessary, in maintaining borderline patients in outpatient psychotherapy. This is particularly the case when borderline patients remain financially and/or emotionally dependent on their parents.

Family therapy with borderlines has been developed along at least three theoretical lines. The first is the psychodynamic, particularly in terms of object relations and systems theory. Everett et al. (1989) have the most complete discussion of this approach in their book, *Treating the Borderline Family: A Systemic Approach.* They specify six treatment goals: (1) increasing the family's ability to reduce the systemic splitting process; (2) increasing family members' capacities for owning split-off objects and moving toward interacting with others as a "whole person"; (3) reducing oppositional and stereotypic behavior of all family members; (4) "resetting" an external boundary for both unclear and intergenerational systems; (5) "resetting" an internal boundary for spousal, parent–child, and sibling subtypes; (6) permitting a clearer alliance between the parents and limiting reciprocal intrusiveness of children and parents. Five treatment strategies for accomplishing these goals in an outpatient family treatment setting are (1) developing and maintaining a therapeutic structure; (2) reality testing in the family; (3) interactional disengagement; (4) intervening in the intergenerational system; and (5) solidification of the marital alliance and sibling subsystem.

Another treatment orientation is the structural family approach developed by Minuchin (1974). Schane and Kovel (1988) describe severe borderline pathology in terms of a spousal subsystem that is internally overinvolved and contemporarily distant and disengaged from the family system. In effect, borderline females have a systems equivalent of object splitting wherein family subsystems are organized around dichotomous extremes: collusion and sabotage; loyalty and scapegoating; inclusion and rejection; nurturance and neglect; and symbiosis and abandonment. It is this structural pattern of family interaction that is the focus of systemic change. Lachar (1992) provides an extensive discussion of an integrated object relations and self psychology approach to the marital treatment of the borderline patient. She provides a detailed treatment protocol and several case reports illustrating this method.

A third option is the relationship enhancement therapy approach for borderline families and couples. Relationship enhancement was developed by Guerney (1977). It integrates social skills training, psychodynamic principles, and interpersonal therapy techniques. Since borderline patients have major deficits in self-differentiation and communication, relationship enhancement's focus on skill building in some areas seems promising with couple and family settings, particularly for mild to moderately dysfunctional borderline patients (Waldo & Harman, 1993). The clinician functions largely as a coach to develop the necessary relational skills, usually in 2-hour sessions. Waldo and Harmon (1993) report a case of time-limited intervention that was successful. A 12-month follow-up showed that the changes had been maintained. These authors also describe and illustrate the use of two therapists working conjointly with couples in which one partner presents with borderline personality disorder (Waldo & Harman, 1998).

Lachkar (1999) offers additional insight into the treatment of couples in which one partner has a borderline personality structure while the other partner presents with a narcissistic pattern. Solomon (1999) also addresses the treatment of the borderline-narcissistic couple from a somewhat different psychoanalytic perspective.

Medication

Psychotropic medications have been commonly employed in the treatment of borderline patients. To date, several random controlled pharmacological trials have been published involving the treatment of borderline personality disorder (Koenigsberg, Woo-Ming, & Siever, 2002).

A full gambit of medications have been tried with this patient population: low-dose neuroleptics, tricyclic antidepressants, anticonvulsants, and most recently, selective serotonin reuptake inhibitors. Given that the diagnosis of borderline personality disorder encompasses a heterogeneous group of patients often with intractable symptoms, both clinicians and patients have held high—and even magical—expectations for medication as a cure, or a palliative, at the very least. Not surprisingly, pharmacologic treatment of borderline pathology can be difficult and frustrating for both clinician and patient.

The basic treatment strategy has been to match a medication to specific target symptoms. Pharmacological and neurobiological research suggests that the borderline disorder encompasses three clusters of symptoms: affective instability, impulsive aggressivity, and transient psychotic phenomenon (Coccaro & Kavoussi, 1991). It appears that affective instability is related to brain abnormalities in adrenergic and cholinergic systems. It has been shown that agents like lithium carbonate and carbamazepines are effective in modulating affects. Abnormalities in central nervous system serotonergic function resulting in impulsivity seem to respond to serotonergic agents like fluoxetine (Prozac). Finally, abnormalities in central dopaminergic systems may account for transient psychotic symptoms. Thus, low-dose neuroleptics have been shown to be effective with this symptom cluster.

The possible efficacy of serotonin reuptake inhibitors specifically with borderline pathology such as dysphoria and impulsive-aggressive behavior has been the subject of a number of clinical trials. Fluoxetine (Prozac) appears to be effective in treating symptoms related to depressed mood and impulsive aggressivity (Coccaro, 1993). Markowitz et al. (1991) report similar results in a prospective, nonblinded study. Double-blind, placebo-controlled trials should help confirm the efficacy of this class of medication for borderline pathology. There are some potential complications or disadvantages with pharmacotherapy in the treatment of borderline patients. First is the matter of noncompliance either related to side effects or to secondary gain. Medications can serve as leverage to control the prescribing clinician or other caregivers. Demands for frequent changes in dose or type of medication, overdosing, and failure to take the medication as prescribed are means of transference acting out. Second, borderline patients may appear to others to have improved from medication but report they feel worse, or vice versa. Gunderson (1989) suggests that this apparent paradox may be caused by the patient believing that symptomatic improvement will result in undesirable consequences, such as loss or abandonment of dependent gratifications.

Perhaps the most clinically useful contributor to the literature is Klein (1989a), who skillfully describes the integration of pharmacotherapy within an individual psychotherapy context. He provides three guidelines for the effective utilization of medication: careful attention to diagnostic precision; evaluation of objective signs rather than subjective symptoms when determining when and which medication to use; and controlled awareness of the risks to therapeutic medication. Seven cases illustrate these guidelines. Although it is now somewhat dated, Klein's chapter should be required reading for medical and nonmedical clinicians involved in the treatment of borderline patients.

Medication Protocol. Begin with an SSRI at antidepressant dosages. If that SSRI fails, try another. If there is a partial response, an adjunctive atypical psychotic agent or a mood stabilizer such as valproate or carbamazepine can be considered. For individuals in whom rejection sensitivity is prominent, a trial of an MAOI is reasonable, particularly if the individual has a history of medication compliance. Naltrexone may be a useful adjunctive for individuals with self-harming behavior (Reich, 2002). Koenigsberg et al. (2002) suggests a somewhat similar strategy.

Combined and Integrated Treatment Approaches

There is considerable consensus that combined treatment is essential, or at least preferable, for borderline pathology given its severity and apparent treatment resistance. Clearly, differences exist between the prognosis and treatability of the high-functioning borderline (i.e., GAF over 65) and the low-functioning borderline (i.e., GAF below 45). Reports of treatment success using only traditional individual psychoanalytic psychotherapy may be possible with the highest-functioning borderline individual but are not likely with lower-functioning borderline individuals. In line with the basic premise of this book, the lower the patient's functioning and motivation and readiness for treatment, the more treatment must be integrated and combined.

The most common recommendation for combined treatment is to prescribe both individual therapy and group therapy. There is currently no consensus on which theoretical approaches to combine or whether both should be combined or sequenced. The earliest recommendation of combined treatment was by Tacbacnik (1965), who advocated concurrent dynamic individual psychotherapy and dynamic group therapy. On the other hand, Horowitz (1977, 1980) advocates sequencing dynamic group and individual therapy in which the group experience prepares the patient to productively utilize individual therapy. Clarkin et al. (1991) also recommend combined individual and group modalities but favor individual behavior treatment with long-term manual-guided group treatment.

Others recommend combining individual therapy and family therapy. These include Kernberg (1984), who describes the indications for concurrent as well as sequential utilization of these modalities.

Berger (1987) recommends combined psychotherapy and pharmaco-therapy because of difficulty treating with only one modality. He notes that combined treatment can be complicated by the borderline's tendency to idealize one treatment and negate the other. Koenigsberg (1993) offers a very thoughtful review of combining medications and psychotherapy, highlighting the indications and contraindications for this treatment decision. He also describes the complications inherent in combined treatment strategy but believes these can be addressed by special structuring of treatment, attention to countertransference issues, and vigilance for splitting. Koenigsberg contends that combining medication and psychotherapy has considerable value for seriously symptomatic patients, those prone to treatment noncompliance, or those susceptible to intractable affective storms and psychotic regression.

Lazarus (1985), the developer of multimodal therapy, endorses the combined use of several modalities, concurrently or sequential, for a variety of difficult patients, including borderline individuals. Vaccani (1989) describes treating alcohol-abusing borderline personality disorder with psychotherapy, family therapy, group therapy, and Alcoholics Anonymous meetings. Nehls and Diamond (1993) describe the modalities for lower-functioning borderlines in a community-based setting. The modalities that are coordinated and continuous include individual therapy, group therapy, medication, drug and alcohol services, psychosocial rehabilitation, crisis intervention, and crisis houses.

CHAPTER 5

Dependent Personality Disorder

The concept of dependency is well established in the psychological literature. Whereas early psychoanalytic theory emphasized the oral character and structural basis of dependency, social learning theory considered dependency to be acquired by learning and experience, and ethological theory posited that attachment or affectional bonding is the basis for dependency. All three theories have contributed to the concept of dependent personality disorder as defined by DSM. The basic feature of the disorder is abnormal dependency that causes subjective distress and/or functional impairment. However, the definition and criteria have changed in the different versions of DSM. In DSM-I, passive dependency personality was characterized by helplessness, denial, and indecisiveness, and was considered a subtype of the passive-aggressive personality. DSM-II listed passive dependent personality as "Other Personality Disorders of Specific Types" and gave no description or criteria. Convinced that a "passive-dependent" type was needed to counterbalance the "active-dependent" or histrionic personality disorder, dependent personality disorder was added to DSM-III (Hirschfield, Shea, & Weise, 1991), which gave three criteria (expanded to nine in DSM-III-R), of which the essential feature was a pervasive pattern of dependent and submissive behavior. DSM-IV emphasizes the excessive need to be taken care of, leading to submissive and clinging behavior and fear of separation.

No reliable data are currently available on the exact prevalence of dependent personality disorder, yet it "is among the most frequently reported Personality Disorders encountered in mental health clinics" (American Psychiatric Association, 2000, p. 723). In terms of gender, this disorder is commonly believed to be more common among women than men. In women the dependent style often takes the form of submissiveness, whereas in men it is more likely to be autocratic, as when the husband and boss depends on his wife and secretary to perform essential tasks he himself cannot accomplish. In either case, this disorder is likely to lead to anxiety and depression when the dependent relationship is threatened (Gunderson, 1989).

DSM-IV-TR addressed the gender differences issue in the "Specific Culture, Age and Gender Features" section. This section was revised "to remove the suggestion that reported gender differences is largely artifactual" (American Psychiatric Association, 2000, p. 842). More specifically, it was noted, "In clinical settings, this disorder has been diagnosed more frequently in females, although some studies report *similar* prevalence rates among males and females (p. 723, italics added). In part, this change was based on Bornstein's research (1997). Bornstein (1995) has also noted that dependent personality disorder has much higher rates of comorbidity with eating, anxiety, and somatization disorders than noted in DSM-IV. In addition, the current diagnostic criteria do not sufficiently recognize the dependency-related cognitions believed to be central to this disorder (Widiger & Bornstein, 2001).

This chapter describes the characteristic features of dependent personality disorder and its related personality style. Five clinical formulations of the disorder and psychological assessment indicators are highlighted. A variety of treatment approaches, modalities, and intervention strategies are also described.

DESCRIPTION OF DEPENDENT PERSONALITY DISORDER

Dependent personality disorder can be recognized by the following descriptors and characteristics: style vs. disorder, triggering event, behavioral style, interpersonal style, cognitive style, affective style, attachment style, and optimal criterion.

Style vs. Disorder. The dependent personality can be thought of as spanning a continuum from healthy to pathological, with dependent personality style at the healthy end and dependent personality disorder at the pathological end. Table 5.1 compares and contrasts differences between the dependent style and the disorder.

Table 5.1
Comparison on Dependent Personality Style and Disorder

Personality Style	*Personality Disorder*
When making decisions, individuals are comfortable seeking out the opinions and advice of others but ultimately make their own decisions	Unable to make everyday decisions without an excessive amount of advice or reassurance from others; allow others to make the most of their important decision
Carefully promote harmony with important persons in their life through being polite, agreeable, and tactful	Agree with people even when they believe they are wrong, because of fear of being rejected
Although they respect authority and prefer the role of team member, they can initiate and complete tasks on their own	Have difficulty initiating projects or doing things on their own
Thoughtful and good at pleasing others. Occasionally, they will endure personal discomfort in accomplishing a good deed for the key people in their lives	Volunteer to do things that are unpleasant or demeaning in order to get other people to like them
Tend to prefer the company of one or more individuals to being alone	Feel uncomfortable or helpless when alone, or go to great lengths to avoid being alone
Tend to be strongly committed to relationships and work hard to sustain them	Feel devastated or helpless when close relationships end; and frequently preoccupied with fears of being abandoned
Can take corrective action in response to criticism	Easily hurt by criticism or disapproval

Triggering Event. The typical situation, circumstance, or event that most likely triggers or activates the characteristic maladaptive response of dependent personality disorder (Othmer & Othmer, 2002), as noted in behavioral, interpersonal, cognitive, and feeling styles, is "expectations of self-reliance and/or being alone."

Behavioral Style. The behavioral style of dependent personalities is characterized by docility, passivity, and nonassertiveness.

Interpersonal Style. In interpersonal relations, they tend to be pleasing, self-sacrificing, and clinging, and constantly require the assurance of others.

Their compliance and reliance on others lead to a subtle demand that others assume responsibility for major areas of their lives.

Cognitive Style. The cognitive style of dependent personalities is characterized by suggestibility. They easily adopt a Pollyanna-type attitude toward life. Furthermore, they tend to minimize difficulties, and because of their naiveté, they are readily persuadable and others easily take advantage of them. In short, this style of thinking is uncritical and unperceptive.

Affective Style. Their emotional or affective style is characterized by insecurity and anxiousness. Because they lack self-confidence, they experience considerable discomfort at being alone. They tend to be preoccupied with the fear of abandonment and disapproval of others. Their mood tends to be one of anxiety or fearfulness, as well as having a somber or sad quality.

Attachment Style. The preoccupied attachment dimension is characterized by a sense of personal unworthiness and a positive evaluation of others. These individuals tend to be very externally oriented in their self-definitions. This preoccupied attachment style is common in individuals with dependent personality disorder (Lyddon & Sherry, 2001).

Optimal DSM-IV-TR Criterion. Of all the stated DSM-IV-TR criteria for dependent personality disorder, one criterion has been found to be the most useful in diagnosing this disorder. The belief is that by beginning with this criterion, the clinician can test for the presence or absence of the criterion and quickly diagnose the personality disorder (Allnutt & Links, 1996). The optimal criterion for this disorder is "needs others to assume responsibility for most major areas of his or her life."

Case Study: Dependent Personality Disorder

Ms. C. is a 38-year-old single woman with panic symptoms that began approximately 3 years earlier. Once the panic attacks began, Ms. C. moved back into her parents' home and has become nearly totally housebound, fearing that "panic could strike anytime." She described both of her parents as caring, concerned, and "my best friends," on whom she is overly reliant. She looks to them to support her financially and emotionally, and to make decisions for her. Ms. C. has also become progressively habituated to the Valium that she was prescribed for panic symptoms.

Case Study: Dependent Personality Style

Mr. B. has been a social worker at a foster care agency for the past 7 years. He finds his job fulfilling and is well liked by the other staff members, as well as the children and prospective parents with whom he works. He is a very concerned, caring, and a gentle person. A year ago, he began dating Sandra, one of the pediatricians who consults to the agency. Their relationship has been happy and fulfilling for both of them, probably because of Mr. B.'s efforts. He cannot get over the fact that a doctor would be interested in being with him, and he expresses his appreciation in numerous ways. He cannot spend enough time with her or do enough things for her. He idealizes her, makes every effort to make her feel comfortable and secure, and regularly seeks her opinions and advice. Yet he insists that he has a mind of his own; after much deliberation and soul searching, he bought an expensive sports car even though Sandra thought it was extravagant.

DSM-IV-TR Description and Criteria

Table 5.2 presents the DSM-IV-TR description and criteria.

Table 5.2
DSM-IV-TR Criteria for Dependent Personality Disorder (301.6)

A pervasive and excessive need to be taken care of that leads to submissive and clinging behavior and fears of separation, beginning by early adulthood and present in a variety of contexts, as indicated by five (or more) of the following:

(1) has difficulty in making everyday decisions without an excessive amount of advice and reassurance from others
(2) needs others to assume responsibility for most major areas of his or her life
(3) has difficulty expressing disagreement with others because of fear of loss of support or approval. Note: Do not include realistic fears of retribution.
(4) has difficulty initiating projects or doing things on his or her own (because of a lack of self-confidence in judgment or abilities rather than a lack of motivation or energy)
(5) goes to excessive lengths to obtain nurturance and support from others, to the point of volunteering to do things that are unpleasant
(6) feels uncomfortable or helpless when alone because of exaggerated fears of being unable to care for himself or herself
(7) urgently seeks another relationship as a source of care and support when a close relationship ends
(8) is unrealistically preoccupied with fears of being left to take care of himself or herself

FORMULATIONS OF DEPENDENT PERSONALITY DISORDER

Psychodynamic Formulation

Early psychoanalytic writers posited that dependent personalities were formed in the oral phase of psychosexual development. Contemporary formulations view the development of dependency as a function of parental—particularly maternal—overinvolvement and intrusiveness throughout all phases of development. These individuals often present histories of parental reward for maintaining loyalty, and subtle parental rejection whenever they attempted separation and independence. They would react with crying and clinging behavior while being immobilized by fear and dread of abandonment. Their submissive stance is the result of multiply determined unconscious factors. Gabbard (1990) notes that dependent personalities typically seek to be cared for by others because of their underlying anxiety, which often masks aggression. Thus, dependency may be viewed as a compromise formation defending against hostility. Furthermore, dependent behavior can also be used to avoid reactivation of past traumatic experiences.

Biosocial Formulation

Millon and Everly (1985) speculate that dependent personalities exhibited fearful, withdrawing, or sad temperaments as infants. Accordingly, such behaviors were likely to elicit overly protective behavior from caretakers. Millon (1981) notes that these dependent individuals tend to have ectomorphic—thin and frail—or endomorphic—heavy and cumbersome—body types that contribute to low-energy thresholds and a lack of physical vigor.

Environmental factors such as parental overprotection, competitive deficits, and social role programming appear to interact with these biological predispositions, resulting in the dependent personality pattern. Parental overprotection often precludes the development of autonomous coping behavior, such as assertiveness, problem solving, and decision making. Hend, Balker, and Williamson (1991) report that families of individuals with dependent personality disorders are characterized by low expressiveness and high control, as compared with families in clinical and normal control groups, which is indicative of the pervasive reinforcement of dependent behavior. Outside the parental relationship, these children often experience social humiliation and doubts about their efficacy in interpersonal situations. Through such repeated experiences, they learn, particularly as adolescents, that it is better to remain submissive than to strive to be competitive. Furthermore, cultural and social norms seem to reinforce passive dependent behavior patterns among women and endomorphically and ectomorphically built men. Finally, dependent personality patterns are self-perpetuating through reinforcement of dependent behaviors; avoidance of growth-promoting activities—that is, those that might be challenging, threatening, or anxiety producing; and self-detraction, by which they not only convince others that they are inferior, defective, and incapable of independence but also themselves (Millon & Davis, 1996).

Cognitive-Behavioral Formulations

According to Beck et al. (1990), the dependent personality is rooted in basic assumptions about the self and the world. These individuals typically view themselves as helpless and inadequate, and the world as too dangerous for them to cope with things alone. Accordingly, they conclude that they must rely on someone else who is stronger and more adequate to take care of and protect them. They must pay a considerable price for this security: (1) they must relinquish responsibility and subordinate their own needs; (2) they must relinquish opportunities to learn such skills as assertiveness, decision making, and problem solving; and (3) they must contend with fears of rejection and abandonment if their clinging relationship ends.

The main cognitive distortion of such dependent individuals is dichotomous thinking with respect to independence. For example, they believe that they are either totally connected to another and dependent or totally alone and independent, with no gradation between. Also, they believe that things are either right or wrong, and that there is either absolute success or absolute failure. Another cognitive distortion observed among dependent personalities is catastrophizing, particularly regarding relationships. Common cognitive distortions are "I never would be able to do that," "I can't," and "I'm too dumb to do that."

Turkat (1990) suggests a behavioral formulation for this disorder that centers on a pervasive fear of decision making and an inability to act assertively. Since these individuals have not previously learned either of these skills, these become basic therapeutic tasks, after their overwhelming anxiety is effectively managed.

Interpersonal Formulation

According to Benjamin (1996), persons with dependent personality disorder experienced sufficient caring and attention as infants to enable them to bond with others. They also learned to rely on others, and expect that others will be there to meet their needs. However, the parents of potential dependent-disordered individuals did not wean this level of nurturing when it was developmentally appropriate to do so. Subsequently, these individuals learned compliant dependent behavior, as well as to avoid autonomy at all costs. As a result, they developed poor self-concepts by default, and as adults continue to view themselves as inadequate and overly tolerant of the blaming of others.

Because they have not learned to take care of self and life's demands, they must depend on others. Since they have limited coping resources, they must tolerate abuse, which is the price of the needed caretaking. Typically, dependent individuals-in-training were mocked by peers and siblings for their incompetence. As a result, their feelings of inadequacy and incompetence were reinforced and reconfirmed. In short, these individuals are characterized by marked submissiveness to a dominant other person, who presumably will provide unending nurturance and guidance. Such a relationship is maintained even if it means tolerating abuse, since dependent-disordered individuals believe themselves to be incompetent and unable to survive without the dominant other.

Integrative Formulation

The following integrative formulation provides a biopsychosocial explanation for how dependent personality disorder develops and is maintained. Biologically, these individuals are characterized by a low energy level. Their temperament is described as melancholic. As infants and young children, they were characterized as fearful, sad, or withdrawn. In terms of body types, they tend to have more ectomorphic or endomorphic builds (Millon, 1981).

Psychologically, dependent personality–disorders individuals can be understood and appreciated in terms of their view of themselves, their worldview, and their life goal. The self-view of these individuals tends to be a variant of the theme: "I'm nice but inadequate (or fragile)." Their view of self is self-effacing, inept, and self-doubting. Their view of the world is some variant of the theme: "Others are here to take care of me, because I can't do it for myself." Their life goal is characterized by some variant of the theme: "Therefore, cling and rely on others at all costs."

The social features of this personality disorder can be described in terms of parental, familial, and environmental factors. The dependent personality is most likely to have been raised in a family in which parental overprotection and pampering were prominent. It is as if the parental injunction to the child was, "I can't trust you to do anything right (or well)." Contact with siblings and peers may engender feelings of unattractiveness, awkwardness, or competitive inadequacy, especially during the preadolescent and adolescent years.

These feelings can have a devastating impact on the individual and further confirm his or her sense of self-deprecation and doubt. Dependent personality disorder becomes self-perpetuating through a process that involves a sense of self-doubt, an avoidance of competitive activity, and the availability of self-reliant individuals who are willing to take care of and make decisions for the dependent person in exchange for that person's self-sacrificing and docile friendship (Sperry & Mosak, 1993). Table 5.3 summarizes these characteristics.

ASSESSMENT OF DEPENDENT PERSONALITY DISORDER

Several sources of information are useful in establishing a diagnosis and treatment plan for personality disorders. Observation, collateral information, and psychological testing are important adjuncts to the patient's self-report in the clinical interview. This section briefly describes some characteristic observations that the clinician makes and the nature of the rapport likely to develop in initial encounters with specific personality-disordered individuals. Characteristic response patterns on various objective (i.e., MMPI-2 and MCMI-II) and projective (i.e., Rorschach and TAT) tests are also described.

Table 5.3
Characteristics of Dependent Personality Disorder

Triggering Event	Expectations of self-reliance and/or being alone.
Behavioral Style	Docile, passive, nonassertive, lack of self-confidence.
Interpersonal Style	Pleasing; self-sacrificing; clinging, compliant; expect others to take responsibility.
Cognitive Style	Suggestible: Pollyanna-like about interpersonal relations; overprotective—the "too good parent."
Feeling Style	Pleasant but anxious, timid, or sad when stressed.
Temperament	Low energy level; fearful, sad, or withdrawn during infancy; melancholic.
Attachment Style	Preoccupied.
Parental Injunction	"You can't do it by yourself."
Self-View	"I'm nice but inadequate (or fragile)." Self-doubting.
Worldview	"Others are here to take care of me" (because I can't do it myself)
Maladaptive Schemas	Defectiveness; self-sacrifice; approval-seeking.
Optimal DSM-IV-TR Criteria	Needs others to assume responsibility for most major areas of his or her life.

Interview Behavior and Rapport

In the initial interview, individuals with dependent personality disorders will commonly wait for the clinician to initiate the conversation. After an opening statement by the clinician, these patients can present an adequate description of their current situation but then will retreat to silence. Predictable comments are: "I don't know what to say. I've never seen a therapist before," or "Ask me questions so that I'll know what's important to talk about." When the clinician responds and asks other questions, the cycle may repeat itself. Nonetheless, interviewing these individuals can be enjoyable, and establishing rapport is relatively easy.

After some initial anxiety, they will begin to trust the clinician and the therapeutic process. So long as the clinician provides pleasant advice and support, and shows empathy for their indecisiveness and failures, the interview flows smoothly. However, when the clinician attempts to explore the detriments engendered by their submissiveness, they become uncomfortable and want support. If the dependency is not pursued with an empathic ear, they will change therapists. If pursued sympathetically, they will cooperate and meet their clinician's expectations. They answer questions to the point and will clarify and elaborate on demand. They can tolerate abrupt transitions and will allow deep feelings to be probed. But they cannot tolerate confrontation and interpretation of their dependency (Othmer & Othmer, 2002).

Psychological Testing Data

The Minnesota Multiphase Personality Inventory (MMPI-2), the Millon Clinical Multiaxial Inventory (MCMI-II), the Rorschach Psychodiagnostic Test, and the Thematic Apperception Test (TAT) can be useful in diagnosing dependent personality disorder, as well as the dependent personality style or trait.

On the MMPI-2, the most likely profile is 2-7/7-2 (depression-psychasthenia), which characterizes individuals who are passive, dependent, and docile. A high score on scale 3 (hysteria) is common, as is a mildly elevated K (correction) scale. Passivity and naiveté are reflected in a high L (lie) scale, while the F (frequency) scale is in the average range. Acceptance of the stereotypical female role is reflected by a low scale 5 (masculinity-femininity). Lack of resistance to coercion from authority shows in a low scale 4 (psychopathic deviate). A low scale 9 (hypomania) reflects passivity and lack of initiative (Meyer, 1995).

On the MCMI-II, a high score on scale 3 (dependent) would be anticipated. An elevation on scale A (anxiety) is common, particularly when these individuals feel insecure about placing their welfare in the hands of others (Choca et al., 1997).

With regard to the Rorschach, if dependent personalities feel accepted by the examiner and believe that the examiner expects a high number of responses, they will produce an extensive record. Otherwise, fewer-than-average responses can be expected. Most common are A (animal), M (human movement), and P (popular) responses. Finally, C (color) tends to be used more often than F (form) in determining responses (Meyer, 1995).

Generally speaking, TAT responses of dependent personalities are not particularly distinctive. However, themes of dependency and compliance are common on card 2 (Bellak, 1997).

TREATMENT APPROACHES AND INTERVENTIONS

Treatment Considerations

The differential diagnoses for dependent personality disorder include histrionic personality disorder and avoidant personality disorder. Common Axis I diagnoses associated with dependent personality disorder include anxiety disorders, particularly simple and social phobias, and panic disorders with or without agoraphobia. Other common DSM-IV-TR disorders include hypochondriasis, conversion disorders, and somatization disorders. The experience of losing a supportive person or relationship can lead to a number of affective disorders, including dysthymia and major depressive episodes. Finally, because persons with dependent personality disorders can have lifelong training in assuming the "sick role," they are especially prone to the factitious disorders.

In general, the long-range goal of psychotherapy with a dependent personality is to increase the individual's sense of independence and ability to function interdependently. At other times, the clinician may need to settle for a more modest goal—that is, helping the individual become a "healthier" dependent personality. Treatment strategies typically include challenging the individual's convictions or dysfunctional beliefs about personal inadequacy and learning ways in which to increase assertiveness. A variety of treatment methods and modalities can be used to achieve these goals, as noted in the following section. To date, no controlled treatment outcome studies have been completed for dependent personality disorder (Crits-Christoph & Barber, 2002).

Individual Psychotherapy

For the various individual psychotherapeutic modalities, there are reports of successful treatment for dependent personality disorder. Although no large-case series or controlled treatment trials have been published yet, several case reports suggest that positive treatment outcomes are common. Treatment tends to be shorter and less difficult than for other personality disorders, such as borderline, narcissistic, or antisocial personality disorder.

Psychodynamic Psychotherapy Approach

A central purpose of psychodynamic psychotherapy is to help patients cope better with previous separations and object losses. Patients enter therapy with the unconscious wish to reinstate earlier relationships and bring them to a more satisfactory resolution. Accordingly, the clinician comes to symbolize the object losses, and therapy succeeds if the clinician becomes a better object than the objects of the patient's childhood. The clinician gratifies certain fundamental wishes that the parent-object did not adequately gratify, as well as provides a more reasonable and benign model for identification. If therapy is a success, the internalization of the objects will be more positive and less laden with anger and guilt, thereby making separation a genuine maturational event (Strupp & Binder, 1984). A major dilemma in the psychotherapy with patients with dependent personality disorders is that they do not readily relinquish the new object and tend to cling tenaciously to the clinician.

In this form of resistance, the patient leans dependently on the clinician as an end in itself, rather than as a means to an end. Thus, as therapy unfolds, these patients may forget what complaint or symptom brought them into treatment, and their only purpose becomes the maintenance of their attachment to the clinician. Dreading termination, they tend to experience a reexacerbation of their initial symptoms. They will endeavor to make the clinician collude in their avoidance of making decisions or asserting themselves in the hope of continuing their dependency. The clinician, however, must frustrate these wishes and prompt independent thoughts and actions in these patients. By conveying that the anxiety produced by this frustration is tolerable and productive, the clinician encourages the patient toward achieving insight and independence (Gabbard, 1994).

In long-term psychodynamic psychotherapy, the emergence of a dependent transference toward the clinician is thus promoted, which is then dealt with in a way to promote emotional growth. Patients are told that extra sessions may be allowed early in therapy, particularly during periods of heightened anxieties. This assurance of readily available support aids in developing a trusting relationship with and transferring dependent wishes onto the clinician. The clinician must encourage patients to express feelings and wishes and to bear the anxiety of making decisions dealing with episodes of anxiety and accepting pleasurable experiences. Furthermore, the clinician will need to clarify and interpret the transference elements, as well as support the patients in finding more self-reliant ways of coping when they plead with the clinician to take a more directive role in their lives.

During the final stage of therapy, the clinician gradually increases the level of expectation for self-initiated behavior and autonomous decision making. The clinician reinforces the patient's increased ability to cope with crises without extra sessions and to self-soothe and self-manage episodes of heightened anxiety. This requires resolution of the patient's wish to be dependent and instead to accept a more self-reliant position in the therapeutic relationship (Hill, 1970). Finally, it should be noted that individuals with dependent personality disorders commonly create countertransference problems in their clinicians related to dependency conflicts. Thus, clinicians must anticipate countertransference contempt or disdain toward dependent patients (Gabbard, 1994).

Time-Limited Dynamic Psychotherapy

Kantor (1992) notes that long-term analytic psychotherapy is arduous and time-consuming, and should be recommended primarily when patients are highly motivated and the dependency is ego syntonic. Otherwise, the treatment may become interminable because of such resistances as unwillingness to work hard in treatment, since this means terminating therapy, which they anticipate will be unbearable. Generally speaking, long-term psychotherapy with motivated patients requires two to four sessions a week over 3 or more years to work through a dependent transference.

For these and other reasons, time-limited dynamic psychotherapy has been advocated as the treatment of choice for most of these patients (Flegenheimer, 1982; Gunderson, 1989). Knowing at the outset that treatment will end after 12, 16, or 20 sessions means that these patients must confront their deepest anxieties about loss and individuation, as well as their fantasies about unlimited nurturance and timelessness (Mann, 1973). Such time-limited therapies are most likely to succeed when three conditions are present: a circumscribed, dynamic conflict or focus; a patient who can quickly form a therapeutic alliance; and little or no tendency to act out or regress to severe dependency (Strupp & Binder, 1984; Luborsky, 1984). Time-limited therapy is less successful with dependent individuals who have limited ego strengths or greater degrees of separation anxiety (Gabbard, 1994). For such patients, Wallerstein (1986) suggests a supportive treatment approach in which sessions are tapered down to one every few months, provided there is no threat to termination.

Flegenheimer (1982) has critically reviewed six different brief dynamic psychotherapy approaches: those of Sifneos, Alexander, Mann, Malan, Davanloo, and Wolberg. He believes that Mann's, Alexander's, and Wolberg's approaches are tailor-made for the many dependent personality-disordered individuals. Passive, indecisive patients are likely to feel comfortable with the paternalistic stances of Alexander or Wolberg, where the clinician initially takes charge, gives advice, and makes decisions. The approach enables these patients to try new behaviors because they are "told to." The positive response to new behaviors engenders and reinforces those new patterns of behavior. Likewise, more passive dependent patients tend to do well with Mann's approach, wherein a termination date is set at the first session. The dependency of the patient allows the "golden glow" of Mann's first phase of therapy to develop to the fullest, setting the stage for subsequent disillusionment and preparing for a meaningful separation experience.

Mann's approach (1973) requires little modification of the standard analytically oriented approach and the least amount of confrontation of the briefer psychotherapies. Not surprisingly, this rather gentle technique tends not to engender major resistances in dependent patients.

Time-limited approaches are advocated as the starting point for treatment of most dependent patients. For those who have multifocal conflicts or otherwise fail to improve in briefer therapies, longer-term dynamic therapies, supportive therapy, or psychoanalysis would be treatment options.

Cognitive-Behavioral Therapy Approach

Beck et al. (1990) provide an extended description of the cognitive therapy approach for individuals for dependent personality disorders. The basic goal of therapy is increased autonomy and self-efficacy. Autonomy is defined as the capability to act independently of others, along with the capability to develop close and intimate relationships. Because dependent individuals are squeamish about the word *independent* and fear that competence will lead to abandonment, achieving these goals must be accomplished with considerable delicacy.

Since these individuals often come to treatment anticipating that clinicians will solve their problems and make their decisions, it is necessary to allow some dependence initially in order to engage them. The structured collaborative nature of cognitive therapy encourages the dependent individual to play an active role in the treatment process, beginning with the agenda and goal setting. The use of guided discovery and Socratic questioning early in treatment helps these individuals to begin to face their own solutions and decisions, reducing overreliance on the therapist and others.

As therapy proceeds, progress toward goals can be utilized as powerful evidence to challenge the dependent individual's assumptions of personal helplessness. Challenging the dichotomous belief about independence—that one is either totally dependent and helpless or totally independent and isolated—helps to modify the distorted notion that autonomy is a commitment to total alienation. Besides challenging and disputing automatic beliefs and maladaptive schemas concerning dependency and helplessness, therapists are encouraged to utilize behavioral methods such as assertiveness training and behavioral experiments, as well as to modify the very structure of therapy.

This modification can be accomplished in several ways, such as by gradually changing to a group format or concurrent individual and group therapy, "weaning" sessions by scheduling them less frequently toward the end of the therapy, or setting a specific termination date early in treatment and focusing therapy as preparation for termination. Since termination typically evokes rejection and abandonment schemas in these individuals, offering the option of one or two booster sessions—late in the course of treatment—following termination can ease the transition. In short, the cognitive treatment of dependent personality disorders begins with a collaborative relationship in which the therapist allows a measure of dependency, which is gradually replaced with guided discovery, and challenges the dichotomy beliefs of independence. As treatment proceeds, schema reconstruction and modification of the structure of treatment, along with behavioral methods, are utilized to achieve treatment goals.

A more behaviorally oriented approach to this disorder is based on the formulation that the dependent personality is hypersensitive to independent decision making (Turkat, 1990). The corresponding behavioral strategy consists of bidirectional anxiety management procedures focused on independent decision making. Since individuals with dependent personality disorder are often undersocialized, social skills training may be indicated. Assertive communication and friendship and dating skills are often minimal in lower-functioning dependent patients. Fay and Lazarus (1993) offer cognitive-behavioral protocols in assertiveness, friendship, and dating skills.

Structured Skill Treatment Interventions. While research shows that medication can modulate or normalize dysregulated behaviors, a similar modulating effect has also been noted for social skills training (Lieberman, DeRisi, & Mueser, 1989). Thus, it appears that social skills training is a relatively potent bottom-up treatment strategy for normalizing limbic system–mediated behaviors that reflect specific skill deficits in personality-disordered individuals. When such skills deficits are present, Sperry (1999) contends that structured skill training intervention is a potent and effective strategy in treatment. Various structured intervention strategies for modifying a personality-disordered individual's affective, behavioral, and cognitive temperament styles are described and illustrated for the treatment of dependent personality disorder (Sperry, 1999).

Cognitive Coping Therapy. Cognitive coping therapy is an active, directive, didactic, and structured approach for treating personality-disordered individuals (Sharoff, 2002). It is a complete and self-contained approach to treatment that begins with assessing an individual's coping skills—in terms of skill chains, subskills, and microskills—then increasing skill competence in targeted areas as needed. Five key skill areas with representative treatment modalities are (1) *cognitive skills*—problem solving, self-instruction training, and self-management; (2) *emotion skills*—emotional containment and compartmentalization; (3) *perceptual skills*—perspective taking, thought stopping, and psychological distance taking; (4) *physiological skills*—meditation and relaxation training; and (5) *behavior skills*—communication and assertiveness training. Sharoff (2002) describes a detailed protocol and clinical example for using this structured approach with a complex and difficult dependent personality disorder case.

Schema Therapy. Schema therapy is an elaboration of cognitive therapy that has been developed by Young (1999; Young et al., 2003) specifically for personality disorders and other difficult individual and couples problems. Schema therapy involves identifying maladaptive schemas and planning specific strategies and interventions. Four main strategies are cognitive, experiential, behavioral, and the therapeutic relationship itself. Cognitive restructuring—modification of maladaptive schemas—is an important cognitive strategy but is combined with imagery exercises, empathic confrontation, homework assignments, and "limited reparenting" (i.e., a form of corrective emotional experience; Young, 1999).

Maladaptive schemas typically associated with dependent personality disorder are *defectiveness*—that is, the belief that one is defective, bad, unwanted, or inferior in important respects; *dependence*—that is, the belief that one is unable to competently complete everyday responsibilities without considerable help from others; *approval-seeking*—that is, the belief that one must constantly seek to belong and be accepted at the expense of developing a true sense of self; and *self-sacrifice*—that is, the belief that one must meet the needs of others at the expense of one's own gratification (Bernstein, 2002).

Interpersonal Approach

Benjamin (1996) explains that psychotherapeutic interventions for persons with dependent personality disorders can be planned and evaluated in terms of whether they enhance collaboration, facilitate learning about maladaptive patterns and their roots, block these patterns, enhance the will to change, and effectively encourage new patterns.

Benjamin notes that the dependent individual's apparent attitude of friendly cooperation actually complicates the development of a collaborative therapeutic alliance. Essentially, eliciting more and better help from clinicians is the agenda for dependent individuals. They see no reason to collaborate with clinicians against their maladaptive pattern of dependency. The clinician's challenge at the onset of treatment is to engage with the position opposite their usual one: stop submitting, learn about being independent, and separate. Initially, this seems impossible for these individuals, because with their histories of intense enmeshment, they cannot understand what it means to be differentiated. They believe that there are only two options: to control others or to submit to others. Since they believe that controlling represents bossiness, aggressivity, and bullying of others, they reject it in favor of submission. However, if they are helped to understand that separation and competence, rather than control, are the opposite of submission, they can change. Blocking maladaptive patterns in dependent individuals often requires the assistance of their significant others, such as family members. The paradoxical suggestion that others restrict their offers of help at times when dependent individuals are functioning well is a way to reward independent behavior. Such suggestions must be followed with other interventions that change the strong wish to be dependent and strengthen the wish to become more competent and independent.

Essentially, dependent individuals must first recognize their dependent pattern and the high price they pay to maintain it, then explore alternatives. To the extent that they can collaborate against "it" and face the present-day meaning of this pattern, they may decide to change. As this occurs, the implementation of a new pattern is relatively straightforward. Benjamin points out that standard behavioral techniques such as assertiveness communication and feeling identification and expression can be quite effective.

Group Therapy

Group treatment has been shown to be successful in the treatment of dependent personality disorders. Two considerations are involved in deciding whether group treatment will be an effective format. The first consideration relates to the patient's degree of impairment; where motivation and potential for growth exist, a more interactional psychotherapy group may be indicated. Such a context provides a therapeutic milieu for exploring the inappropriateness of passive dependent behavior and for experimenting with greater assertiveness (Yalom, 1995). However, if dependent traits reflect severe personality impairment or the absence of prosocial behavior such as assertive communication, decision making, and negotiation, an ongoing supportive problem-solving group or a social skills training group might be indicated. The second consideration refers to whether referral should be made to a homogeneous group, with treatment targeted at dependency issues shared by all group members, or a heterogeneous group, where group members have different personality styles or disorders. Francis et al. (1984) provide selection criteria for both types of group formats. Clinical lore suggests that dependent patients tend to get "lost" in heterogeneous groups. Yalom (1995) seems to be describing the dependent personality in his discussion of the "silent patient" in groups. Yet time-limited assertiveness training groups that are homogeneous and have clearly defined goals have been shown to be very effective (Lazarus, 1981).

Two studies involving the treatment of dependent patients have been reported in the literature. Montgomery (1971) utilized homogeneous group formats for dependent patients who were previously being seen in an individual format in a clinical setting. The patients were described as clinging and dependent, and as expecting magical cures and medication. Engagement within the group provided the patients with the opportunity to redirect their attention-seeking behavior from regressive to more socially adaptive purposes. Montgomery reports that all but 3 of 30 patients eventually discontinued medication. Sadoff and Collins (1968) reported group therapy for dependent patients who also stuttered. Weekly group treatment that emphasized dynamic interpretation was shown to be effective. Positive changes in stuttering and dependency were reported.

Marital and Family Therapy

The professional literature on family therapy interventions with dependent personality disorders is almost nonexistent. Harbir (1981) notes that individuals with dependent personality disorders are usually brought to family therapy by their parents. They are frequently older adolescents or young adults between the ages of 20 and 35 who present with a neurotic or psychotic symptom. Harbir describes a prototypical case of a 29-year-old man with a diagnosis of dependent personality who essentially was totally dependent on his parents for his maintenance. A more functional younger sister had moved out on her own the previous year. Although he did some part-time work at home for his father, he neither made his own meals, cleaned his own room, nor washed his own clothes. He was content to live the rest of his life with his parents, if they would permit it. There was no clear-cut presenting problem, other than the identified patient's unwillingness to work outside the home. Clearly, the son, mother, and father were deeply enmeshed, although the son was much more dependent on the mother than the father, and vice versa. Structural techniques were employed by the clinician to decrease the intensity of the mother–child interaction. Essentially, various tasks were prescribed that encouraged the father and son to form a separate relationship. Tasks that encouraged social activities outside the family also were prescribed. Since the son had developed few peer relationships, these tasks initially were quite difficult for both the son and his parents.

After 1 year of family treatment, the son was able to emancipate sufficiently and could work and socialize outside the home. Could these results have been accomplished in individual therapy? Perhaps, but it was not likely in that time frame, and without some cooperation from the parents. Changing the enmeshed family relationship tends to be anxiety-provoking for all parties, and thus there is considerable resistance from other family members when only one member of the family is in therapy.

Very little has been published on marital therapy with persons with dependent personality disorders. Malinow (1981a) notes that dependent patients can function adequately if their marital partners consistently meet their needs, but they typically become symptomatic and impaired when that support is withdrawn or withheld. Turkat (1990) believes that it is useful to engage the cooperation of the marital partner in treatment for two reasons: (1) because of the negative impact on the relationship as the dependent individual becomes less anxious and more independent, and (2) because the patient's progress can be facilitated if the partner collaborates in accomplishing the treatment goals. Barlow and Waddell (1985) describe a time-limited couples group for the treatment of agoraphobia. Most of the symptomatic partners exhibited features of the dependent personality. In group, the nonsymptomatic partners took the roles of "coach" and "confidant," collaborating on treatment goals. Taking on these roles meant relinquishing the role in which they reinforced their partner's agoraphobia and dependency. During the course of this 10-session treatment protocol, not only did panic and agoraphobia symptoms remit but the marital relationship shifted from dependency to more interdependency.

A common marital relational pattern is the dependent/narcissistic couple in which one partner presents with dependent personality disorder and the other partner presents with narcissistic personality disorder. Nurse (1998) provides a detailed rationale and treatment protocol for working with such couples based on Millon's theory of personality disorders (Millon & Davis, 1996).

Medication

To date, dependent personality disorder has not been subject to controlled pharmacological trials (Koenigsberg, Woo-Ming, & Siever, 2002). Nevertheless, such individuals who present for treatment often exhibit Axis I diagnoses, particularly anxiety and depressive disorders. When appropriate, a concurrent anxiety or depressive disorder would be treated with a variety of psychotropic agents. Mavissakalian (1993) reviewed the indications for the use of psychotropic agents with various anxiety disorders, as well as for combining cognitive-behavioral interventions with medication. Similarly, Rush and Hollon (1991) reviewed the indications for medication and cognitive-behavioral interventions for various depressive disorders.

However, if medication is not warranted for an Axis I disorder, caution should be exercised in considering medication for Axis II dependent personality disorder. Anxiolytics can be abused and antidepressants should be used with caution for reactive symptoms (Reid, 1989; Reid, Balis, & Sutton, 1998). Nevertheless, if anxiety is prominent but without impulsivity, begin with an SSRI. If no response, try another SSRI (Reich, 2002).

Combined and Integrated Treatment Approaches

In many ways, the dependent personality is an "orphan" in the clinical literature, and this certainly is evident in the area of combined and integrative treatment. In the section on medication, reference was made to combined behavioral therapy for Axis I anxiety and depressive disorders concurrent with Axis II dependent personality disorder. The reader is referred to Mavissakalian (1993) and Rush and Hollon (1991) for excellent overviews of this literature.

Another type of combined treatment involves utilizing different modalities simultaneously. Barlow and Waddell's (1985) effort to combine behavior therapy in a group setting with couples was previously described. Not surprisingly, the results of combining modalities are noteworthy. Lazarus (1981, 1985) provides further documentation of the overall efficacy and cost-effectiveness of multimodal interventions.

Little has been written regarding integrative treatment. However, clinical practice is replete with efforts to utilize anxiety-reducing strategies in both dynamic and cognitive therapies. Glantz and Goisman (1990) describe a unique integration of relaxation techniques with object-relations psychodynamic psychotherapy with dependent patients. A breath-controlling and progressive muscle relaxation strategy was used to merge split self-representations in the course of exploration psychotherapy. The technique was introduced after signs of split self-representation had been identified. Patients were taught the technique and it was prescribed as an intersession treatment task. Once they were able to relax adequately in session, they were asked for visual images of first one and then another of the conflicting self-representations. After clear images had been elicited and discussed, they were encouraged to merge the images. Twenty-four of the 27 personality-disordered patients in the study, many of whom were dependent personalities, responded with greater compliance, improved interpersonal relationships, and reduced resistance.

Handler (1989) reports integrating Ericksonian hypnotic methods with psychodynamically oriented psychotherapy in the treatment of a woman diagnosed with dependent personality disorder and somatoform disorder. The results were positive and were sustained over a 2-year period.

CHAPTER 6

Histrionic Personality Disorder

Histrionic personality disorder has a long history dating back some four thousand years when it was designated as "hysteria" (Veith, 1977). The modern roots of the histrionic personality, however, are traceable to Freud's description of cases of "hysterical neurosis," which today would be classified as a type of somatoform disorder. DSM-I had no category for hysterical personality, although some of its traits were encompassed by the diagnostic category "emotionally unstable personality." DSM-II listed hysterical personality with histrionic personality disorder in parentheses. In DSM-III it was designated as histrionic personality disorder, and because of considerable overlap with borderline personality disorder, several changes in criteria were made in DSM-III-R (Pfohl, 1991). DSM-IV has further modified criteria to better distinguish histrionic from borderline. Nonetheless, psychodynamically oriented clinicians remain dissatisfied as the new criteria do not allow for the higher-functioning type of patient. Thus, psychoanalytic writers prefer to use the designation hysterical personality disorder for higher-functioning individuals and histrionic personality disorder for more primitive, lower-functioning individuals who clearly meet DSM-IV criteria (Gabbard, 1994). This disorder appears to be more common in women than men. Prevalence rates are estimated to be 2 to 3 percent in the general population and 10 to 15 percent in clinical settings.

This chapter describes the characteristic features of histrionic personality disorder and its related style. Five clinical formulations of the disorder and psychological assessment indicators are highlighted. A variety of treatment approaches, modalities, and intervention strategies are also described.

DESCRIPTION OF HISTRIONIC PERSONALITY DISORDER

Histrionic personality disorder can be recognized by the following descriptors and characteristics: style vs. disorder, triggering event, behavioral styles, interpersonal style, cognitive style, affective style, attachment style, and optimal criterion.

Style vs. Disorder. Histrionic personality can be thought of as spanning a continuum from healthy to pathological, wherein the histrionic personality style is on the healthy end and the histrionic personality disorder is on the pathological end. Table 6.1 compares and contrasts histrionic personality style and disorder.

Triggering Event. The typical situation, circumstance, or event that most likely triggers or activates the characteristic maladaptive response of histrionic personality disorder (Othmer & Othmer, 2002), as noted in behavioral, interpersonal, cognitive, and feeling styles, is "opposite sex relationships."

Behavioral Style. The behavioral style is characterized as charming, dramatic, and expressive, while also being demanding, self-indulgent, and inconsiderate. Persistent attention-seeking, mood lability, capriciousness, and superficiality further characterize behavior.

Interpersonal Style. Interpersonally, these individuals tend to be exhibitionistic and flirtatious in their manner, with attention-seeking and manipulativeness being prominent. They also tend to have empathic deficits like narcissistic personality–disordered individuals.

Cognitive Style. The cognitive or thinking style of this personality can be characterized as impulsive and thematic, rather than being analytical, precise, and field-independent. Their tendency is to be nonanalytic, vague, and field-dependent. They are highly suggestible and rely heavily on hunches and intuition. They avoid awareness of their own hidden dependency and other self-knowledge, and tend to be "other-directed" with respect to the need for

Table 6.1
Comparison of Histrionic Personality Style and Disorder

Personality Style	Personality Disorder
Enjoy compliments and praise	Constantly seeks or demands reassurance, approval, or praise
Charming, engaging, and appropriately seductive in appearance and behavior	Inappropriately sexually seductive in appearance or behavior
Attentive to their appearance and grooming, enjoying clothes, style, and fashion	Overly concerned with physical attractiveness
Lively and fun-loving, often impulsive but can delay gratification	Expresses emotion with inappropriate exaggeration; self-centered and little tolerance for gratification
Enjoy being the center of attention and can rise to the occasion when all eyes are on them	Uncomfortable in situations where they cannot be the center of attention.
Sensation oriented, emotionally demonstrative, and physically affectionate; react emotionally but appropriately	Display rapidly shifting and shallow expression of emotion
Utilize a style of speech that is appropriately global and specific	Utilize a style of speech that is excessively impressionistic and lacking in detail

approval from others. Therefore, they can easily dissociate their real or inner self from their public or outer self.

Affective Style. Their emotional or feeling style is characterized by exaggerated emotional displays and excitability including irrational outbursts and temper tantrums. Although they are constantly seeking reassurance that they are loved, they respond with only superficial warmth and charm and are generally emotionally shallow. Finally, they are exquisitely rejection-sensitive.

Attachment Style. The preoccupied attachment dimension is characterized by a sense of personal unworthiness and a positive evaluation of others. These individuals tend to be rather externally oriented in their self-definitions. Preoccupied attachment style is common in individuals with histrionic personality disorder.

Optimal DSM-IV-TR Criterion. Of all the stated DSM-IV-TR criteria for histrionic personality disorder, one criterion has been found to be the most useful in diagnosing this disorder. The belief is that by beginning with this criterion, the clinician can test for the presence or absence of the criterion and quickly diagnose the personality disorder (Allnutt & Links, 1996). The optimal criterion for this disorder is "uncomfortable in situations in which he or she is not the center of attention."

The following two case examples further illustrate differences between histrionic personality disorder (Ms. P.) and histrionic personality style (Mr. M.).

Case Study: Histrionic Personality Disorder

Ms. P. is a 20-year-old female undergraduate student who requested psychological counseling at the college health services for "boyfriend problems." Actually, she had taken a nonlethal overdose of minor tranquilizers the day before coming to health services. She said she took the overdose in an attempt to kill herself because "life wasn't worth living" after her boyfriend had left the afternoon before. She is an attractive, well-dressed woman adorned with makeup and nail polish, which contrasts sharply with the very casual fashion of most coeds on campus. During the initial interview she was warm and charming, maintained good eye contact, yet was mildly seductive. At two points in the interview she was emotionally labile, shifting from smiling elation to tearful sadness. Her boyfriend had accompanied her to the evaluation session and asked to talk to the clinician. He stated the reason he had left the patient was because she made demands on him that he could not meet and that he "hadn't been able to satisfy her emotionally or sexually." Also, he noted that he could not afford to "take her out every night and party."

Case Study: Histrionic Personality Style

Mr. M. is a 41-year-old literary agent who spent the early years of his career representing nonfiction writers to major publishing houses. He was quite successful for several years but also became somewhat disenchanted with his behind-the-scene efforts. Although he has made several of his clients extraordinarily wealthy and famous, he dreamed of the time when he too would be financially independent and in the limelight. When cable TV licenses became available, he sensed the opportunity to fulfill his dream. He would become president of his own station and host his own talk show. After all, he had several high-visibility clients who he could get to be guests on his show. He set out to garner financing for his plan. With his charming manner and alluring vision, he quickly intrigued several backers and got the station launched. The only problem was he had not thought much about the production side of the enterprise. He quickly arranged for interviews for an executive producer. William T. was the fourth person he interviewed. Mr. M. knew as soon as William walked in that he was right for the job. After a 10-minute interview, William was hired. Mr. M's hunch about both William and the success of the talk show proved to be right.

DSM-IV-TR Description and Criteria

DSM-IV-TR offers a description and criteria for histrionic personality disorder (Table 6.2).

FORMULATIONS OF HISTRIONIC PERSONALITY DISORDER

Psychodynamic Formulation

Gabbard (1990) argues that histrionic personality disorder must be distinguished from hysterical personality disorder. The latter has a central place in the tradition of psychoanalytic thinking and refers to a higher-functioning, healthier group of patients than the group characterized by DSM-IV criteria. Histrionic females typically lack maternal nurturance and turn to their fathers for gratification of their dependence needs. They learn that they can

Table 6. 2
DSM-IV-TR Criteria for Histrionic Personality Disorder (301.50)

A pervasive pattern of excessive emotionality and attention seeking, beginning by early adulthood and present in a variety of contexts, as indicated by at least five of the following:

(1) is uncomfortable in situations in which he or she is not the center of attention
(2) interaction with others is often characterized by inappropriate sexually seductive or provocative behavior
(3) displays rapidly shifting and shallow expression of emotions
(4) consistently uses physical appearance to draw attention to oneself
(5) style of speech that is excessively impressionistic and lacking in detail
(6) self-dramatization, theatricality, and exaggerated expression of emotion
(7) suggestibility, i.e., easily influenced by others or circumstances
(8) considers relationships to be more intimate than they actually are

Reprinted with permission from the *Diagnostic and Statistical Manual of Mental Disorders, Fourth Edition–Text Revision.* Copyright 2000. American Psychiatric Association.

gain their father's attention through flirtatious and exhibitionistic displays of emotion. As the individual matures, she learns she must repress her genital sexuality to remain "daddy's little girl."

Similarly, histrionic males will have also experienced maternal deprivation and turned to their fathers for nurturance. If their father is emotionally unavailable, they may develop a passive, effeminate identification or hypermasculine one in reaction to anxiety about effeminacy. The individual may not become homosexual, but his heterosexual relationships are means of reassuring himself relative to underlying genital inadequacy. These men will be disappointed with all women since they cannot measure up to mother. Some will choose a celibate lifestyle to maintain their loyalty to their mother, while others will indulge in macho behavior such as body building and Don Juanism—that is, compulsive seduction of women—to reassure themselves that they are "real men" (Kellerman & Burry, 1989).

Biosocial Formulation

Millon (1981) and Millon and Davis (1996) note that individuals with histrionic personality disorders often display a high degree of emotional lability and responsiveness during infancy and early childhood, which may be attributed to low excitability thresholds for limbic and posterior hypothalamic nuclei. However, environmental factors seem to play the major role in the development of this pathology. Millon and Everly (1985) list three such factors: parental reinforcement of attention-seeking behavior; histrionic parental role models; and reinforcement of interpersonally manipulative behavior. In effect, as children these individuals learned to employ cuteness, charm, attractiveness, and seduction to secure parental reinforcement. Furthermore, this disorder is self-perpetuated through short-lived relationships, preoccupation with externals, and massive repression. Specifically, by sealing off and repressing aspects of their inner worlds, histrionic individuals deny themselves opportunities to develop psychologically.

Cognitive-Behavioral Formulation

Beck and Freeman (1990) describe a cognitive therapy view of histrionic personality disorder based on specific underlying assumptions and cognitive distortions. Two underlying assumptions are posited: "I am inadequate and unable to handle life by myself" and "I must be loved by everyone to be worthwhile."

Believing they are incapable of caring for themselves, histrionic individuals actively seek the attention and approval of others and expect others to take care of them and their needs. Believing they must be loved and approved by others promotes rejection sensitivity. Finally, feeling inadequate and desperate for approval, they are under considerable pressure to seek attention by "performing" for others. These beliefs also give rise to a thinking style characterized as impressionistic, global, and unfocused, which is not conducive to a differentiated sense of self. Not surprisingly, this global, exaggerated thinking style engenders common cognitive distortions (Beck, 1976) such as dichotomous thinking, overgeneralization, and emotional reasoning.

Taking a more behavioral tact, Turkat (1990) differentiates histrionic personality disorder into two types: (1) the controlling type in which the basic motivation is achieving total control through the use of manipulative and dramatic ploys and (2) the reactive type in which the basic motivation is seeking reassurance and approval. Turkat does not believe the controlling type is amenable to behavior treatment. Unable to read others' emotions and interventions accurately, these individuals remain shallow, self-centered, and uncomfortable when immediate reinforcement is not immediately forthcoming from others. In short, they suffer from a primary deficit in empathy.

Interpersonal Formulation

Benjamin (1996) notes that persons with histrionic personality disorder were likely to be loved for their good looks and entertainment value, rather than for competence or personal strength. They learned that physical appearance and charm could be used to control important others. The household of histrionic personalities tended to be a shifting stage. Unpredictable changes stemmed from parental instability possibly associated with alcohol or substance use. The chaos in these families was more likely to be dramatic and interesting rather than primitive and life-threatening as with borderline personalities. On the other hand, the help-seeking histrionic subtypes were likely to be nurtured for being ill. They learned that complaints and disabilities were an effective way to elicit warm concern. Along with encouragement of denial, these families rewarded sickness. Finally, they exhibit a strange fear of being ignored, together with a wish to be loved and taken care of by important others who can be controlled through charm or sickness. In short, a friendly trust is accompanied by a secretly disrespectful agenda of forcing delivery of the desired nurturance and love. Inappropriate seductive behaviors and manipulative suicide attempts exemplify such coercions.

Integrative Formulation

The following integrative formulation may be helpful in understanding how histrionic personality disorder develops and is maintained. Biologically and temperamentally, histrionic personality disorder appears to be quite different from the dependent personality disorder. Unlike the dependent personality, histrionic personality is characterized by a high energy level and emotional and autonomic reactivity. Millon and Everly (1985) noted that histrionic adults tended to display a high degree of emotional lability and responsiveness in their infancy and early childhood. Their temperament then can be characterized as hyperresponsive and externally oriented for gratification.

Psychologically, histrionic personality disorder has the characteristic view of self, worldview, and life goal. The self view of the histrionic will be some variant of the theme: "I am sensitive and everyone should admire and approve of me." The worldview will be some variant of: "Life makes me nervous, so I am entitled to special care and consideration." The life goal is some variant of the theme: "Therefore, play to the audience, and have fun, fun, fun." It should be noted that although there are expectations of special entitlement in the histrionic personality, these expectations are somewhat different than in narcissistic personality disorder. Both are sensitive to minor slights and are easily angered when ignored. However, these slights tend to be easily attenuated in the histrionic as the deflection of self-esteem involves only a threat to dependency, while for the narcissist these slights are a threat to the integrity of the self. Thus, it is more likely that the narcissist will employ splitting, projective identification, and other primitive defenses than the histrionic (Kellerman & Burry, 1989).

In addition to biological and psychological factors, social factors, such as parenting style and injunction, and family and environmental factors influence the development of the histrionic personality. The parental injunction for the histrionic personality involves reciprocity: "I'll give you attention if you do X." A parenting style that involves minimal or inconsistent discipline helps ensure and reinforce the histrionic pattern. The histrionic child is likely to grow up with at least one manipulative or histrionic parent who reinforces the child's histrionic and attention-seeking behavior. Finally, the following sequence of self- and system perpetuants are likely to be seen in histrionic personality disorder: denial of one's real or inner self; a preoccupation with externals; the need for excitement and attention seeking, which leads to a superficial charm and interpersonal presence; and the need for external approval. This, in turn, further reinforces the dissociation and denial of the real or inner self from the public self, and the cycle continues.

Table 6.3
Characteristics of Histrionic Personality Disorder

Triggering Event	Opposite sex relationships.
Behavioral Style	Charming/excitement-seeking; labile, capricious, superficial.
Interpersonal Style	Attention-getting/manipulative; exhibitionistic/flirtatious.
Cognitive Style	Impulsive, thematic, field-dependent; avoid awareness of their hidden dependencies.
Feeling Style	Exaggerated emotional display.
Temperament	Hyperresponsive infantile pattern externally oriented for gratification.
Attachment Style	Preoccupied.
Parental injunction	"I'll give you attention when you do what I want."
Self -View	"I need to be noticed"; externally oriented for gratification.
Worldview	"Life makes me so nervous, so I'm entitled to special care and consideration."
Maladaptive Schemas	Approval-seeking; emotional deprivation; defectiveness.
Optimal DSM-IV-TR Criteria	Uncomfortable in situations in which they are not the center of attention.

ASSESSMENT OF HISTRIONIC PERSONALITY DISORDER

Several sources of information are useful in establishing a diagnosis and treatment plan for personality disorders. Observation, collateral information, and psychological testing are important adjuncts to the patient's self-report in the clinical interview. This section briefly describes some characteristic observations that the clinician makes and the nature of the rapport likely to develop in initial encounters with specific personality-disordered individuals. Characteristic response patterns on various objective (i.e., MMPI-2 and MCMI-III) and projective tests (i.e., Rorschach and TAT) are also described.

Interview Behavior and Rapport

Interviewing histrionic personality–disordered individuals can be enjoyable while challenging. Initially these individuals may be more interested in admiration and approval than in a therapeutic relationship. Rapport, therefore, may be difficult to establish. Exaggerated emotionality, vagueness, superficiality, and phoniness are common in the first encounter. With a male clinician, histrionic females may be flirtatious and seductive. But with a female clinician they are more likely to engage in a power struggle. To elicit sufficient information to complete a diagnostic evaluation usually requires the clinician to overcome their vagueness and dramatic exaggerations. Open-ended and unstructured questions are not useful, since these individuals easily become sidetracked. It is preferable to pursue a main theme such as a work problem or an interpersonal conflict and elicit concrete examples, while curbing rambling and contradictions. Confronting contradictions typically results in anger and loss of rapport. Instead, the clinician should express empathy and encouragement. It is predictable that when these individuals feel that empathy and understanding are slipping away, they will return to dramatization (Othmer & Othmer, 2002).

Psychological Testing Data

The Minnesota Multiphase Personality Inventory (MMPI-2), the Millon Clinical Multiaxial Inventory (MCMI-II), the Rorschach Psychodiagnostic Test, and the Thematic Apperception Test (TAT) can be useful in diagnosing histrionic personality disorder as well as the histrionic personality style or trait.

On the MMPI-2, the 2-3/3-2 (depression-hysteria) profile is most commonly found. When clinically distressed, these individuals are likely to have elevations on 2 greater than 70. If not, scale 3 will be more elevated. The 3-4/4-3 (hysteria-psychopathic deviant) and 4-9/9-4 (psychopathic deviant-hypermania) patterns are also noted in these individuals (Graham, 2000). Scales 4, 7 (psychasthenia), and 8 (schizophrenia) may also be moderately elevated, with scale 4 reflecting their tendency to be overdramatic and self-absorbed, while self-doubt and anxiety raise the 7 score, and impulsive emotionality elevates the 8. Scale 5 is also likely to be elevated in males—but quite low in females—reflecting the association of hysteria with traditional feminine role behavior (Meyer, 1995).

On the MCMI-III, elevations on scale 4 (histrionic) are expected. Because these individuals are attention seekers, scales 1 (schizoid) and 2 (avoidant) tend to be very low, while H (somatization) may be high, since somatization can be used as an attention-getting device, as can N (bipolar-manic; Choca & Denburg, 1997).

On the Rorschach, these individuals provide a low number of responses, as well as a low number of W (whole), M (human movement), C (pure color), and Y, YF, or T (shading) responses. Occasionally, these individuals will give a "blood" response to a color card.

On the TAT, these individuals typically produce stories containing dependency and control themes. Their stories may also become personalized, generating some affective display. Occasionally, blocking occurs on cards with sexual or aggressive percepts. Rarely, primitive splitting may be noted in characters that are all good or all bad on incongruous juxtapositions (Bellak, 1997).

TREATMENT APPROACHES AND INTERVENTIONS

Treatment Considerations

The differential diagnosis of histrionic personality disorder includes narcissistic personality disorder and dependent personality disorder. In addition, Axis II combines histrionic-borderline disorder, which is a decompensated version of histrionic personality disorder. Associated DSM-IV Axis I diagnoses are in order of occurrence: dysthymia; acute anxiety syndromes such as simple and social phobias; and somatoform disorders, particularly conversion reactions and hypochondriasis. Other disorders are obsessive-compulsive disorder and dissociative disorders, particularly fugue states. Finally, major depression and bipolar disorders are common in decompensated histrionic personality disorder.

The treatment of histrionic personality disorder may present a considerable challenge to the clinician. General treatment goals include helping the individual integrate gentleness with strength, moderating emotional expression, and encouraging warmth, genuineness, and empathy. Because the histrionic personality can present as dramatic, impulsive, seductive, and manipulative with potential for suicidal gestures, the clinician needs to discuss the matter of limits early in the course of therapy regarding professional boundaries and personal responsibilities. To date, no controlled treatment outcome studies have been completed for histrionic personality disorder (Crits-Christoph & Barber, 2002).

Individual Psychotherapy

This section will briefly review the major psychotherapeutic approaches for treating histrionic personality disorder in an individual psychotherapy format. Later sections will describe other treatment formats such as group therapy, couples therapy, and pharmacotherapy. The individual treatment approaches are psychodynamic psychotherapy, brief dynamic psychotherapy, cognitive-behavioral therapy, and interpersonal psychotherapy.

Psychodynamic Psychotherapy Approach

Gabbard (1990) is quite optimistic about the responsiveness of higher-functioning individuals with histrionic personality disorder to psychoanalytically oriented psychotherapy. He reports that such individuals readily develop a therapeutic alliance and perceive the therapist as helpful. On the other hand, Gabbard believes that treatment with lower-functioning individuals with this personality disorder should employ therapeutic strategies utilized for borderline personality disorder.

Winer and Pollack (1989) indicate the basic dynamic in all presentations of histrionic personality–disordered individuals is the excessive, unresolved effort to have all of their needs met by someone else. The general goal of dynamically oriented therapies is to examine the origins of the pattern and explore the neurotic strategies—seductiveness, temper tantrums, charm, or illogical thinking—these individuals employ in order to fulfill their needs.

The classical psychoanalytic method emphasizes therapist neutrality and abstinence, and requires that the patient have sufficient ego strength to regress in a controlled manner. The transference that develops is analyzed with mutative interpretations and presumably lends to enduring personality change. Thus, proper handling of transference, particularly erotic transference, is important. Gabbard (1990) notes that mishandling of erotic transference is probably the most frequent cause of treatment failure with these individuals. However, with more disturbed and unstable histrionic personality–disordered individuals, resolving transference distortions by interpretation must be undertaken with great caution. In fact, some researchers (Khan, 1975; Havens, 1976) suggest that erotic transference not be allowed to develop too firmly or to be interpreted. Rather, counterprojective techniques are advised. These are direct or subtle, verbal or nonverbal responses that communicate to the patient that the therapist is not a transference figure of childhood (Havens, 1976).

Brief Dynamic Psychotherapy

Although long-term psychoanalytically oriented psychotherapy is considered the mainstay of dynamic treatment (Quality Assurance Project, 1991) time-limited individual psychotherapy may also be quite useful, particularly with higher-functioning histrionic individuals. The approaches of Malan (1976) and Sifneos (1972, 1984) seem quite promising. The short-term-anxiety-provoking psychotherapy (STAPP) approach developed by Sifneos may be a particularly good fit for higher-functioning histrionic individuals who present with satisfactory impersonal relationships, psychological mindedness, the ability to easily engage and interact with a therapist, and a circumscribed presenting complaint. On the other hand, Mann's (1973, 1984) time-limited approach, which requires patients to quickly engage and disengage from therapy "without suffering unduly," may pose considerable difficulty for these individuals who characteristically develop intense and sticky transference with their therapist (Chadoff, 1989). Winston and Pollack (1991) describe brief adaptive psychotherapy (BAP) as particularly effective with histrionic individuals. BAP has an ego psychological orientation that focuses on maladaptive patterns of beliefs and behaviors. The maladaptive pattern is thoroughly assessed as its underlying elements are explored in detail with particular attention to transference and resistance.

Cognitive-Behavioral Therapy Approach

According to Beck, Freeman, and associates (1990), cognitive therapy is particularly appropriate in treating histrionic personality–disordered individuals provided they remain in treatment. Although usually cooperative and motivated for therapy, the histrionic's global, diffuse thinking style is quite different from the systematic, structural nature of cognitive therapy. Thus, these individuals initially find treatment difficult and frustrating as they learn to focus attention on a single issue at a time, then monitor their thoughts and feelings. There are a number of necessary conditions for successful cognitive treatment of this disorder. Since these individuals are generally dependent and demanding in relationships, the use of collaborative and guided discovery is particularly well suited. Taking an active role and utilizing questioning is quite helpful in stemming the histrionic individual's view of clinicians as rescuers and saviors. Setting limits that are clear and firm, while rewarding assertive requests within these limits and demonstrating caring in other ways, is another necessary condition of treatment. The next condition is establishing treatment goals. These goals must be meaningful and perceived as urgent by these individuals and must be specific and concrete enough that short-term as well as long-term benefits can become realities. This counters the histrionic individual's tendency to set broad, vague, noble-sounding goals. An important key to keeping these individuals in therapy is achieving one or more of the specific short-term goals that were collaboratively established.

The mainstay of treatment with these individuals involves challenging automatic thoughts; the self-monitoring of cognition, which is helpful in

controlling their impulsivity; and the restructuring, modification, and interpretation of maladaptive schemas. Challenging their most basic assumption,
such as "I am inadequate and have to rely on others to survive," is aided by
cognitive-behavioral methods such as assertion, problem solving, and behavioral experiments that can increase their self-efficacy and help them feel more
competent.

Another central belief that must be modified is that the loss of a relationship is always disastrous. Fantasizing about the reality of what would happen
if a relationship would end, and recalling how they survived before that relationship began, can help these individuals "decatastrophize" their beliefs about
rejection. The behavioral approach with the controlling type of histrionic personality (Turkat, 1990) has not been shown to be effective (Turkat & Maisto,
1985; Turkat, 1990). The reactive type is more amenable to change, specifically with empathy training. Turkat (1990) describes this intervention, which
consists of social skills training in active listening, paraphrasing, and reflec-
tion. The goal is to teach these patients to focus increasingly on others' needs
and feelings. Role-playing with video feedback has been particularly effective.
The use of dramatic behavioral experiments and training in problem-solving
skills are also advocated by Beck and Freeman (1990).

In short, an effective cognitive therapy approach to histrionic personality
disorder will be systematic and structural—including firm limit setting and
specific treatment goals—and will include cognitive—disputation of automatic
thoughts and schemas, restructuring of basic maladaptive beliefs and schemas—
as well as behavioral methods.

Structured Skill Treatment Interventions. While research shows that medication can modulate or normalize dysregulated behaviors, a similar modulating effect has also been noted for social skills training (Lieberman, DeRisi, &
Mueser, 1989). Thus, it appears that social skills training is a relatively potent
bottom-up treatment strategy for normalizing limbic system–mediated behaviors that reflect specific skill deficits in personality-disordered individuals.
When such skill deficits are present, Sperry (1999) contends that structured
skill training interventions is a potent and effective strategy in treatment. Various structured intervention strategies for modifying a personality-disordered
individual's affective, behavioral, and cognitive temperament styles are described and illustrated for histrionic personality disorder (Sperry, 1999).

Schema Therapy. Schema therapy is an elaboration of cognitive therapy that
has been developed by Young (1999) and Young et al. (2003) specifically for
personality disorders and other difficult individual and couples problems.
Schema therapy involves identifying maladaptive schemas and planning specific strategies and interventions. Four main strategies are cognitive, experi-

ential, behavioral, and the therapeutic relationship itself. Cognitive restructuring—modification of maladaptive schemas—is an important cognitive strategy but is combined with imagery exercises, empathic confrontation, homework assignments, and "limited reparenting," (i.e., a form of corrective emotional experience; Young, 1999).

Maladaptive schemas typically associated with histrionic personality disorder include *emotional deprivation*—that is, the belief that one's desire for emotional support will not be met by others; *defectiveness*—that is, the belief that one is defective, bad, unwanted, or inferior in important respects; and *approval-seeking*—that is, the belief that one must constantly seek to belong and be accepted at the expense of developing a true sense of self (Bernstein, 2002).

Interpersonal Approach

Benjamin (1996) writes that psychotherapeutic interventions with histrionic personality–disordered individuals can be planned and evaluated in terms of whether they enhance collaboration, facilitate learning about maladaptive patterns and their roots, block these patterns, enhance the will to change, and effectively encourage new patterns.

Benjamin notes that it is essential to establish a therapeutic alliance facilitating collaboration with the histrionic individual based on knowledge of the basic pattern, wishes, and fears of that individual. It is essential that the therapist communicate warmth and competent support while not reinforcing the histrionic's dependent, needy position. The working contract is with the individual's observing ego while the "enemy" is the damaging pattern. A major task of beginning treatment is transforming the histrionic's view of treatment as making fantasies come true to a place where personal development can be facilitated.

The task of learning to recognize patterns is complicated in that histrionic individuals have not sufficiently developed an observing ego to help them recognize and reflect on patterns. In fact, they've come to believe that if they became competent, they would be left alone and no one would care for them. Whereas the female histrionic can internalize the female clinician's modeling of benign and constructive examination of patterns, the male clinician must help the individual look at her fears that if she becomes competent the clinician will decide she is unattractive and stop treatment.

Next, the clinician focuses the histrionic individual's attention on potentially destructive patterns of acting out based on underlying fears and wishes. By providing gentle challenges, the clinician protects these individuals from their own past. The goal is to expand options and enhance awareness in light of what is being learned about patterns. The therapist does not block patterns with advice giving but rather reviews options. Developing the will to change patterns is enhanced if these patterns can be uncovered and clearly connected in an experiential way to the past. This often facilitates the individual's "decision" to give up the goals that drive the patterns. Finally, Benjamin advocates traditional techniques from other approaches that can be utilized to build new patterns and ways of functioning, once the "unconscious underbrush" has been cleared away.

Group Therapy

The literature on histrionic personality is quite interesting with regard to treatability of this disorder in group settings. There are clear warnings in the older psychoanalytic literature about the impact of these patients on other group members. Slavson (1939) cautioned that their changeability and unpredictability would engender stress and anxiety in a group. Thus, he believed these patients should be treated only in individual therapy. On the other hand, contemporary clinicians like Gabbard (1990, 1994) contend that histrionic patients who are appropriate for individual dynamic psychotherapy are also appropriate for dynamic group psychotherapy. In fact, Gabbard finds these patients are highly valued by other group members for their ability to express affects directly, and because of their concern for other group members.

The group treatment format has a number of advantages over individual treatment. First, a group setting frustrates the wish and demand these patients have for the exclusive attention of the therapist, and so challenges the approval-seeking posture of these patients. Thus, the risk that an eroticized transference will develop is relatively small as compared with individual therapy.

Second, their global cognitive style and associated defenses of repression and denial can be more effectively treated in a group setting. Group members will confront the distorted manner in which histrionic patients view themselves and others by their style, omission of details, and focus on affects over thought.

Finally, histrionic patients tend to form positive maternal transference and expect the group to make up for the maternal nurturance they missed as children (Gabbard, 1990). While this transference is particularly challenging for the clinician in individual therapy, it is considerably diluted in a group treatment format.

Relatively little has been published about the effectiveness of group treatment of histrionic patients. But one study is encouraging. Cass et al. (1972) reported behavioral group treatment significantly modified inappropriate passivity, manipulativeness, and acting out, which was replaced by more effective assertive interpersonal behavior.

The question of indication and contraindication has been addressed by some writers. Halleck (1978) notes that histrionic patients who cannot participate in a group process without monopolizing or disrupting it should be excluded. Gabbard (1990) cautions that individuals might still be candidates for group therapy if they are concurrently in individual psychotherapy. Sheidlinger and Porter (1980) indicate that combined treatment (i.e., individual plus group therapy) may be the treatment of choice for such histrionic patients.

Marital and Family Therapy

There are no reports of family therapy, per se, with histrionic patients. However, there are a number of case reports on marital therapy with these patients. Typically, the marriage consists of an obsessive-compulsive husband and a histrionic wife, wherein the obsessive-compulsive spouse tends to assume increasing responsibility while the histrionic spouse becomes increasingly helpless (Berman, 1983). Treatment may be sought following some primitive outburst that can include some threat of self-destructive behavior, typically during separation or divorce. The loss of a stable dependent figure is a major stressor for the histrionic patient, who may exhibit aggressive attention-seeking behavior, increased affective display and seductiveness, and/or possible promiscuity, in an effort to make the other spouse jealous (Harbir, 1981).

The general goal of treatment is to facilitate changing this pattern in both spouses. This is better accomplished in a couples format rather than in individual sessions. Harbir (1981) offers a treatment protocol for couples wherein divorce and child custody are issues. Nichols (1996) describes the interactional patterns and symptomatology of individuals with histrionic personality disorders and antisocial personality disorders in close interpersonal relationships, as well as a suggested treatment plan protocol and strategies for dealing with such couples in a therapeutic context.

An integrative marital therapy approach involving dynamic, cognitive-behavioral, and systemic interventions is described by Sperry and Maniacci (1996) for couples in which one partner presents with histrionic personality disorder and the other with obsessive-compulsive personality disorder. Three phases of the treatment process are discussed and illustrated: establishing a therapeutic alliance, restoring balance to the couple relationship, and modifying individual partner dynamics. The first two phases involve conjoint couples sessions, while much of the third phase involves individual sessions (Sperry & Maniacci, 1996).

Medication

To date, histrionic personality disorder has not been subject to controlled phar-macological trials (Koenigsberg, Woo-Ming, & Siever, 2002). However, from a target symptom or dimensional—that is, trait cluster—perspective there are promising indications for the effective utilization of psychotropics in the treat-ment of certain histrionic personalities.

The most obvious indications for medication are when concurrent Axis I presentations are noted. When severe depression is the presenting symptom, antidepressants are probably indicated. The choice of cyclic or serotonergic blocker is made based on specific depressive features and side effect profiles.

When the presentation involves exquisite rejection sensitivity, craving for attention, demanding behavior, hyperphagia, and hypersomnia when de-pressed, the depressive hysteroid dysphoria subtype may exist (Liebowitz & Klein, 1979, 1981). Monoamine oxidase inhibitors (MAOIs) have been found to be the medications of choice.

When no obvious Axis I is present but dimensional cluster symptoms are noted—that is, affective constability, compulsivity, or cognitive-perceptual dis-organization—specific agents may be indicated (Siever & Davis, 1991). Lower-functioning histrionic individuals are characterized by affective instability and some impulsivity (Siever & Davis, 1991). Sertraline, a serotonergic blocker, has demonstrated some efficacy with such patients (Kavoussi, Liu, & Coccaro, 1994).

Medication Protocol. For the lower-functioning and more problematic histri-onic individuals, the following protocol is suggested: Begin with an SSRI at antidepressant dosages. If that SSRI fails, try another. If there is a partial re-sponse, an adjunctive atypical psychotic agent or a mood stabilizer, such as valproate or carbamazepine, can be considered. For individuals in whom re-jection sensitivity is prominent, a trial of an MAOI is reasonable, particularly if the individual has a history of medication compliance. Naltrexone may be a useful adjunctive for individuals with self-harming behavior (Reich, 2002).

Combined and Integrated Treatment Approaches

The basic premise of this book is that symptomatic and lower-functioning personality-disordered individuals are less likely to respond to a single-treatment approach or modality. Since personality disorders are biopsychosocial phenomena (Pies, 1992), combined or integrative tailored treat-ment is indicated, particularly for the more symptomatic and severe presentations. Stone (1992) advocates combined treatments, wherein two or more approaches or modalities are utilized concurrently or in tandem.

Previously it was mentioned that concurrently combining individual psychotherapy with group therapy was indicated for histrionic patients who monopolized or were disruptive in group settings (Sheidlinger & Porter, 1980). It has also been noted that behavioral techniques may be integrated with psychodynamic or cognitive approaches. Finally, medications may be a useful adjunct to psychotherapy, either concurrently or in tandem, if specific Axis I or Axis II symptoms or trait clusters are prominent.

Horowitz (1997) discusses guidelines for the psychotherapeutic treatment for histrionic personality disorder that integrates cognitive and psychodynamic principles and methods. This personality disorder is formulated in terms of levels: states of mind, defensive control processes, and schemas. A phase-oriented treatment plan is linked to these three formulation levels. Specific psychotherapeutic guidelines for each of these phases are described.

CHAPTER 7

Narcissistic Personality
Disorder

Narcissistic personality disorder has been the subject of widespread interest among mental health professionals. Prior to DSM-III, this disorder had not been in DSMs or in the *International Classification of Disorders* (ICD). Narcissistic personality has been dubbed one of the neurotic personalities of our time (Sperry, 1991). The widespread usage of the term *narcissistic personality* by psychodynamically oriented clinicians was a major impetus for the inclusion of narcissistic personality disorder in DSM-III (Gunderson, Ronningstam, & Smith, 1991). This diagnostic category seems to have been accepted easily by clinicians and researchers, and there has been little change in diagnostic criteria from DSM-III to DSM-III-R to DSM-IV, to DSM-IV-TR.

Prevalence estimates of this disorder in the general population are less than 1 percent. In clinical populations the range is between 2 and 16 percent. However, the number of individuals exhibiting significant narcissistic traits is estimated to be a large percentage of the general population (Stone, 1993).

This chapter describes the characteristic features of this disorder and its related personality style, five different clinical formulations, psychological assessment indicators, and a variety of treatment approaches and intervention strategies.

DESCRIPTION OF NARCISSISTIC PERSONALITY DISORDER

Narcissistic personality disorder can be recognized by the following descriptors and characteristics: styles vs. disorder, triggering event, behavioral style, interpersonal style, cognitive style, affective style, attachment style, and optimal criterion.

Style vs. Disorder. The narcissistic personality is quite common in Western culture, particularly among certain occupations and professions such as law, medicine, entertainment and sports, and politics. The narcissistic personality can be thought of as spanning a continuum from healthy to pathological, with the narcissistic personality style on the healthy end and the personality disorder on the pathological end. Table 7.1 compares and contrasts differences between the narcissistic style and disorder.

Triggering Event. The typical situation, circumstance, or event that most likely triggers or activates the characteristic maladaptive response of narcissistic personality disorder (Othmer & Othmer, 2002), as noted in behavioral, interpersonal, cognitive, and feeling styles, is "evaluation of self."

Behavioral Style. Behaviorally, narcissistic individuals are seen as conceited, boastful, and snobbish. They appear self-assured and self-centered, and they tend to dominate conversation, seek admiration, and act in a pompous and exhibitionistic fashion. They are also impatient, arrogant, and thin-skinned or hypersensitive.

Interpersonal Style. Interpersonally, they are exploitive and use others to indulge themselves and their desires. Their behavior is socially facile, pleasant, and endearing. However, they are unable to respond with true empathy to others. When stressed, they can be disdainful, exploitive, and generally irresponsible in their behavior.

Cognitive Style. Their thinking style is categorized by cognitive expansiveness and exaggeration. They tend to focus on images and themes rather than on facts and issues. In fact, they take liberties with the facts, distort them, and even engage in prevarication and self-deception to preserve their own illusions about themselves and the projects in which they are involved. Their cognitive style is also marked by inflexibility. In addition, they have an exaggerated sense of self-importance and establish unrealistic goals of power, wealth, and ability. They justify all of this with their sense of entitlement and exaggerated sense of their own self-importance.

Table 7.1
A Comparison of the Narcissistic Personality Style and Disorder

Personality Style	*Personality Disorder*
Although emotionally vulnerable to negative assessments and feelings of others they can handle these with style and grace	Reacts to criticism with feelings of rage, stress, or humiliation (even if not expressed).
Shrewd in dealing with others, utilizing the strengths and advantages of others to achieve their own goals	Interpersonally exploitive, taking advantage of others to achieve their own ends
Can energetically sell themselves, their ideas, and their projects	Grandiose sense of self-importance
Tend to be able competitors who love getting to the top and enjoy staying there	Believe their problems are unique and understood only by other special people
Can visualize themselves as the best or most accomplished in their field	Preoccupied by fantasies of unlimited success, power, brilliance, beauty, or ideal love
Believe in themselves, their abilities, and their uniqueness but do not demand special treatment or privilege	Have a sense of entitlement and unreasonable expectations of especially favorable treatment
Accept accomplishments, praise, and admiration gracefully and with self-possession	Require constant attention and admiration
Possess a keen awareness of their thoughts and feelings, and have some awareness of those of others	Lack of empathy; inability to recognize and experience how others feel
Expect others to treat them well at all times	Preoccupied with feelings of envy

Affective Style. Their emotional or affective style is characterized by an aura of self-confidence and nonchalance that is present in most situations except when their narcissistic confidence is shaken. Then they are likely to respond with rage at criticism. Their feelings toward others shift and vacillate between overidealization and devaluation. Finally, their inability to show empathy is reflected in their superficial relationships with minimal emotional ties or commitments.

Attachment Style. Individuals with an other-view that is negative and a self-view that vacillates between positive and negative exhibit a composite fearful–dismissing style of attachment. They tend to view themselves as special and entitled but are also mindful of their need for others who can potentially hurt them. Accordingly, they use others to meet their needs while being wary and dismissive of them. The fearful–dismissing attachment style is common in individuals with narcissistic personality disorder.

Optimal DSM-IV-TR Criterion. Of all the stated DSM-IV-TR criteria for narcissistic personality disorder, one criterion has been found to be the most useful in diagnosing this disorder. The belief is that by beginning with this criterion, the clinician can test for the presence or absence of the criterion and quickly diagnose the personality disorder (Allnutt & Links, 1996). The optimal criterion for this disorder is "has grandiose sense of self-importance."

The following two case examples illustrate the differences between narcissistic personality style (Mr. J.) and narcissistic personality disorder (Mr. C.).

Case Study: Narcissistic Personality Disorder

Mr. C. is a 41-year-old male who presented for therapy after his wife of 6 years threatened to leave him and because his employer was pressuring him to resign his position as a sales executive for a condominium project. Apparently, Mrs. C. had told her husband that he loved himself "a hundred times more than you love me." Mr. C. dismissed this by saying he needed to buy $600 suits because his job demanded that he look his best at all times and that he was "tall, dark, handsome, and sexy—all any woman could want in a man." Mr. C. denied that he used scare tactics, exaggerated claims, or other pressure selling techniques with customers: "Sure, I'm a bit aggressive, but you don't get into the millionaire's club by being a wimp." He added that his employer would "go belly up without me," and that he was too important to be dismissed for such petty reasons.

Case Study Example: Narcissistic Personality Style

Mr. J. is chairman of his state's Democratic party and caucus. Throughout most of his career, Mr. J. has been incredibly successful and effective. He is extroverted, witty, and charming interpersonally, and astute, visionary, and effective in mobilizing support for his party's political agenda. However, in graduate school a political science professor had criticized a first draft of his master's thesis, evaluating his arguments as weak and saying that his conclusions were only partially substantiated by the research cited. Prior to this, Mr. J. had held the professor in high esteem, but he questioned the professor's competence after this criticism. Nevertheless, he swallowed his pride and reworked the thesis according to the professor's suggestion so that he could graduate. A short time after graduation, Mr. J. lost his first job as a speech writer for a state senator because the opinions and conclusions cited in his drafts were not sufficiently well documented. Fortunately, Mr. J. took these lessons to heart and found others to research his own speeches when he ran for office. Mr. J. recognized that this was not one of his strengths and he could delegate it while focusing on his real strengths, which were envisioning policy and political agendas and galvanizing support for them.

DSM-IV-TR Description and Criteria

According to DSM-IV-TR, narcissistic personality disorder is described as a pervasive pattern of grandiosity (in fantasy or behavior), need for admiration, and lack of empathy, beginning by early adulthood and present in a variety of contexts. It is indicated by at least five of nine criteria listed in Table 7.2.

Table 7.2
DSM-IV-TR Criteria for Narcissistic Personality Disorder (301.81)

(1) a grandiose sense of self-importance (e.g., exaggerates achievements and talents, expects to be recognized as superior without commensurate achievements)
(2) preoccupation with fantasies of unlimited success, power, brilliance, beauty, or ideal love
(3) believes that he or she is "special" and unique and can only be understood by, or should associate with, other special or high-status people (or institutions)
(4) requires excessive admiration
(5) a sense of entitlement, i.e., unreasonable expectations of especially favorable treatment or automatic compliance with his or her expectations
(6) is interpersonally exploitative, i.e., takes advantage of others to achieve his or her own ends
(7) lack of empathy: unwilling to recognize or identify with the feelings and needs of others
(8) is often envious of others or believes that others are envious of him or her
(9) arrogant, haughty behaviors or attitudes

Reprinted with permission from the *Diagnostic and Statistical Manual of Mental Disorders, Fourth Edition–Text Revision.* Copyright 2000. American Psychiatric Association.

FORMULATIONS OF NARCISSISTIC PERSONALITY DISORDER

Psychodynamic Formulation

Freud (1914/1976) described the original psychoanalytic formulation of narcissistic personality. For Freud, parental overevaluation or erratic, unreliable caretaking in early life disrupted the development of object love in the child. As a result of this fixation or arrest at the narcissistic phase of development, Freud posited that narcissists would be unable to form lasting relationships. In other words, the etiology of narcissistic personality disorder is that it is the outcome of insufficient gratification of the normal narcissistic needs of infancy and childhood. The contrary hypothesis is that the disorder stems from narcissistic overgratification during childhood, and because of this fixation, it interferes with the normal maturation and integration of the superego, leading to difficulties in regulation of self-esteem (Fernando, 1998). Another common belief is that the disorder arises from faulty parenting or disturbed object relations. Imbesi (2000) suggests this hypothesis is the common etiology of most personality disorders and instead proposes that the caretaker's failure to provide optimal frustrating experiences necessary to foster the development of a more realistic self-image in the child is the etiology of the narcissistic personality.

In the past, the formulations of the narcissistic personality by Kohut and Kernberg have become the dominant models. Kohut (1971, 1977) believed the narcissist is developmentally arrested at the stage that requires specific responses from individuals in their environment to maintain cohesive selves—that is, the structures of the grandiose self and the idealized parental image are not integrated. He described the formulation of self-object transferences—both mirroring and idealizing—that re-create the situation with parents that was not fully successful during childhood. When such responses are not forthcoming (an empathic deficit), the narcissistic is prone to fragmentation of the self (narcissistic injury).

Unlike Kohut, who worked with high-functioning professionals in psychoanalysis, Kernberg (1975, 1984) based his conceptualization of narcissistic pathology on his work with inpatients as well as outpatients. He views the narcissist's grandiosity and exploitation as evidence of oral rage, which he believes results from the emotional deprivation caused by an indifferent and covertly spiteful mother figure. Concurrently, some unique attribute, talent, or role provides the child with a sense of being special, which supplies an emotional escape valve in a world of perceived threat or indifference. Thus, grandiosity and entitlement shelter a "real self" that is "split off"—that is, outside consciousness. Parenthetically for Kernberg, the real self contains strong but unconscious feelings of envy, deprivation, fear, and rage. Finally, Kernberg (1975) views defensive structure of the narcissist as remarkably similar to the borderline, differentiating the two on the basis of the narcissist's integrated but pathological grandiose self.

Biosocial Formulation

According to Millon and Everly (1985), narcissistic personality disorder primarily arises from environmental factors, since the role of biogenic factors is unclear. The principal environmental factors are parental indulgence and overvaluation, learned exploitive behavior, and only-child status. Essentially, then, children are pampered and given special treatment by the parents such that they learn to believe the world revolves around them. They become egotistical in their perspectives and narcissistic in their expressions of love and emotion. Not surprisingly, they come to expect special treatment from others outside the home. When special treatment is not forthcoming, the children experiment with demanding and exploitive tactics, subsequently developing considerable skill in manipulating others so as to receive the special consideration they believe they deserve. At the same time, they come to believe that most others are inferior, weak, and exploitable. Furthermore, Millon and colleagues (Millon & Everly, 1985; Millon & Davis, 2000) indicate that parental overindulgence is particularly likely with only children. Finally, the narcissistic pattern is self-perpetuated through the illusion of superiority, a lack of self-control manifested by disdain for situations and persons who do not support the individual's exalted beliefs, deficient social responsibility, and self-reinforcement of the narcissistic pattern itself.

Cognitive-Behavioral Formulation

According to Beck, Freeman, and Associates (1990) narcissistic personality disorder stems from a combination of schemas about the self, world, and future. The central schema is the superior/special schema that develops from direct and indirect messages from parents, siblings, and significant others, as well as by experiences that mold beliefs about personal uniqueness and self-importance. The schema of being superior can be shaped by flattery, indulgence, and favoritism. Similarly, the schema of being special can be shaped by experiences of rejection, limitations, exclusion, or deficits. The common denominator for such beliefs about self is that individuals perceive themselves as different from others in significant ways. The actual presence of some culturally valued or devalued talent or attribute tends to elicit social responses that reinforce the superior/special schema. Feedback that could modify this schema may be lacking or distorted. Being insulted from negative feedback may contribute to the narcissist's vulnerability to criticism and evaluation. Behavior is affected by difficulty in cooperation and reciprocal social intervention and by excesses in self-indulgent, demanding, and aggressive behavior. Problems emerge when this self-schema is overactive and not balanced by more integrative judgments.

Interpersonal Formulation

Benjamin (1996) explains that persons with narcissistic personality disorder typically were raised in an environment of selfless noncontingent love and adoration. Unfortunately, this adoration was not accompanied by genuine self-disclosure. As a result, the narcissist-to-be learned to be insensitive to others' needs and views. The adoring parent was likely to have been consistently differential and nurturant to the narcissist-in-training. As a result, the adult narcissist holds the arrogant expectation that others will continue to provide these emotional supplies. Along with this nurturance and adoration is the ever-present threat of a fall from grace. As such the narcissistic individual who is simply "normal" and ordinary creates unbearable disappointment for the parent(s). Thus, the burden of being special or perfect can be overwhelming for the narcissistic individual. Since this individual's self-concept derives from an internalization of unrealistic adoration and nurturance, the substitution of criticism or disappointment for love can be particularly devastating. Thus, the narcissistically disordered individual can dish it out but is not well equipped to take it. In short, there is extreme vulnerability to criticism or being ignored, together with a strong wish for love, support, and admiration from others. Noncontingent love and presumptive control of others is expected and even demanded. If support is withdrawn or lack of perfection is evident, the self-concept degrades into severe self-criticism. Totally devoid of empathy, these individuals tend to treat others with contempt and rage if entitlement fail.

Integrative Formulation

The following integrative formulation may be helpful in understanding how the narcissistic personality is developed and maintained. Biologically, narcissistic personalities tend to have hyperresponsive temperaments (Millon, 1981).

As young children they were viewed by others as being special in terms of looks, talents, or promise. Often as young children they had early and exceptional speech development. In addition, they were likely keenly aware of interpersonal cues.

Psychologically, the narcissists' view of themselves, others, the world, and life's purpose can be articulated in terms of the following: "I'm special and unique, and I am entitled to extraordinary rights and privileges whether I have earned them or not." Their worldview is a variant of the theme: "Life is a banquet table to be sampled at will. People owe me admiration and privilege." Their goal is, "Therefore, I'll expect and demand this specialness." Common defense mechanisms utilized by the narcissistic personality involve rationalization and projective identification.

Socially, predictable parental patterns and environmental factors can be noted for the narcissistic personality. Parental indulgence and overevaluation characterize the narcissistic personality. The parental injunction was likely: "Grow up and be wonderful—for me." Often they were only children and may have sustained early losses in childhood. From an early age they learned exploitive and manipulative behavior from their parents. This narcissistic pattern is confirmed, reinforced, and perpetuated by certain individual and systems factors. The illusion of specialness, disdain for others' views, and a sense of entitlement lead to an underdeveloped sense of social interest and responsibility. This, in turn, leads to increased self-absorption and confirmation of narcissistic beliefs (Sperry & Mosak, 1996).

ASSESSMENT OF NARCISSISTIC PERSONALITY DISORDER

Several sources of information are useful in establishing a diagnosis and treatment plan for personality disorders. Observation, collateral information, and psychological testing are important adjuncts to the patient's self-report in the clinical interview. This section briefly describes some characteristic observations that the clinician makes and the nature of the rapport likely to develop in initial encounters with specific personality-disordered individuals. Characteristic response patterns on various objective (i.e., MMPI-2 and MCMI-III) and projective tests (i.e., Rorschach and TAT) are also described.

Interview Behavior and Rapport

Interviewing narcissistic personality–disordered individuals is singularly different from interviewing other personality-disordered individuals. Through-

Table 7.3
Characteristics of Narcissistic Personality Disorder

Triggering Event	Evaluation of self.
Behavioral Style	Conceited, boastful, snobbish; self-assured, self-centered, pompous; impatient, arrogant, thin-skinned.
Interpersonal Style	Disdainful, exploitive, irresponsible; socially facile but without empathy; use others to indulge themselves.
Cognitive Style	Cognitive expansiveness and exaggeration; focus on images and themes: take liberties with facts; persistent and inflexible.
Feeling Style	Self-confidence—narcissistic rage.
Temperament	Active and responsive; special talents, attractiveness, early language development.
Attachment Style	Fearful and dismissing.
Parental Injunction	"Grow up and be wonderful—for me."
Self-View:	"I'm special and unique, and I'm entitled to extraordinary rights and privileges whether I've earned them or not."
Worldview	"Life is a banquet table to be sampled at will. People owe me admiration and privilege. Therefore, I'll expect and demand this specialness."
Maladaptive Schemas	Entitlement; defectiveness; emotional deprivation; insufficient self-control; unrelenting standards.
Optimal DSM-IV-TR Criteria	Have grandiose sense of self-importance.

out the interview, these individuals give clinicians the impression that the interview has only one purpose: to endorse their self-promoted importance (Othmer and Othmer, 2002). These individuals typically present as self-assured, pretentious, and unwilling to adapt to the basic cultural differences customary to the patient role. They behave as though they are indifferent to the clinician's perspective (Soloff, 1985). As long as the clinician plays the expected role, he or she is idealized as a marvelous clinician. However, confronting their grandiosity early in the treatment process will inevitably lead to rage and possibly premature termination. They prefer open-ended questions that permit them extended descriptions of their many talents, accomplishments, and future plans. Rapport is established after a considerable period of mirroring and soothing. Typical clinician countertransferences in the initial interviews are boredom, frustration, and anger. To the extent that the clinician can patiently wait through this period of mirroring, the work of confronting and interpreting their grandiosity can begin.

Psychological Testing Data

This section describes typical themes and patterns noted for the narcissistic personality on the Minnesota Multiphase Personality Inventory (MMPI-2), the Millon Clinical Multiaxial Inventory (MCMI-III), the Rorschach Psychodiagnostic Test, and the Thematic Apperception Test (TAT). These data have been useful in diagnosing narcissistic personality disorder as well as the narcissistic personality style or trait.

On the MMPI-2 a 4-9 (psychopathic deviant-hypomania) profile or an elevation on scale 4 is most likely. Since they develop only superficial relationships, a low score on 0 (social introversion) might also be noted (Graham, 2000). And since they often fit stereotypic sexual roles, scale 5 (masculinity-femininity) may be low, particularly in narcissistic males. If they also tend to be suspicious or irritable, an elevation on scale 6 (paranoia) may be noted (Meyer, 1995).

On the MCMI-III, an elevation on scale 5 (narcissistic) is expected. Scales 4 (histrionic), 6A (antisocial), and 6B (sadistic) could also be elevated. During periods of stress, elevations on P (paranoid) and DD (delusional disorder) may be noted. Since these individuals are adverse to admitting psychic distress or personal weakness, elevations on scales A (anxiety), D (dysthymia), and S (schizotypal) are not likely (Choca & Denburg, 1997).

On the Rorschach, these individuals are likely to produce records with a high number of C (pure color) and CF (color form) responses. They seldom respond directly to shading (Y, YF, or FY) but often make texture (T, TF, or FT) responses (Meyer, 1995). Responses that reflect the ornate, the exotic, or the expensive are characteristic of narcissism (Shafer, 1954).

On the TAT, these individuals tend to avoid the essential features of the cards and thus their stories may be void of meaningful content. Cards that demand a response to potentially anxiety-producing fantasy, such as 13 MF, may yield a superficially avoidant story or are with blatant shocking or lewd content (Bellak, 1997).

TREATMENT APPROACHES AND INTERVENTIONS

Treatment Considerations

Included in the differential diagnosis of narcissistic personality disorder are these other Axis II personality disorders: histrionic personality disorder, antisocial personality disorder, and paranoid personality disorder. The most common Axis I syndromes associated with narcissistic personality disorder are acute anxiety reactions, dysthymia, hypochondriasis, and delusional disorders.

In terms of treatment goals, a decision needs to be made as to whether the treatment is short term and crisis oriented or long term and focused on personality restructuring. Crisis-oriented psychotherapy usually focuses on alleviation of the symptoms such as anxiety, depression, or somatic symptoms associated with the narcissistic injury or wound. The goals of longer-term therapy often involve restructuring of personality. These goals include increasing empathy, decreasing rage and cognitive distortions, and increasing the individual's ability to mourn losses. The following sections describe various treatment approaches and individual, group, marital and family, medication, and combined integrative formats. To date, no controlled treatment outcome studies have been completed for narcissistic personality disorder (Crits-Christoph & Barber, 2002).

Individual Psychotherapies

Alone, or in conjunction with group or marital and family therapy, individual psychotherapy is viewed by many as the basic treatment of choice for individuals with narcissistic personality disorder. Because of their empathic deficit and proclivity to devalue others, psychotherapy with these individuals can be very trying. Giving little, treating others shabbily, and demanding much tends to frustrate the natural inclination of therapists to respond empathically. And although the literature is divided on whether to utilize confrontation or mirroring techniques, both approaches must be part of the therapist's armamentarium. Generally speaking, higher-functioning narcissistic personalities eventually do well in psychotherapy as their sense of entitlement gives way to emulation. On the other hand, lower-functioning narcissistic personalities have fewer of the necessary personality assets and relational skills for changing, and unless the therapeutic process addresses these deficits, these individuals may predictably leave treatment precipitously to avoid the humiliation of admitting how ill-equipped they are to achieve realistic treatment goals. Psychodynamic, cognitive-behavioral, and interpersonal approaches are reviewed.

Psychodynamic Psychotherapy Approach

This section will briefly outline the various psychodynamic approaches: psychoanalysis, psychoanalytic psychotherapy, supportive psychotherapy, and brief psychoanalytic psychotherapy.

Psychoanalysis. Although Freud (1914/1976) was not optimistic about the treatability of the narcissistic personality, Kernberg (1984) and Kohut (1977) believe that higher-functioning narcissistic personality–disordered individuals are particularly suited for psychoanalysis. Kernberg views the core of the disorder as involving anger, envy, and distorted self-sufficiency, so he emphasizes an active interpretation and confrontation of the individual's defenses. Kohut, on the other hand, views the core of the disorder as stunted development of the grandiose self. He believes that through the establishment of a self-object transference, both mirroring and idealizing, missing elements of the self-structure can be added. When a correct empathic interpretation is made, the individual reintegrates by way of the reestablishment of the self-object transference—cohesion—and the disappearance of figmentation. In short, then, Kernberg's goal of psychoanalysis is to effect a significant personality change so that envy and rage no longer overwhelm the individual and lead to a protective need to withdraw to a self-sufficient position. For Kohut, the goal is to heal the individual's incomplete self-structure and increase self-esteem through transmuting internalization—that is, taking in of missing functions from the self-object analyst. The process of psychoanalysis for both Kohut and Kernberg is expected to take several years since significant personality change is the goal.

Psychoanalytic Psychotherapy. In what he calls expressive psychotherapy, Kernberg (1984) describes a modified psychoanalytic treatment as an alternative to psychoanalysis and supportive psychotherapy. In expressive psychotherapy the therapeutic effort focuses on the negative transference in which early manifestations of anger toward the therapist are explored and interpreted. Also included are the defenses of splitting, projection, and projective identification. Masterson (1981) and Rinsley (1982) further emphasize the value of this approach in the development of a therapeutic alliance. Masterson also emphasizes the importance of exploring the individual's exquisite sensitivity to the therapist's empathic failures and the importance of therapeutically exploring this vulnerability. Although Kohut did not describe a psychotherapeutic treatment of narcissistic personality disorder, Goldberg (1973) and Chessick (1985) have shown that self-object transference does become established in psychotherapy and can be interpreted in light of Kohut's approach. Goldberg (1989) describes the use of mirroring idealizing and twinship transference in a self psychology approach of the narcissistic patient.

Psychoanalytically oriented psychotherapy of narcissistically disordered individuals typically involves one to three sessions a week for 2 or more years. Kantor (1992) offers a number of proactive suggestions for use in the course of psychotherapy. Among them is the use of predictive interpretation. He points out how painful therapy will be as the individual feels forced to abandon entitlement and grandiosity. Forewarning the individual will make it less likely that he or she will leave therapy precipitously.

Supportive Psychotherapy. According to Kernberg (1984), supportive psychotherapy emphasizes an avoidance of working with the negative transference, and instead focuses on supporting the individual in expanding ego functions, skills, and capacities. In Kernberg's opinion, rapid symptomatic improvement is more likely in supportive psychotherapy than in more expressive approaches. The reader is referred to Kernberg's (1984) chapter on "Supportive Psychotherapy" for an extended discussion of treatment goals and techniques. Kantor (1992) recommends palliation as the goal of supportive psychotherapy wherein the disordered narcissistic personality is maintained while reducing or eliminating destructive sequelae. He recommends a number of palliative strategies such as teaching the individual to become a better narcissist. For instance, Kantor shows the individual how excessive self-adoration actually interferes with the ability to receive more realistic, wanted, and needed adoration from others.

Brief Psychoanalytically Oriented Psychotherapy. Not surprisingly, the least explored treatment modalities of the psychodynamic therapies are the shorter-term and brief approaches. Until recently, a self-deficit disorder like the narcissistic personality was considered unamenable except with long-term treatment. However, as economic realities collide with ideology, this view may be changing somewhat. Kernberg (1984) describes a short-term crisis intervention for narcissistic personality disorder until the individual is ready and motivated for long-term treatment. Lazarus (1982) and Binder (1979) report utilizing a brief approach for increasing the individual's self-esteem and self-cohesion, again as preparation for longer-term treatment.

Klein (1989b) describes a shorter-term treatment that is not a preparation for longer-term therapy. Admittedly, the goals are not ego repair but are more limited. They include learning, or an increased awareness and anticipation of personal vulnerability to injury, shame, and disappointment; containment—or an increased ability to modulate affects, especially narcissistic rage; and adaptation—that is, seriously taking into account those aspects of reality previously ignored and their destructive consequences. Interpretation of narcissistic vulnerability and clarification of the need for containment of defensive devaluation and withdrawal are the cornerstones of this approach. Klein, a colleague of Masterson, describes two selection criteria: (1) an acute interruption of narcissistic "supply lives" (i.e., interpersonal rejection or disappointment), resulting in narcissistic injury amenable to a substitute "supply line" (i.e., the therapist's mirroring); and (2) when the narcissistic injury makes conscious a persistent vulnerability (often experienced as depression or somatic preoccupation), and these individuals are motivated to learn more adaptive ways of managing their environment.

Klein specifically excludes individuals who present or are referred with chronic, nonspecific, vague, or ego-syntonic symptoms from his brief approach. He describes a course of time-limited treatment (i.e., 6 months) with a young male, which effected symptom relief and circumscribed improvement in functioning. Oldham (1988) describes a 24-session treatment strategy as a dynamically informed directive approach with limited, focused treatment goals. Marmar and Freeman (1988) also describe a brief dynamic approach.

Cognitive-Behavioral Therapy Approach

Beck, Freeman, and Associates (1990) provide an in-depth discussion of the cognitive therapy approach to narcissistic personality–disordered individuals. Early in the course of therapy with these individuals, three treatment objectives must be met: developing a collaborative working relationship, socializing the individuals to the cognitive theory and model of treatment, and agreeing on treatment goals. Forming a collaborative relationship is challenging in that narcissistic individuals are deeply invested in being special and superior, and usually have a limited capacity for working collaboratively. Establishing and maintaining firm treatment guidelines and limits in a neutral, matter-of-fact tone is necessary. It should be pointed out that sticking to an agreed-upon agenda allows the therapist to more effectively address the narcissistic individual's important concerns. Similarly, the therapist can approach other counterproductive behaviors in therapy by appealing to the individual's self-interest.

Because disclosing shortcomings and weaknesses is alien to the narcissist's style, behavioral interventions are usually easier to implement earlier in treatment since they require less self-disclosure than most cognitive techniques. The rhythm of treatment with narcissistic individuals alternates focus between increasing responsibility for behavior, decreasing cognitive distortions and dysfunctional affects—such as rage reactions—and developing healthier attitudes and beliefs. The challenge of treatment with these individuals is to tailor treatment for the three components of grandiosity, hypersensitivity to criticism, and emphatic deficits. Cognitive techniques are useful in revising their distorted self-view, particularly with dichotomous, black-white thinking. Furthermore, magical restructuring methods wherein a realistic and pleasure fantasy replaces a grandiose one are useful.

Systematic desensitization and role reversal can be used to address hypersensitivity. Working with empathy deficits is a major focus of treatment and involves several techniques. After bringing these deficits to the attention of the individual, emotional schemas related to the feelings and reactions of others are activated, usually through role-plays including role reversal. Then alternative ways of relating to others can be discussed, and new statements of belief, such as "others' feelings count too," are formulated. The use of significant others in therapy, such as in couples sessions, has been found useful in developing and practicing empathy and in reinforcing changes, as well as helping the significant other cope more affectively with the narcissistic individual.

In summary, cognitive therapy with narcissistic personality–disordered individuals can be most challenging; nevertheless, they can make significant changes. Beck indicates that the best predictors of success are the degree of narcissism and the therapist's ability to withstand the individual's demands for approval and special treatment. To the extent that a collaborative working relationship is established, limits are set and maintained regarding the control of therapy and special treatment, and schemas of regarding grandiosity, hypersensitivity, and empathy are changed, and associated behaviors and affects modulated, positive treatment outcomes are likely.

Structured Skill Treatment Interventions. While research shows that medication can modulate or normalize dysregulated behaviors, a similar modulating effect has also been noted for social skills training (Lieberman, DeRisi, & Mueser, 1989). Thus, it appears that social skills training is a relatively potent bottom-up treatment strategy for normalizing limbic system–mediated behaviors that reflect specific skill deficits in personality-disordered individuals. When such skill deficits are present, Sperry (1999) contends that structured skill training intervention is a potent and effective strategy in treatment. Various structured intervention strategies for modifying a personality-disordered individual's affective, behavioral, and cognitive temperament styles are described and illustrated for narcissistic personality disorder (Sperry, 1999).

Schema Therapy. Schema therapy is an elaboration of cognitive therapy developed by Young (1999) and Young et al. (2003) specifically for personality disorders and other difficult individual and couples problems. Schema therapy involves identifying maladaptive schemas and planning specific strategies and interventions. Four main strategies are cognitive, experiential, behavioral, and the therapeutic relationship itself. Cognitive restructuring—involving the modification of maladaptive schemas—is an important cognitive strategy but is combined with imagery exercises, empathic confrontation, homework assignments, and "limited reparenting" (i.e., a form of corrective emotional experience; Young, 1999).

Maladaptive schemas typically associated with narcissistic personality disorder include *entitlement*—that is, the belief that one is superior to others and not bound by the rules and norms that govern normal social interaction; *emotional deprivation*—that is, the belief that one's desire for emotional support will not be met by others; *defectiveness*—that is, the belief that one is defective, bad, unwanted, or inferior in important respects; *unrelenting standards*—that is, the belief that striving to meet unrealistically high standards of performance is essential to being accepted and avoiding criticism; and *insufficient self-control*—that is, the belief that one is incapable of self-control and frustration tolerance (Bernstein, 2002). Young et al. (2003) provide a detailed treatment protocol for treating narcissistic personality disorder.

Interpersonal Approach

Benjamin (1996) writes that psychotherapeutic interventions with narcissistic personality–disordered individuals can be planned and evaluated in terms of whether they enhance collaboration, facilitate learning about maladaptive patterns and their roots, block these patterns, enhance the will to change, and effectively encourage new patterns.

Facilitating collaboration with narcissistic individuals is rooted in accurate, consistent empathy. Consistent empathy provides the affirmation and soothing needed to learn self-regulation. Through the experience of being accurately mirrored, they are able to internalize this empathic affirmation of self. Another important aspect of collaboration involves the individual's learning to tolerate his or her faults. This is facilitated through modeling as the therapist acknowledges errors, such as an occasional minor lapse in understanding the individual. In therapy, narcissistic individuals must learn to recognize and block the patterns of entitlement, grandiosity, and envy of others' success. Gentle confrontations embedded in strong support are utilized for this purpose. To accomplish this successfully, the therapist must master the delicate art of pushing the edge of awareness without destroying the therapeutic relationship. Couples therapy can be useful in the recognition and blocking of maladaptive patterns.

Once these individuals understand their maladaptive patterns and choose to relinquish the quest for unattainable or maladaptive goals, new learning is relatively easy. According to Benjamin, the basic focus of interpersonal learning is empathy. Empathy can effectively be taught in couples therapy. Role-playing and other empathy training approaches can be particularly useful. Benjamin contends that when utilizing role-playing, it is important that a collaborative and benign use of the individual's exact words and inflections be employed, as inexact mirroring can elicit rage and withdrawal.

Group Therapy

There is growing literature in the treatment of narcissistic personality–disordered individuals in group therapy formats. Many of the recent reports are based on object relations and/or self psychology approaches (Leszcz, 1989). Outcome research demonstrates that group therapy is as effective as any other therapy in treating narcissistic personality disorder (Alonzo, 1992). A number of factors contribute to the effectiveness of groups. First, peer rather than therapist feedback is likely to be more acceptable to the individual. Second, transference is likely to be less intense than in individual therapy. Working through intense affects is more possible because of the individual's positive attachments within the group and because of peer group scrutiny of the individual's disavowed affects. Third, group membership provides the narcissist individual with three unique needs: mirroring of needs, objects for idealization, and opportunities for peer relationships (Grotjahn, 1984). Finally, the group provides individuals with opportunities to increase their capacity to empathize with others, as well as enhance self-esteem and self-cohesion.

Most of the recent reports suggest that groups consisting exclusively of narcissistic individuals can have successful therapeutic outcomes. Alonzo (1992) notes that while narcissistic pathology undermines the usual forces that lead to group cohesion, a properly run group can function as a container for splitting and oscillation of self-love and hate. She also notes that a high dropout rate is common in groups for narcissistic personality–disordered individuals, with up to 50 percent of the individuals dropping out in ongoing rather than time-limited groups. Alonzo recommends intermittent individual therapy focused on helping individuals remain in the group.

Horowitz (1987) describes the indications and contraindications for group treatment of narcissistic individuals. He notes four indications: demandingness, egocentrism, social isolation and withdrawal, and socially deviant behavior. Even though these traits may be taxing to both the therapist and group members, Horowitz believes individuals with such traits are quite amenable to group treatment. Finally, Stone and Whiteman (1980) note that attention to the unique needs of the individual might warrant a deemphasis on interpretations geared to the entire group, with a focus on an individual member's needs or capacities that are different from those of the group.

Marital and Family Therapy

The early family therapy literature emphasized the treatment of adolescents in families with severe narcissistic pathology (Shapiro, 1982; Berkowitz et al.,

1974). Typically, such families identify the adolescent as the patient and project onto him or her their own devalued view of themselves. Not surprisingly, when the adolescent attempts to separate and individualize, the parent's rage and projections intensify. In a family therapy format, the therapist functions to contain displaced, projected, and acted-out impulses and affects. Furthermore, the therapist must acknowledge, work through, and redirect these responses so that the family has an opportunity to restore previously severed communication and mutual support during this critical phase of adolescent development.

More recent applications of family therapy to narcissistic personality disorder treat entire family systems for one or both parents/spouses. Jones (1987) advocates the family systems approach to the narcissistic family. He suggests several strategies, particularly determining the dilemma the family faces regarding change by analyzing the metaphorical themes that paradoxically bind the family to resist change. Subsequently, the therapist must join—rather than challenge or confront—the family's resistance. Such an empathic relationship is useful in understanding how resistance can be lowered. Usually, family sessions are scheduled weekly for 90 minutes with all family members. Such family treatment has been described for 1 year or longer.

Considerably more has been published about marital therapy with the narcissistic spouse or couple. Berkowitz (1985) has described a couples therapy protocol based on Kohut's view of narcissistic vulnerability, self-object needs, and projective identification. The couple is seen conjointly in weekly sessions—usually 75 to 90 minutes—with the goal of "owning" projections and internalizing needed self-object functions. Lachkar (1986, 1992) describes a common spousal bond: the narcissist dominated by mirroring needs and the others by fears of abandonment. She describes a psychoanalytic treatment approach—combining both object relations theory and self psychology—in which the therapist functions as a self-object so that the exhibitionistic/bonding expectations can become channeled into more realistic goals. Therapy is envisioned as involving three developmental phases: fusion, separation, and interaction. It should be noted that Lachkar views conjoint marital therapy as a precursor to individual psychotherapy or psychoanalysis of one or both spouses. Furthermore, she adds that in conjoint work the therapeutic alliance must be joined by the spouse who is predominantly narcissistic because of the individual's tendency to flee, become isolated, and withdraw from therapy.

Solomon (1989) describes marital therapy wherein one or both spouses meet criteria for narcissistic personality disorder. Elucidating a self psychology perspective of narcissism in marriage, she describes a conjoint treatment protocol wherein marital therapy session functions as a "holding environment." Furthermore, she believes that distorted conscious and unconscious communication is central to marital conflict and its resolution. Finally, she describes the therapist's empathic self as the basic tool of treatment. Masterson and Orcutt (1989) describe a conjoint approach to working with the narcissistic couple.

Relationship enhancement therapy has recently been adapted to couples therapy with narcissistic spouses (Snyder, 1994). It is a unique blending of object relationship theory, social learning theory, interpersonal theory, and system theory that provides a psychoeducational format for incorporating skill training in either individual psychotherapy or conjoint couple therapy.

Relationship enhancement couples therapy focuses on the learning and application of four interpersonal care skills: empathy, effective expression, discussion mode switching between empathic and expressor roles, and problem solving/conflict resolution. The therapist explains, demonstrates, and coaches each skill in the conjoint session, and the spouse then practices these skills during and between sessions with progressively difficult issues. Not surprisingly, the empathic skills and the subjective aspect of the expressor skill are notably deficient for the narcissistically vulnerable couple. Furthermore, the therapist provides a "holding environment" in which narcissistic vulnerability is minimally acted out and instead is experienced and addressed productively. As a result, both spouses learn to express feelings with less risk of shaming the other and are more able to empathize with the other spouse's feelings, which previously evoked defensive reactions. Snyder (1994) provides a detailed case example of this promising approach.

There have been a number of recent developments in couples therapy wherein one or both partners present with narcissistic personality issues or the full-blown personality disorder. Kalojera et al. (1999) provide a detailed rationale and treatment strategy for approaching such couples from a self psychology perspective that incorporates systemic dynamics. These authors present a useful flow chart of the process of relational work with such couples and a detailed case example illustrating the application of this approach.

Lachkar (1999) offers additional insight into the psychoanalytic treatment of couples in which one partner has a narcissistic personality structure while the other partner presents with a borderline personality pattern or meets criteria for borderline personality disorder. Solomon (1999) also addresses the treatment of the narcissistic-borderline couple from a somewhat different psychoanalytic perspective. Another common relational pattern is the dependent/narcissistic couple. Nurse (1998) provides a detailed rationale and treatment protocol for working with such couples based on Millon's theory of personality disorders (Millon & Davis, 1996).

Medication

To date, narcissistic personality disorder has not been subject to controlled pharmacological trials (Koenigsberg, Woo-Ming, & Siever, 2002). Nevertheless, there is a small literature defining the use of psychopharmacological agents for the treatment of this disorder. Klein's (1975) discussion of the use of monoamine oxidase inhibitors in hysteroid dysphoria might have relevance to narcissistic personality disorder since both disorders share an exquisite sensitivity to criticism. More recently, Siever (1993) has reported preliminary data showing that selective serotonergic reuptake inhibitors such as fluoxetine and sertroline have been effective in reducing the target symptom of interpersonal sensitivity and reactivity.

Abramson (1983) described the successful use of lorazepam as an adjunct to individual psychotherapy for the treatment of narcissistic rage in three individuals adjudged to meet the criteria for narcissistic personality disorder. On the other hand, Reich (1988) reported that research showing a strong negative association among a cohort of individuals with panic disorder and narcissistic personality disorder who were treated with benzodiazepines. Other medications may be successfully utilized with narcissistic individuals with specific target symptoms. An episode of major depression would certainly be a reasonable indication for a tricyclic or newer class of antidepressants, particularly if insomnia were also present.

Medication Protocol. Begin with an SSRI at antidepressant dosages. If that SSRI fails, try another. If there is a partial response, an adjunctive atypical psychotic agent or a mood stabilizer, such as valproate or carbamazepine, can be considered. For individuals in whom rejection sensitivity is prominent, a trial of an MAOI is reasonable, particularly if the individual has a history of medication compliance. Naltrexone may be a useful adjunctive for individuals with self-harming behavior (Reich, 2002).

Combined and Integrative Treatment Approaches

As noted previously, there is seldom a single treatment of choice—be it a specific method (e.g., mirroring) or a general approach (e.g., psychoanalysis)—that can ensure positive treatment outcomes with personality-disordered individuals. Rather, depending on the individual's overall level of functioning, temperamental patterns, defensive style, and skill deficits, a focused, specific, and sequentially coordinated tailored treatment protocol is usually necessary to accomplish treatment goals and objectives in a timely manner.

Several treatment approaches and interventions applicable to narcissistic personality disorder have been described by orientation (i.e., psychodynamic, cognitive, behavior/psychoeducational, interpersonal) or format (i.e., individual, group, marital/family, or medication). This final section offers another treatment perspective: an integrative and combined approach. Again, as described before, the highest-functioning individuals who meet either DSM-IV-TR or dynamic criteria for a personality disorder are more likely to have fewer rather than many troubling temperamental patterns, skill deficits, and defensive styles. And, repeating the basic premise of the book, higher-functioning personality-disordered individuals with fewer skill deficits are more likely to benefit from a single approach than lower-functioning individuals with more skill deficits. Those with under- or overmodulated temperament patterns require an integrative, tailored, and combined sequential approach.

The following are specific treatment strategies and methods aimed at the treatment targets of cognitive style and content, behavioral style, emotional style, and relational style that I have found useful in my clinical and consulting practice. These strategies are based on the composite model in Figure 7.1.

FIGURE 7.1. Composite Model of Narcissistic Personality Disorder

This basic stress-diathesis model has narcissistic vulnerability and expectations as the diathesis and the underempathic behavior of others as the stressor. Generally speaking, the psychodynamic approaches have largely emphasized the dimensions of narcissistic vulnerability and narcissistic frustration, particularly focusing on the interpretation of vulnerability regarding grandiosity and entitlement and soothing and mirroring frustrations to reduce narcissistic rage. The cognitive therapy approaches have focused largely on modifying narcissistic vulnerability (self- and worldview), narcissistic expectation, and cognitive distortions. The behavioral and psychoeducational approaches have espoused skill training at several levels, including empathy training (as in relationship enhancement therapy). Finally, the interpersonal approaches emphasize empathy training and appropriate responding to the unempathic behavior of others. Thus, no single approach formally impacts each level of the model.

I have found it valuable to continually emphasize the dimensions of narcissistic vulnerability throughout the course of treatment with considerable attention given to the four temperamental styles: cognitive, emotional, relational, and behavioral. For cognitive style in which the narcissistic individual tends to cognitively distort and utilize the defenses of splitting and projective identification, cognitive restructuring and cognitive awareness training (Beck, Freeman, & Associates, 1990) are useful. With regard to emotional style wherein narcissistic rage is prominent, anger-control training (Turkat, 1990) is indicated. Since empathic deficits greatly affect relational style, empathy training and increasing intimacy-promoting behavior (Snyder, 1994) are indicated. And, because narcissistic individuals tend to be impatient and may have difficulty taking responsibility, problem solving and behavior contracting (Beck, Freeman, & Associates, 1990) have been found useful.

Efforts to effect change in schemas, especially self-view and worldview, with psychodynamic interpretation and both cognitive restructuring methods are usually necessary. I have found that a successful course of therapy may encompass up to 100 or more sessions. When individual psychotherapy can be combined with group therapy or couples therapy, I have noted that treatment can be greatly facilitated, with usually only 30 or so sessions needed. I am much less optimistic about long-term treatment for the lower-functioning narcissist unless group and/or couples therapy are mandatory. See Figure 7.2.

Medication seems to be particularly useful when exquisite sensitivity to criticism or impulsivity and anger control are problematic. In these situations, fluoxetine has proved to be particularly valuable.

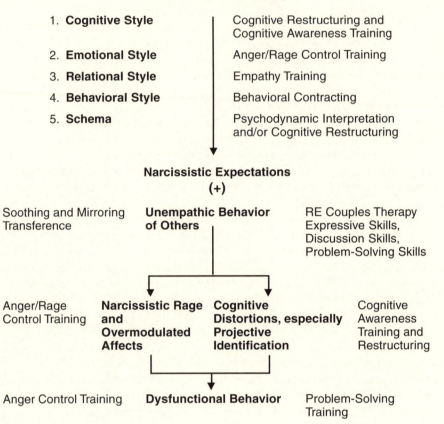

FIGURE 7.2. Targeted Treatment Interventions for Narcissistic Personality Disorder

CHAPTER 8

Obsessive-Compulsive Personality Disorder

Obsessive-compulsive personality disorder has been distinguished from obsessive-compulsive disorder (OCD) in DSM-III, DSM-III-R, and DSM-IV (Pfohl & Blum, 1991). Whereas individuals with OCD are plagued with recurring unpleasant thoughts and are driven to perform ritualized behavior that is ego-dystonic, individuals with obsessive-compulsive personality disorder exhibit traits that are adaptive, seldom distressing, and ego-syntonic. Despite these diagnostic differences, some clinicians, particularly psychodynamically oriented ones, note significant similarities between the two. Nemiah (1980) observes that many individuals presenting for psychotherapy with obsessive-compulsive neurotic symptoms also have an underlying obsessive-compulsive character structure, while Munich (1986) notes that obsessive-compulsive symptoms are often transitory phenomena during the psychoanalytic treatment of individuals with a diagnosed obsessive-compulsive personality disorder. Nevertheless, a distinction is made by DSM-III between Axis I and Axis II obsessive-compulsive presentations, and treatment strategies for both appear to differ significantly. The estimated prevalence is that about 1 percent of the general population would meet criteria for this disorder. This compares with between 3 and 10 percent of individuals in clinical settings.

In terms of DSM-IV-TR changes to obsessive-compulsive personality disorder, the "Associated Features and Disorders" section was updated to clarify the relationship between obsessive-compulsive disorders and obsessive-compulsive personality disorders. Presumably, this clarification was necessary because of the prevailing belief that the disorders are often comorbid or that they are essentially variants of the same disorder, as in Freud's famous case of the Rat Man, or in Melvin Udall, the main character in the movie *As Good As It Gets*. The revised text notes, "the majority of individuals with Obsessive-Compulsive Disorders do not have a pattern of behavior that meets criteria for Obsessive-Compulsive Personality Disorders" (p. 727). What, if any, are the treatment implications of this distinction? One study found that the presence of obsessive-compulsive personality disorder predicted poorer response to the pharmacological treatment of obsessive-compulsive disorder when an SSRI—either clomipramine or fluvoxamine—was used (Cavedini et al., 1997).

This chapter describes the characterizing features of obsessive-compulsive personality disorder and its related personality style. It also describes five clinical formulations, psychological assessment indicators, and a variety of treatment approaches, modalities, and intervention strategies.

DESCRIPTION OF OBSESSIVE-COMPULSIVE PERSONALITY DISORDER

Obsessive-compulsive personality disorder can be recognized by the following descriptors and characteristics: style vs. disorder, triggering event, behavioral style, interpersonal style, cognitive style, affective styles, attachment style, and optimal criterion.

Style vs. Disorder. The obsessive-compulsive personality can be thought of as spanning a continuum from healthy to pathological, with the obsessive personality style on the healthy end and obsessive-compulsive personality disorder on the pathological end. Table 8.1 compares and contrasts differences between the obsessive compulsive style and disorder.

Triggering Event. The typical situation, circumstance, or event that most likely triggers or activates the characteristic maladaptive response of obsessive-compulsive personality disorder (Othmer & Othmer, 2002), as noted in behavioral, interpersonal, cognitive, and feeling styles, is "authority; unstructured situations, and/or demands of intimate and close relations."

Behavioral Style. Behaviorally, this disorder is characterized by perfectionism. Individuals with this disorder are likely to be workaholics. In addition to

Table 8.1
Comparison of the Obsessive-Compulsive Personality Style and Disorder

Personality Style	*Personality Disorder*
Desire to complete tasks and projects without flaws or errors	Perfectionism that interferes with task completion
Take pride in doing all job or tasks well, including the smallest details	Preoccupation with details, rules, lists, order, organization, or schedules to the extent that the major point of the activity is lost
Tend to want things to be done "just right" and in a specific manner, but have some tolerance for things being done another way	Unreasonable insistence that others submit exactly to their way of doing things, or unreasonable reluctance to allow others to do things because of the conviction that they will not do them correctly
Dedicated to work and working hard; capable of intense, single-minded effort	Excessive devotion to work and productivity to the exclusion of leisure activities and friendships (not accounted for by obvious economic necessity)
Carefully consider alternatives and their consequences in making decisions	Indecisive: decision making either avoided, postponed, or protracted (but not due to excessive need for advice or reassurance from others)
Tend to have strong moral principles and strongly desire to do the right thing	Overconscientious, scrupulous, and inflexible about matters of morality, ethics, or values
No-nonsense individuals who do their work without much emotional expenditure	Restructured expression of affection
Generally careful, thrifty, and cautious but able to share from their abundance	Lack of generosity in giving time, money, or gifts when no personal gain is likely to result
Tend to save and collect objects; reluctant to discard objects that formerly had or someday may have value	Unable to discard worn-out or worthless objects even when they have no sentimental value

dependability, they tend to be stubborn and possessive. They tend to be indecisive and procrastinating.

Interpersonal Style. Interpersonally, these individuals are exquisitely conscious of social rank and status and modify their behavior accordingly. That is, they tend to be deferential and obsequious to superiors, and haughty and autocratic to subordinates and peers. They can be doggedly insistent that others do things their way without an appreciation or awareness of how others react to this insistence. At their best, they are polite and loyal to the organizations and ideals they espouse.

Cognitive Style. Their thinking style can be characterized as constricted and rule-based. They have difficulty establishing priorities and perspective. They are "detail" people and often lose sight of the larger project. In other words, they "can't see the forest for the trees." Their indecisiveness and doubts make decision making difficult. Their mental inflexibility is matched by their nonsuggestible and unimaginative style, suggesting they have a restricted fantasy life. Like passive-aggressive individuals, obsessive-compulsive individuals have conflicts between assertiveness and defiance, and pleasing and obedience, but for different reasons.

Affective Style. Their affective or emotional style is characterized as grim and cheerless. They have difficulty with the expression of intimate feelings such as warmth and tenderness. They tend to avoid the "softer" feelings, although they may express anger, frustration, and irritability quite freely. This grim, feeling-avoidant demeanor shows itself in stilted, stiff relationship behaviors.

Attachment Style. The preoccupied attachment dimension is characterized by a sense of personal unworthiness and a positive evaluation of others. These individuals tend to be very externally oriented in their self-definitions. This preoccupied attachment style is common in individuals with obsessive-compulsive personality disorder.

Optimal DSM-IV-TR Criterion. Of all the stated DSM-IV-TR criteria for dependent personality disorder, one criterion has been found to be the most useful in diagnosing this disorder. The belief is that by beginning with this criterion, the clinician can test for the presence or absence of the criterion and quickly diagnose the personality disorder (Allnutt & Links, 1996). The optimal criterion for this disorder is "shows perfectionism that interferes with task completion." The following case examples further illustrate the differences between obsessive-compulsive personality disorder (Mr. Z.) and obsessive-compulsive personality style (Mr. C.).

Case Study: Obsessive-Compulsive Personality Disorder

Mr. Z. is a 39-year-old business executive who wanted to begin a course of psychotherapy because his "whole world was closing in." He gave a history of longstanding feelings of dissatisfaction with his marriage, which had worsened in the past 2 years. He described his wife's increasing demands for time and affection from him, which he believed were a weakness she had. His professional life also had become conflicted when his partner of 10 years wanted to expand their accounting firm to another city. Mr. Z. believed this proposal was fraught with dangers and had come to the point of selling out his share of the business to his partner. He knew he had to make some decisions about his marriage and his business but found himself unable to do so. He hoped therapy would help with these decisions. He presented as neatly dressed in a conservative three-piece blue suit. His posture was rigid and he spoke in a formal and controlled tone with constricted affect. His thinking was characterized by preoccupation with details and was somewhat circumstantial.

Case Study: Obsessive-Compulsive Personality Style

Mr. C. is a 41-year-old assistant vice president of personnel for a public utility. He rose through the ranks because of his loyalty and accomplishments above and beyond the call of duty. Because of his thoroughness and attention to detail, he has saved his corporation nearly $3 million in the past 2 years on insurance and health benefits for the employees of the utility. Most evenings, Mr. C. takes a briefcase of work home with him. Although he does not really mind this intrusion into his family life, his wife of 18 years does. Accordingly, they have reached an agreement that Mr. C. will spend at least 2 hours with his wife and three kids before turning to his briefcase.

DSM-IV-TR Description and Criteria

Unlike the Axis I obsessive-compulsive disorder, ritualistic compulsions and obsessions do not characterize obsessive-compulsive personality disorder. DSM-IV-TR offers the description and criteria in Table 8.2.

Table 8.2
DSM-IV-TR Criteria for Obsessive-Compulsive Personality Disorder (301.4)

A pervasive pattern of preoccupation with orderliness, perfectionism, and mental and interpersonal control, at the expense of flexibility, openness, and efficiency, beginning by early adulthood and present in a variety of contexts, as indicated by at least four of the following:

(1) preoccupation with details, rules, lists, order, organization, or schedules to the extent that the major point of the activity is lost
(2) perfectionism that interferes with task completion (e.g., inability to complete a project because one's own overly strict standards are not met)
(3) excessive devotion to work and productivity to the exclusion of leisure activities and friendships (not accounted for by obvious economic necessity)
(4) overconscientiousness, scrupulousness, and inflexibility about matters or morality, ethics, or values (not accounted for by cultural or religious identification)
(5) inability to discard worn-out or worthless objects even when they have no sentimental value
(6) reluctant to delegate tasks or to work with others unless they submit exactly to his or her way of doing things
(7) adopts a miserly spending style toward both self and others; money is viewed as something to be hoarded for future catastrophes
(8) rigidity and stubbornness

Reprinted with permission from the *Diagnostic and Statistical Manual of Mental Disorders, Fourth Edition–Text Revision.* Copyright 2000. American Psychiatric Association.

FORMULATIONS OF OBSESSIVE-COMPULSIVE
PERSONALITY DISORDER

Psychodynamic Formulation

Early psychoanalytic writers formulated the obsessive-compulsive personality as a regression from the oedipal phase to the anal phase of development. Because of a punitive superego, these obsessive-compulsive individuals employed intellectualization, isolation of affect, undoing, development, and reaction formation as defenses. Presumably, these individuals experienced difficulty expressing aggression as a result of power struggles with maternal figures over toilet training.

However, contemporary writers formulate this pattern as being much broader than anal fixation. As children, these individuals were not sufficiently valued or loved by their caretakers and subsequently developed overwhelming doubt. Salzman (1980) believes the obsessive pattern is basically a device for preventing any thought or feeling that could produce shame, loss of pride or status, or a feeling of deficiency or weakness, irrespective of whether the feelings are hostile, sexual, or otherwise. He views obsessive compulsivity as a neurotic strategy that protects these individuals from exposure to any thoughts or feelings that could endanger their physical or psychological existence. This overriding need to control their inner and outer world requires them to lead overly structured and manageable lives. They tend to maintain doubts, are willing to make commitments, and strive for perfection. Thus, it is necessary for them to know everything to predict the future and prepare for every exigency. To maintain the fiction of perfection, they must never make an error or admit any deficiency. Furthermore, their tendency to procrastinate is related to their tendency to doubt as a means of guaranteeing their omniscience when life forces a decision or choice. As such, they are deeply ambivalent, which allows them to maintain security, but at the price of productivity and positive feelings and attitudes.

These individuals find both anger and dependency consciously unacceptable, so they defend against these feelings with defenses like reaction formation and isolation of affect as well as differential and obsequious behaviors. Intimacy poses major concerns for these individuals, who fear being overwhelmed by powerful wishes to be taken care of while also experiencing the frustration of those wishes along with the fear of being out of control. In addition, these individuals harbor the secret conviction that if they could become perfect, they would finally receive the parental approval and esteem they missed in early life. Finally, psychodynamic writers have noted the unique cognitive style of obsessive-compulsive individuals (Shapiro, 1965; Horowitz, 1988; Horowitz et al., 1984) characterized by drivenness, careful attention to detail and lack of spontaneity, and ruminative thinking.

Biosocial Formulation

To date there is no research evidence that biological predisposing factors underlie this disorder (Millon & Davis, 1996). Nonetheless, clinical observations suggest that many obsessive-compulsive individuals display an anhedonic temperament and tend to be first born. Certain environmental factors may be etiologic: parental overcontrol, learned compulsive behavior, and responsibility training. Rather than being overprotective, parents of obsessive compulsive individuals overcontrol with firmness and punitiveness. This attempt is to prevent their children from causing trouble for themselves or others, and is punitive when the child misbehaves or fails to meet expectations.

These children learn compulsive behavior directly and indirectly within the family matrix. They learn to avoid punishment by accepting and meeting the demands and expectations of perfectionistic and punitive parents. Furthermore, they learn compulsivity by imitating the compulsive behaviors modeled by one or both parents. As a result, they do not develop the ability to generate options and explore alternatives and thus fail to function autonomously.

Obsessive-compulsive individuals are regularly exposed to conditions that teach them to overvalue a sense of responsibility to others. They are taught to feel guilt when these responsibilities are not met and shame when they act impulsively or even playfully. Instead they learn to be polite, pleasing, and loyal to superiors. These influences typically yield individuals who are hard-driving, perfectionistic, and seemingly polite and pleasing, individuals who lead rather restrictive, tentative, colorless lives.

This obsessive-compulsive pattern is self-perpetuated through an interaction of cognitive and behavioral rigidity, strict adherence of roles, regulations, and social convention, and a tendency to be highly self-critical. While their cognitive rigidity serves to reduce anxiety associated with flexibility and ambivalence, they tend to lead overstructured, one-sided lives. Self-criticism serves to keep them in line, while striving for perfection reduces opportunities for risk taking and adventure.

Cognitive-Behavioral Formulation

Guideno and Liotti (1983) provide a cognitive formulation of this personality pattern based on three maladaptive schemas: perfectionism, the need for certainty, and the belief that there is an absolute correct solution for human problems. Guideno and Liotti note that these individuals received contradictory messages from at least one parent.

Beck and Freeman (1990) identified some schemas held by obsessive-compulsive individuals: *Perfection*—"To be worthwhile I must avoid making mistakes, because to make a mistake is to fail, which would be intolerable"; "If the perfect course of action is unclear, it is better to do nothing." *Control*—"I must be perfectly in control of myself and my environment, because loss of control is intolerable and dangerous"; "Without my rules and rituals, I'll collapse into an inert pile"; "Magical rituals or obsessive ruminations prevent the occurrence of catastrophes."

Beck and Freeman also describe typical automatic thoughts of obsessive-compulsive individuals: "I need to get this assignment done perfectly"; "I have to do this project myself or it won't be done right"; "That person misbehaved and should be punished"; and "I should keep these old reports because I might need them some day." In addition to these schemas and automatic thoughts, individuals with this personality pattern often utilize the cognitive distortions of dichotomous thinking and magnification or catastrophizing.

Turkat (1990) and Turkat and Maisto (1985) suggest a behavioral formulation of this pattern. These individuals are noted to have been reared in families that emphasized productivity and rule-following at the expense of emotional expressivity and interpersonal relationships. Accordingly, these individuals did not acquire adequate levels of empathy skills or skills in interacting with others as an emotional basis.

Interpersonal Formulation

According to Benjamin (1996), persons diagnosed with obsessive-compulsive personality disorder were likely raised in an atmosphere of unreasonable and relentless coercion to perform correctly and follow rules regardless of personal cost. As a consequence, the obsessive-compulsive individual has an unbalanced devotion to perfection of self and others. Their parents typically held extremely high expectations for self-control and perfection; they not only punished their children for not being perfect but gave them little or no reward for success. Subsequently, these children focused primarily on avoiding mistakes and self-criticism by trying hard to be good and right. Furthermore, there tended to be little warmth in these households. Laughter, hugging, holding, and other signs of affection were seldom if ever modeled. Expression of feelings was considered dangerous. The adult consequence of this lack of warmth and demand for perfection is social correctness albeit unaccessibility of feelings. Finally, there is a fear of making mistakes and a penchant for rule following. A quest for order underlies blame and inconsiderate control of others, with control alternating with blind obedience to authority of principle. This stance is supported by excessive self-discipline, restraint of excessive of feelings, self-criticism, as well as neglect of the self.

Integrative Formulation

The following integrative formulation may be helpful in understanding how obsessive-compulsive personality disorder is likely to be developed and maintained. Biologically, these individuals were likely to have exhibited an anhedonic temperament as infants (Millon, 1981). Firstborn children have a greater propensity for developing a compulsive style than other siblings (Toman, 1961).

Psychologically, these individuals view themselves, others, the world, and life's purpose in terms of the following themes. They tend to view themselves with some variant of the theme: "I'm responsible if something goes wrong, so I have to be reliable, competent, and righteous." Their worldview is some variant of the theme: "Life is unpredictable and expects too much." As such, they are likely to conclude, "Therefore, be in control, right, and proper at all times."

Socially, predictable patterns of parenting and environmental conditioning are noted for this personality. The parenting style they experienced could be characterized as both consistent and overcontrolled. As children they were trained to be overly responsible for their actions and to feel guilty and worthless if they were not obedient, achievement oriented, or "good." The parental injunction to which they were most likely exposed was "You must do and be better to be worthwhile."

This obsessive-compulsive pattern is confirmed, reinforced, and perpetuated by the following individual and systems factors: Exceedingly high expectations plus harshly rigid behavior and beliefs, along with a tendency to be self-critical, lead to rigid rule-based behavior and avoidance of social, professional, and moral unacceptability. This in turn further reconfirms the harshly rigid behaviors and beliefs of this personality (Sperry & Mosak, 1993).

ASSESSMENT OF OBSESSIVE-COMPULSIVE PERSONALITY DISORDER

Several sources of information are useful in establishing a diagnosis and treatment plan for personality disorders. Observation, collateral information, and psychological testing are important adjuncts to the patient's self-report in the clinical interview. This section briefly describes some characteristic observations that the clinician makes and the nature of the rapport likely to develop in initial encounters with specific personality-disordered individuals. Characteristic response patterns on various objective (i.e., MMPI-2 and MCMI-III) and projective tests (i.e., Rorschach and TAT) are also described.

Interview Behavior and Rapport

The obsessive-compulsive's dynamics of circumstantiability, perfectionism, and ambivalence make interviewing these individuals difficult and challenging. Their preoccupation with and focus on details and need for control lead to a seemingly endless struggle about words, issues, and who is in charge without being able to develop an atmosphere of understanding and cooperation. Open-ended questions lead them to confusion. Instead they want more focused questions but interpret them too narrowly when this kind of question is asked. They may bring a notebook of their medical history, diet and exercise pattern, or even dreams, expecting to review these details with you. And while they may admit that affects and feelings are associated with the details, they are

Table 8.3
Characteristics of Obsessive-Compulsive Personality Disorder

Triggering Event	Authority, unstructured situations, and/or demands of intimate and close relations.
Behavioral Style	Workaholic, dependable, stubborn, possessive; procrastination, indecisive, perfectionistic.
Interpersonal Style	Autocratic to peers and subordinates but deferential to superiors; polite and loyal.
Cognitive Style	Constricted—rule-based, unimaginative; assertive (defiance) vs. pleasing (obedience).
Feeling Style	Grim and cheerless, feeling avoidance.
Temperament	Irritable, difficult, or anxious.
Attachment Style	Preoccupied.
Parental Injunction	"You must do/be better to be worthwhile."
Self-View	"I'm responsible if something goes wrong." See themselves as reliable, competent, righteous.
Worldview	"Life is unpredictable and expects too much. Therefore, be in control, be right and proper, and don't make mistakes."
Maladaptive Schemas	Unrelenting standards; punitiveness; emotional inhibition.
Optimal DSM-IV-TR Criteria	Shows perfectionism that interferes with task completion.

unwilling to admit the value of expressing those affects, much less talking about them. Their ambivalence is difficult to overcome since they cannot accept your assurances that their problems are solvable or that they can tolerate less control in their lives.

The clinician's expression of empathy is problematic for them, since they insist they are objective and have no feelings. Thus, they are perturbed at the expression of empathy and reject it as irrelevant. They may insist that their problems, not their suffering, are important. Yet their problems are unsolvable! The only therapeutic leverage for the clinician is to attempt to get and keep these individuals in touch with their anger and other feelings. But this is difficult as they will attempt to defend or deny affects and put forth even more obstructive obsessive thinking to neutralize such therapeutic leverage. Needless to say, forming a therapeutic alliance is difficult and the interview often consists of aborted attempts, frustrations, and struggles (Othmer & Othmer, 2002).

Psychological Testing Data

The Minnesota Multiphase Personality Inventory (MMPI-2), the Millon Clinical Multiaxial Inventory (MCMI-III), the Rorschach Psychodiagnostic Test, and the Thematic Apperception Test (TAT) can be useful in diagnosing obsessive-compulsive personality disorder as well as the obsessive-compulsive personality style or trait.

On the MMPI-2, look for a moderately high K (correction) scale. Since individuals with obsessive-compulsive features are not inclined to self-disclosure, they seldom leave elevated profiles. However, scales 1 (hypochondriasis) and 3 (hysteria) tend to be elevated. If physical complaints are the focus of the distress scale, 1 may be particularly elevated. An elevation on scale 9 (hypomania) usually reflects the degree to which these individuals are autocratic and dominant in interpersonal relationships. Since scale 7 (psychasthenia) reflects obsessionalism, elevation of this scale usually indicates a complaining and querulous attitude (Meyer, 1995; Graham, 2000).

Expect a high score on scale 7 (obsessive-compulsive) of the MCMI-II. Elevations on scale A (anxiety) are not likely, since these individuals tend to express anxiety somatically. Thus, scale H is likely to be elevated (somatoform; Choca & Denburg, 1997).

Expect an emphasis on Dd (unusual detail) and D (common detail) responses on the Rorschach. Also, a high F+% (form plus) and fewer W (whole) responses and color-based responses. Obsessive-compulsive individuals tend to describe some responses in overly specific detail and make criticisms of the ink blots (Meyer, 1995).

The TAT stories of these individuals tend to be lengthy with a variety of themes. Sometimes the primary theme is lost amid the detailing of their response. This is particularly likely on card 2 and 13 MF (Bellak, 1997).

TREATMENT APPROACHES AND INTERVENTIONS

Treatment Considerations

Included in the differential diagnosis of obsessive-compulsive personality disorder are two other Axis II personality disorders: dependent personality disorder and passive-aggressive personality disorder. The most common Axis I syndromes associated with obsessive-compulsive personality disorder are social phobia disorder, simple phobias, generalized anxiety disorder, and dysthymia (Turner et al., 1991). Other Axis I syndromes are hypochondriasis, somatization disorder, obsessive-compulsive disorder, and psychological factors affecting physical conditions. Occasionally, a brief reactive psychosis may be noted in decompensated obsessive-compulsive individuals.

Obsessive-compulsive disorder (OCD) has a long tradition of treatment dating back to Freud's case of the "Rat Man" and Adler's "Case of Mrs. A." Note that OCD is an Axis I disorder while obsessive-compulsive personality disorder is an Axis II disorder. Since the "Rat Man" exhibited both Axis I and Axis II disorders, many who have read Freud's account of this case and its treatment have incorrectly assumed that both disorders are the same and are treated the same. They are not the same disorder, but in about one-third of cases, both disorders have been shown to be present (Jenike, Baer, & Minichiello, 1990). Baer and Jenike (1992) note that obsessive-compulsive personality disorder is less common in OCD than dependent, avoidant, and personality disorder NOS. When both disorders are present together, treatment has been shown to be much more challenging than if only OCD is present.

What about research support and evidence-based guidelines for the treatment of this disorder? To date, there has been only one treatment outcomes study of this disorder (Barber et al., 2002). It was an open trial of supportive-expressive therapy, which is described below.

Individual Psychotherapy

Psychodynamic Psychotherapy Approach

The therapy of obsessive-compulsive patients involves exposing their extreme feelings of insecurity and uncertainty. As they come to identify their neurotic structure as a defense against recognizing these weaknesses, they can begin to develop a more adaptive security system. At the outset of treatment, these patients are unable to abandon their obsessive-compulsive defense, fearing unspeakable consequences. However, as their self-esteem grows and awareness of their strengths increases, they are able to take the risks of abandoning these patterns and are thus freer to function more productively.

The goal of therapy is to switch from impossible expectations for self and others to more realistically achievable ones. In short, these individuals come to learn that by relinquishing their rigid, inflexible patterns of control and protection, they can actually feel more productive. Doing psychodynamically oriented psychotherapy with obsessive-compulsive patients requires a number of modifications, which involve the clinician's level of activity. The clinician must be active from the beginning through the end of treatment. Clinician passivity, according to Salzman (1989), can lead only to interminable analysis and an atmosphere of confusion. Specifically, free association and a tendency to endless detail and circumstantiality must be controlled and limited.

Because of these patients' need for perfection, they tend to qualify and quantify their descriptions, which obfuscates them instead of clarifying them. The free association process tends to defeat its own purpose. Thus, the clinician must be active to prevent this tangentiality and distraction by attempting to interrupt the irrelevances and avoidances. Of course, the major avoidance is affect. While these patients may talk about feelings and emotions, and even about transference and countertransference, they assiduously avoid the expression of affect. The clinician must, therefore, focus on real feelings and their expression, and limit intellectual discussion of affects.

Another modification from traditional analytic methods involves a focus on recent events. While obsessive-compulsive individuals can discuss anger and hostile behavior associated with past events, they find it very difficult to disclose tender impurities and feelings with recent and here-and-now experiences. Such tender impulses and feelings are viewed as threatening and dangerous, and Salzman (1989) contends this is the essence of obsessive-compulsive defenses. It is the failure to express these feelings, rather than their hostile behavior, that initiates retaliatory behavior from others, which in turn stirs up their wrath and hostile responders.

Finally, the usual instruction to forego major decisions during the course of therapy must be modified. Because of their fear of making mistakes, such instruction can serve to reinforce their pathological pattern. Rather, risk taking and decision making must be promoted. The techniques for dealing with their indecisiveness are clarification and interpretation of their need for absolutes and certainties. If dream material is utilized, the emphasis must be in the here-and-now, and dream content treated as data dealt with in the same manner as their other productions.

The outcome goal of treatment is that these individuals achieve some degree of balance and compromise, and instead of needing to be superhuman, they should be able to function as fallible humans. Because of their anticipatory anxiety, termination issues abound with these patients. It must be clearly understood by both patients and clinicians that anxiety episodes will occur throughout life, and that continuation in therapy is no guarantee against life's distress.

A related goal is superego modification so that these patients can accept that their wish to transcend such feelings as anger, lust, and dependency is doomed to failure and must be integrated rather than disowned. Gabbard (1994) notes that such changes occur through detailed interpretation of conflicts around aggression, sexuality, and dependence.

There is a consensus that long-term psychodynamic treatment is needed with these patients. This is because of their constricted emotionality and their vulnerability to deflation of self-esteem under their rigid exterior. Treatment typically lasts 2 to 3 years of one or two sessions per week. The prevailing wisdom is that dynamic psychotherapy with the ancillary support of medication and behavioral interventions is effective (Salzman, 1989).

Time-Limited Supportive-Expressive Therapy. Supportive-expressive therapy was provided to individuals who had obsessive-compulsive or avoidant personality disorder. Those with obsessive-compulsive personality disorder lost their personality disorder diagnosis in a significantly shorter period of time than those with avoidant personality disorder. While both groups responded to this time-limited therapy on measures of personality disorder, depression, anxiety, general functioning, and interpersonal problems, those with obsessive-compulsive personality disorder no longer met Axis II criteria within the first 17 sessions (Barber et al., 2002).

Cognitive-Behavioral Therapy Approach

Which cognitive-behavioral approach and treatment targets have the best treatment outcomes with obsessive-compulsive personality disorder? Unfortunately, no randomly controlled trials have been published to date that offer the clinician usable and reliable guidelines. Bailey (1998) describes and critiques the two most common cognitive approaches: Young's schema-focused approach and Beck's more traditional approach. Kyrios (1999) describes several cognitive-behavioral treatment targets in treating obsessive-compulsive personality disorder. These include targeting dysfunctional cognitions, restricted behavioral repertoires, negative affective dispositions, and issues related to attachment and identity. Until research-based guidelines are forthcoming, a careful assessment of client and situational attributes and clinician judgment must continue to guide treatment decisions.

Beck, Freeman, and Associates (1990) provide an extended discussion of the cognitive therapy approach with obsessive-compulsive personality–disordered individuals. The general outcome goal in working therapeutically with these individuals is helping them modify and restructure their maladaptive schemas that underlie behaviors and effects. Establishing a collaborative working relationship is the first task of therapy. This can be quite difficult for these individuals because of their rigidity, feeling avoidance and tendency to minimize the importance of interpersonal relationships. Therefore, rapport is based on the individual's respect for the therapist's competence and the belief that the therapist will be respecting and helpful. Efforts to develop a closer emotional relationship early in treatment may result in premature termination.

It is also essential to introduce the obsessive-compulsive individual to the cognitive theory of emotion early in the course of therapy, as well as establishing therapeutic goals. Usually, these goals involve presenting problems. After collaboratively establishing them, they are ranked in the order they are to be addressed. A given problem is monitored between sessions with the dysfunctional thought record, which includes the situation as well as the feelings and thoughts about when the problem occurred. The record is reviewed at the next session, which is the basis for discussing automatic thoughts and the assumptions or schemas underlying the thoughts. In this collaborative relationship, the individual can identify and understand the negative consequences of the schema and ways of refuting them. This process of cognitive disputation and restructuring is particularly useful and well received by obsessive-compulsive individuals because of its structured and problem-centered here-and-now focus.

Several specific strategies and techniques have been found to be particularly useful with these individuals as adjuncts to cognitive therapy. Setting an agenda, prioritizing problems, and utilizing problem-solving and thought-stopping techniques are effective with issues of rumination, procrastination, and indecisiveness. Salzman (1989) reports that flooding, desensitization, response prevention, and satiation training have been used in treating this disorder. Relaxation training is useful with anxiety and psychosomatic symptoms, while behavioral experiments can be used instead of direct disputation of maladaptive beliefs. Because of their difficulty in attending to their emotions and those of others, empathy training and role reversal have been used effectively. In sum, obsessive-compulsive personality disorder is challenging but very treatable. With collaboration, cognitive restructuring, and systematic application of cognitive and behavioral strategies and techniques, the obsessive-compulsive individual's automatic thoughts and schemas that underlie inadaptive behavior and affects can be effectively modified and changed.

Turkat (1990) concludes that behavioral modification alone is not sufficient for effective treatment outcomes with most of these patients. Turkat's treatment regimen involved social skills training to increase pleasure and emotion-related experience and to decrease their overcommitment to work. He notes that while these patients would agree with the clinical formulation and treatment plan, most would not agree to undergo the training. Turkat and Maisto (1985) report similar experiences, leading them to conclude that behavior modification alone is not effective for obsessive-compulsive personality disorder.

Structured Skill Treatment Interventions. While research shows that medication can modulate or normalize dysregulated behaviors, a similar modulating effect has also been noted for social skills training (Lieberman, DeRisi, & Mueser, 1989). Thus, it appears that social skills training is a relatively potent bottom-up treatment strategy for normalizing limbic system–mediated behaviors that reflect specific skill deficits in personality-disordered individuals. When such skill deficits are present, Sperry (1999) contends that structured skill training interventions is a potent and effective strategy in treatment. Various structured intervention strategies for modifying a personality-disordered individual's affective, behavioral, and cognitive temperament styles are described and illustrated for the treatment of obsessive-compulsive personality Disorder (Sperry, 1999).

Schema Therapy. Schema therapy is an elaboration of cognitive therapy that has been developed by Young (1999) and Young et al. (2003) specifically for personality disorders and other difficult individual and couples problems. Schema therapy involves identifying maladaptive schemas and planning specific strategies and interventions. Four main strategies are cognitive, experiential, behavioral, and the therapeutic relationship itself. Cognitive restructuring—particularly modification of maladaptive schemas—is an important cognitive strategy but is combined with imagery exercises, empathic confrontation, homework assignments, and "limited reparenting" (i.e., a form of corrective emotional experience; Young, 1999).

Maladaptive schemas typically associated with obsessive-compulsive personality disorder are *unrelenting standards*—that is, the belief that striving to meet unrealistically high standards of performance is essential to be accepted and to avoid criticism: *punitiveness*—that is, the belief that others should be harshly punished for making errors; and *emotional inhibition*—that is, the excessive inhibition of spontaneous action, feeling, or communication usually to avoid disapproval by others, feelings of shame, or losing control of one's impulses (Bernstein, 2002).

Interpersonal Approach

Benjamin (1996) writes that psychotherapeutic interventions with obsessive-compulsive personality–disordered individuals can be planned and evaluated in terms of whether they enhance collaboration, facilitate learning about maladaptive patterns and their roots, block these patterns, enhance the will to change, and effectively encourage new patterns.

Because of the centrality of control in their lives, obsessive-compulsive individuals find collaboration difficult. These individuals are often inconsistent in their attitudes about control of the therapy, sometimes wanting to take control and other times wanting the clinician to take it. Benjamin suggests breaking through a potential power struggle by describing the obsessive-complusive's typical patterns of control, submission, and self-control and their opposites—affirmation, disclosure, and self-affirmation—and how and why the obsessive-compulsive patterns developed. She notes that these individuals quickly grasp—intellectually—the idea of friendly differentiation as the opposite of hostile control and will develop an interest in collaboration. After this shared goal of openness and warmth has been established, they can begin working at experiencing feeling and changing their relational behaviors. Not surprisingly, the work of learning to let go is not easy.

As these individuals begin seeking connections between early life experiences and present difficulties, they must be helped to develop compassion and empathy for themselves as children. Benjamin notes that couples therapy is a particularly potent format for learning about and changing maladaptive patterns in obsessive-compulsive individuals. Dealing with control and power struggles between partners is aided by reframing and paradoxical injunctions. A paradoxical use of their preference for rule following would involve the clinician "ordering" the obsessive-compulsive individual to collimate with the partner to develop rules for dealing with the problematic relational issues.

Therapeutic efforts to block maladaptive patterns should be targeted to power struggles, feeling avoidance, and perfectionism. With regard to perfectionism, undercutting the need to reach perfection through control usually results in anger reduction. As the obsessive-compulsive individual no longer needs to make others perfect, there is no need to be angry at them. This is also true of the anxiety that arises from the fear of not reaching perfection. Since the individual does not need to be perfect to survive, the individual no longer needs to be anxious about not being perfect. As these individuals come to understand the origins of their quest for perfection and compare their early life situations with the present, they are better able to relinquish their past neurotic strivings. Developing empathy for the self as a child and for the parent at that distant time can strengthen their will to give up their maladaptive patterns.

Cognitive therapy is particularly useful in modifying their constricted cognitive style and self-criticism. Likewise, insight can increase the probability that these individuals will become more comfortable with fallibility and ordinariness.

Group Therapy

Because a major deficit of the obsessive-compulsive personality is the inability to share tenderly and spontaneously with others, group treatment has particular advantages with such patients. Nonetheless, there are certain complications, because of these patients' tendency to be competitive and control situations. Yalom (1995) uses the description "monopolist" to refer to this obsessive-compulsive pattern in group therapy. They can easily dominate a group with their rambling and excessive speech patterns. They may find the affective atmosphere in group psychotherapy particularly overwhelming at first, resulting in either further isolation or detached intellectualization. The group leader may need to intervene and avoid unnecessary power struggles. If this is achieved, these patients may be able to vicariously model the emotional expressiveness of other group members.

Actually, group therapy offers a number of advantages over individual therapy as the obsessive-compulsive personality pattern tends to make the dyadic therapy process tedious, difficult, and unrewarding, particularly during the inevitable "constipated" period of treatment when clinicians commonly err with premature interpretations or behavioral prescriptions (Salzman, 1980; Wells, Glickhauf-Hughes, & Buzzel, 1990).

A group format can diffuse intensity of the patient's impact, particularly in a heterogeneous group (Francis, Clarkin, & Perry, 1984). Group treatment can also reduce transference and countertransference traps because patients are more likely to accept feedback from peers without the same power struggle that often accompanies feedback from the clinician (Gabbard, 1994). Furthermore, group therapy propels these patients into having problems rather than just talking about them (Alonso & Ruton, 1984).

Wells, Glickhauf-Hughes, and Buzzell (1990) note the following contraindications for group therapy for these patients: severe depression or strong suicidal potential, impulsive dyscontrol, strong paranoid propensities, acute crisis, difficulty in establishing trust, fear of relinquishing obsessive-compulsive defenses, the need to establish superiority, and the use of "pseudo insight" to avoid dealing with both hostile and tender feelings.

These authors have described a unique group approach combining interpersonal and psychodynamic principles based on the premise that this personality disorder arises from the unsuccessful resolution of the developmental tasks of autonomy vs. shame and doubt. The process of treatment involves six goals: (1) modifying cognitive style; (2) augmenting decision making and action taking; (3) modifying harsh superego; (4) increasing comfort with emotional expression; (5) resolving control issues; and (6) modifying interpersonal style.

Marital and Family Therapy

The professional literature in this area is particularly limited; however, some of the dynamics and treatment discussed regarding group therapy are relevant in a family treatment context.

Harbir (1981) notes that obsessive-compulsive personality–disordered individuals typically enter family treatment because close family members are angry with their rigidity, procrastination, constricted affect, perfectionism, and somber or joyless outlook. The spouse of an obsessive-compulsive individual may threaten divorce if the individual does not change. Often, such a threat of separation or divorce is the only motivation for treatment. The anxiety of the complaining spouse may be the only leverage for treatment, and the clinician may need to work with that spouse to deal more effectively with the other spouse's obsessive-compulsive personality pattern. Harbir adds that it is not uncommon for an obsessive-compulsive individual to marry an individual with a histrionic personality.

Salzman (1989) cautions that obsessive-compulsive patients who are particularly anxious may not be able to participate in family therapy until their anxiety has been sufficiently ameliorated in individual psychotherapy or combined psychotherapeutic and psychopharmacological treatment. Even when excessive anxiety is not a particular concern, these patients are often tyrants in family sessions. They may immobilize other family members to such an extent that treatment is jeopardized. The use of structural and strategic intervention directed at redistributing power may be particularly advantageous in such situations (Minuchin, 1974).

Regarding treatment outcomes, no controlled research studies have been published. However, Minuchin (1974) and Haley and Hoffman (1976) have reported favorable outcomes with family therapy interventions with obsessive-compulsive personalities and particularly those with permanent eating disorders.

Harbir (1981) and Perry, Francis, and Clarkin (1990) present a case example of marital therapy wherein one partner exhibits an obsessive-compulsive personality and the other a histrionic personality. This case is quite instructive with regard to treatment strategy and technique.

An integrative approach involving dynamic, cognitive-behavioral, and systemic interventions is described for couples in which one partner presents with obsessive-compulsive personality disorder and the other with histrionic personality disorder. Three stages of the treatment process are discussed and illustrated: establishing a therapeutic alliance, restoring balance to the couple relationship, and modifying individual partner dynamics. The first two phases involve conjoint couples sessions, while much of the third phase involves individual sessions (Sperry & Maniacci, 1996).

Medication

Presently, no pharmacological trials on obsessive-compulsive personality disorder, per se, have been reported. This contrasts with numerous drug studies of obsessive-compulsive disorders. Jenike (1990) reports that cyclic antidepressants, serotonergic blockers, monoamine oxidase inhibitors, lithium carbonate, antipsychotics, and anxiolytics, have been effective with OCD.

However, Jenike (1991) reports that medications have little or no effect on obsessive-compulsive personality disorder, and that psychotherapy is the treatment of choice.

Nevertheless, concurrent Axis I conditions, particularly symptoms of anxiety and depression, may be amenable to medication. Salzman (1989) reports that anxiolytics can relieve coexisting anxiety, and antidepressants can relieve secondary depression.

Medication Protocol. For individuals with prominent anxiety but without impulsivity, begin with an SSRI. If no response, try another SSRI. If there is a partial response, a long-acting benzodiazepine or clonazepam can be added or even used as the sole medication following multiple SSRI trials (Reich, 2002).

Combined and Integrated Treatment Approaches

Salzman (1989) elegantly makes the case for a combined/integrated approach to the treatment of obsessive-compulsive disorder, particularly for the more severe cases. He argues that the various treatment modalities and approaches are supplementary rather than mutually exclusive.

Combining treatment should follow a protocol. Since high levels of anxiety or depression may limit participation in psychotherapy, an appropriate medication trial may be useful at the onset of treatment. If rituals or obsessions are prominent, specific behavior interventions—such as response prevention, exposure, habituation, and thought stopping (Salkovskis & Kirk, 1989)—are indicated. The basic dynamics of perfectionism, indecisiveness, and isolation of affect are best reached by psychotherapeutic approaches. Decisions about individual, group, or a marital and module format, or a combination of modalities, are based on severity of the disorder, the particular treatment target, and specific contraindications. For instance, where isolation of affect and perfectionism manifest primarily as a rambling speech pattern, an integrative group therapy approach, such as described by Wells et al. (1990), may greatly delimit resistance and subsequent countertransference that is so common in dynamic treatment formats. Where indecisiveness is a prominent issue, modeling and other behavioral methods, as well as role-playing, might be incorporated in individual treatment formats. In general, the more severe the disorder, the more treatment needs to be tailored and multimodal.

Salzman concludes that a true understanding and appreciation of the obsessive-compulsive personality "requires an integration of psychodynamic, pharmacologic, and behavior therapies, because the resolution of the disabling disorder demands cognitive clarity plus behavioral and physiologic alterations. Each modality alone deals with only a piece of the puzzle. A therapist who can combine all these approaches will be the most effective" (1989, p. 2782).

Developmental Therapy. Developmental approaches to therapy focus on fostering optimal functioning. For individuals with obsessive-compulsive personality style who seek to develop beyond the adequate level of functioning—the current end point of therapy—a developmentally focused therapy utilizes a variety of interventions to facilitate this process (Cortright, 1997; Blocher, 2002; Sperry, 2002). A protocol for conducting developmental therapy for individuals with obsessive-compulsive personality is described and illustrated by Sperry (2002).

CHAPTER 9

Paranoid Personality
Disorder

Paranoid personality disorder is a well-established diagnostic entity. It has been listed in the previous versions of DSM, and references to it are consistently noted throughout the vast literature on schizophrenic and paranoid psychosis. Since the time of Kraeplin, the defining feature of paranoid personality disorder has been a pervasive and unwarranted mistrust and suspiciousness of others. Other clinical features that have been associated with this disorder are hypervigilance, hypersensitivity to criticism, rigidity, antagonism, and aggressiveness. In DSM-III, patients were required to meet three criteria for suspiciousness, two for restricted affect, and two for hypersensitivity. DSM-III-R was less restrictive, requiring any combination of four of seven criteria (Bernstein et al., 1993). Only minor changes were made in DSM-IV criteria to reduce overlap with other disorders, and no changes are noted in DSM-IV-TR. Taking a broader view, Miller et al. (2001) describe some dimensional alternatives to the DSM-IV-TR diagnostic classification of paranoid personality disorder.

Paranoid personality disorder has been described as a paranoid spectrum disorder ranging from paranoid personality disorder through delusional disorder to paranoid schizophrenia. The distinguishing feature of the personality disorder is the lack of clear-cut delusions, hallucinations, or other psychotic features. Nevertheless, the boundaries between paranoid personality disorder and delusional disorder, persecutory style, remain unclearly charted (Manschreck, 1992). Psychoanalytic literature also recognizes the paranoid personality. Following Freud's formulation, based largely on the Schreber case, analytical writers have related paranoid tendencies to the repudiation of latent homosexuality through projection as the common denominator of this disorder (Ahktar, 1990). Others, like Frosch (1985), contend that the common denominator may be humiliating experiences at the hands of significant others of the same sex, which engender in the patient a feeling of having been a helpless victim.

Prevalence of this disorder has been estimated at between 0.5 and 2.5 percent in the general population. In clinical settings, the figures are 10 to 30 percent among inpatients and 2 to 10 percent among outpatients.

This chapter will describe the characteristic features of paranoid personality disorder and its related personality style. Five clinical formulations of the disorder and psychological assessment indicators are highlighted. A variety of treatment approaches, modalities, and intervention strategies are also described.

DESCRIPTION OF PARANOID PERSONALITY DISORDER

Paranoid personality disorder can be recognized by the following descriptors and characteristics: style vs. disorder, triggering event, behavioral style, interpersonal style, cognitive style, affective style, attachment style, and optimal criterion.

Style vs. Disorder. The paranoid personality can be thought of as spanning a continuum from healthy to pathological, with paranoid personality style on the healthy end and paranoid personality disorder on the pathological end. Table 9.1 compares and contrasts differences between the paranoid personality style and disorder.

Triggering Event. The typical situation, circumstance, or event that most likely triggers or activates the characteristic maladaptive response of paranoid personality disorder (Othmer & Othmer, 2002), as noted in behavioral, interpersonal, cognitive, and feeling styles, is "close interpersonal relationships and/ or personal queries."

Behavioral Style. Behaviorally, paranoid individuals are resistive of external influences. They tend to be chronically tense because they are constantly

Table 9.1
Comparison of Paranoid Personality Style and Disorder

Personality Style	*Personality Disorder*
Self-assured and confident in their ability to make decisions and take care of themselves	Reluctant to confide in others because of unwarranted fear that the information will be used against them
Good listeners and observers, keenly aware of subtlety, tone, and multiple levels of meaning	Read hidden meanings or threats into benign remarks or events—e.g., suspect that a neighbor put out trash early to annoy them
Take criticism rather seriously without becoming intimidated	Bears grudges or are unforgiving of insults or slights
Place a high premium on loyalty, fidelity, working hard to earn and maintain loyalty, and never taking it for granted	Question, without justification, the fidelity of spouse or sexual partner, friends, and associates
Careful in dealings with other people, preferring to size up individuals before entering into relationships with them	Expect, without sufficient basis, to be exploited or harmed by others
Assertive and can defend themselves without losing control and becoming aggressive	Are easily slighted and quick to react with anger or to counterattack

mobilized against perceived threats from their environment. Their behavior is also marked by guardedness, defensiveness, argumentativeness, and litigiousness.

Interpersonal Style. Interpersonally, individuals tend to be distrustful, secretive, and isolative. They are deeply suspicious of others' motives. They are also intimacy-avoiders by nature and repudiate nurturant overtures by others.

Cognitive Style. Their cognitive style is characterized by mistrusting preconceptions. They carefully scrutinize every situation and scan the environment for "clues" or "evidence" to confirm their preconceptions rather than objectively focus on data. Thus, while their perception may be accurate, their judgment often is not. The paranoid personalities' prejudices mold the perceived data to fit their preconceptions. Thus, they tend to disregard evidence that does not fit their preconceptions. When under stress, their thinking can take on a conspiratorial or even delusional flavor. Their hypervigilance and need to seek evidence to confirm their beliefs lead them to have a rather authoritarian and mistrustful outlook on life.

Affective Style. Their emotional or affective style is characterized as cold, aloof, unemotional, and humorless. In addition, they lack a deep sense of affection, warmth, and sentimentality. Because of their hypersensitivity to real or imagined slights, and their subsequent anger at what they believe to be deceptions and betrayals, they tend to have few if any friends. The two emotions they experience and express with some depth are anger and intense jealousies.

Attachment Style. Individuals with a fearful attachment style exhibit a sense of personal unworthiness combined with an expectation that other people will be rejecting and untrustworthy. They trust neither their own internal cognitions or feelings nor others' intentions. While they believe themselves to be special and different from others, they guard against threats and unexpected circumstances, since they cannot trust that others will protect them. This fearful attachment style is common in individuals with paranoid personality disorder.

Optimal DSM-IV-TR Criterion. Of all the stated DSM-IV-TR criteria for paranoid personality disorder, one criterion has been found to be the most useful in diagnosing this disorder. The belief is that by beginning with this criterion, the clinician can test for the presence or absence of the criterion and quickly diagnose the personality disorder (Allnutt & Links, 1996). The optimal criterion for this disorder is "suspects, without sufficient basis, that others are exploiting, harming, or deceiving him or her." The following two cases further illustrate differences between paranoid personality disorder (Mr. W.) and paranoid personality style (Janice L.).

Case Study: Paranoid Personality Disorder

Mr. W. is a 53-year-old referred for psychiatric evaluation by his attorney to rule out a treatable psychiatric disorder. Mr. W. has entered into five lawsuits in the past 2½ years. His attorney believes that each suit is of questionable validity. Mr. W. has been described as an unemotional, highly controlled person who is now suing a local men's clothing store "for conspiring to deprive me of my consumer rights." He contends that the store manager consistently issued bad credit reports on him. The consulting psychiatrist elicited other examples of similar concerns. Mr. W. has long distrusted his neighbors across the street and regularly monitors their activity since one of his garbage cans disappeared 2 years ago. He took an early retirement from his accounting job a year ago because he could not get along with his supervisor, who he believed was faulting him about his accounts and paperwork. He contends he was faultless. On examination, Mr. W.'s mental status is unremarkable except for constriction of affect and for a certain hesitation and guardedness in his response to questions.

Case Study: Paranoid Personality Style

Janice L. is a 46-year-old tax attorney for a major corporation. Although she had been reluctant to leave her private law practice, the corporation had courted her for several years. They really needed a skilled and successful female to round out their legal team. They made her an offer she could not refuse, and after ensuring that she could maintain sufficient independence in the job, she accepted. Although she had a loose reporting relationship to the chief counsel and two corporate vice presidents, from the beginning Janice maintained cordial but somewhat distant relationships with them. She attended only those meetings and social gatherings that were absolutely required. She kept small talk to a minimum and went about her work with a single-minded vigor that others came to respect, although they could not quite understand her style. When others began to question her standoffish manner, she replied she was hired "to be a competent litigator, not a social butterfly." In the courtroom she was an awesome sight: cool, calm, and collected. She was totally in charge of examining and cross-examining witnesses and in delivering her opening and closing statements. No stone was left unturned and no verbal or nonverbal cue was missed. She instinctively went for the juggler, as her peers would say, and seldom lost a judgment. There was never a question about her worth or loyalty to the corporation, and in time, her peers and superiors came to accept her unique style.

DSM-IV-TR Description and Criteria

DSM-IV-TR offers the description and criteria for paranoid personality disorder in Table 9.2.

FORMULATIONS OF THE PARANOID PERSONALITY DISORDER

Psychodynamic Formulation

Psychoanalytic formulations of the paranoid personality focus on the phenomenon of projection. Essentially, paranoid individuals inaccurately perceive

Table 9.2
DSM-IV-TR Criteria for Paranoid Personality Disorder (301.0)

A. A pervasive distrust and suspiciousness of others such that their motives are interpreted as malevolent, beginning by early adulthood and present in a variety of contexts, as indicated by at least four of the following:

(1) suspects, without sufficient basis, that others are exploiting or deceiving him or her
(2) preoccupied with unjustified doubts about the loyalty or trustworthiness of friends or associates
(3) is reluctant to confide in others because of unwarranted fear that the information will be used maliciously against him or her
(4) reads hidden demeaning or threatening meanings into benign remarks or events
(5) persistently bears grudges, i.e., is unforgiving of insults, injuries, or slights
(6) perceives attacks on his or her character or reputation that are not apparent to others and is quick to react angrily or to counterattack
(7) recurrent suspicions, without justification, regarding fidelity of spouse or sexual partner

B. Does not occur exclusively during the course of schizophrenia, a mood disorder with psychotic features, or another psychotic disorder, and is not due to the direct effects of a general medical condition

Note: If criteria are met prior to the onset of schizophrenia, add "premorbid," e.g., "paranoid personality disorder (premorbid)."

Reprinted with permission from the *Diagnostic and Statistical Manual of Mental Disorders, Fourth Edition–Text Revision.* Copyright 2000. American Psychiatric Association.

in others that which is true of them, and, as by projecting unacceptable feelings and impulses onto others, they experience a reduction in anxiety and distress (Shapiro, 1965).

The self-representation of the paranoid personality involves the coexistence of a special, entitled grandiose self with a weak, worthless, inferior polar opposite (Gabbard, 1990). Developmentally, individuals with paranoid personality disorder are likely to have grown up in an atmosphere charged with criticism, blame, and hostility, and to have identified with a critical parent. Identification with such critical parents suppresses these individuals' feelings of inadequacy and ensures the continuing importance of the mode of criticalness in the development and functioning of the personality. Through their identifications, paranoid individuals learn hypervigilance, suspiciousness, and blaming. Hypervigilance and suspiciousness prevent self-criticism, while blaming—considered an identification with the aggressor—serves to erase the possible experience of humiliation (Kellerman & Burry, 1989).

Paranoid individuals focus on seeing imperfection in the world around them. This externalization permits a denial of any personal imperfection. Essentially, paranoid individuals feel inferior, weak, and ineffective. Thus, grandiosity and specialness allow them to be understood as a compensatory defense against feelings of inferiority (Gabbard, 1990).

The primary defense mechanisms of this disorder are projection and projective identification. In addition to externalizing threats with projection, projective identification serves to control others in the environment by binding them to paranoid individuals in pathological ways. This need to control others reflects low self-esteem, which is at the heart of paranoid personality disorder. Basically, it sensitizes these individuals to concerns about all passive surrender to all impulses and to all persons (Shapiro, 1965). Finally, rationalization, reaction formation, and displacement are secondary defense mechanisms.

In short, the need to criticize the world and external objects allows paranoid individuals to maintain an anxiety-free existence in the face of personal imperfections and a grave sense of inadequacy. Profound inferiority feelings are projected onto the "inferior" world, which is then related to in a consistently critical manner. The self can then be viewed as "good" and "badness" can be split off and projected outward.

Cognitive-Behavioral Formulation

From the cognitive therapy perspective, paranoid personality disorder is characterized by a pattern of certain assumptions, automatic thoughts, and cognitive distortions. Beck and Freeman (1990) note that individuals with paranoid personality disorders typically view themselves as righteous and mistreated by others. They tend to view others as interfering, devious, treacherous, covertly manipulative, and discriminatory. They may believe that others form secret coalitions against them. Based on the belief that others are against them, these individuals are driven to be hypervigilant and on guard. They tend to be wary, suspicious, and sensitive to cues that would betray the hidden motives of their adversaries. When they confront their adversaries, they often provoke the hostility that they believed already existed. Pretzer (1988) believes that this attribution of the malicious intent of others is the core assumption of this disorder.

Typical automatic beliefs of this disorder are: "Other people can't be trusted"; "People are basically deceptive"; "If people act friendly, they are trying to use me"; and "If people seem distant, it proves they are unfriendly." Finally, individuals with paranoid personality disorder often utilize the cognitive distortions of dichotomous thinking, selective abstraction, and overgeneralization (Freeman et al., 1990).

Turkat and colleagues (Turkat & Maisto, 1985; Turkat & Banks, 1987;

Turkat, 1985, 1986, 1990) have painstakingly studied paranoid personality disorder from the behavioral perspective. Although Turkat (1990) contends there is no single formulation for this disorder, he notes that hypersensitivity to criticism is usually present. He notes that such individuals receive early training to be frightened of what others think of them. These individuals also learn that they are different from others, and that they must not make mistakes. As a result, paranoid individuals become overly concerned about the evaluations of others, constrained to conform to parental expectations, and hypersensitive to others' evaluations. This, of course, often interferes with acceptance by their peers.

Eventually, they are humiliated and ostracized by their peers, in part because they lack the interpersonal skills necessary to overcome this ostracism. Consequently, they excessively engage in ruminating about their isolation and mistreatment by others. From this, they conclude that the reason for this rejection and persecution is that they are special and others are jealous of them. Accordingly, they act in ways to avoid negative evaluations from others, but these attempts lead them to act differently, which invites social criticism. In their isolation they brood about their predicament, which engenders persecutory and grandiose thoughts and further maintains their social isolation. Thus, the paranoid patient is caught in a vicious cycle that perpetuates the disorder.

Biosocial Formulation

In a marked departure from other formulations of paranoid personality disorder, Millon (Millon & Davis, 1996) and Millon and Everly (1985) conceive of paranoid personality disorder as a severe form of character pathology. More specifically, Millon and Everly describe it as syndromal continuation of one of three less severe disorders: narcissistic, antisocial, or compulsive. Based on their clinical research, individuals with paranoid personalities develop in one of these three syndromal patterns based on their unique biogenic and environmental histories. The narcissistic variation of paranoid disorder is largely shaped by parental overvaluation and indulgence. As a result, these individuals fail to adequately learn interpersonal responsibility, cooperation, and interpersonal skills. They are often perceived by others as selfish and egotistical. Furthermore, lack of parental controls can give rise to grandiose fantasies of success, power, beauty, or brilliance. But then they tend to be rejected and humiliated by their peers. These interpersonal rebuffs are followed by increased fantasy and isolation from which a propensity for paranoia emerges.

The antisocial variant of paranoid personality exhibits high levels of activation and impulsive high-energy temperaments. The principal environmental determinant seems to be harsh parental treatment. Consequently, they

develop a deep abiding mistrust of others and manifest a strong self-directedness and arrogance. Because of their tendency to reject both parental and
social controls, they also develop an aggressive, impulsive, hedonistic lifestyle.
Anticipating the attacks of others, paranoid antisocial individuals react irrationally and vindictively. Since they are unable to cope directly with perceived
threats, they often erupt in overt hostility.

Individuals with the paranoid compulsive pattern have developmental
histories quite similar to obsessive-compulsive personality disorder. However,
they exhibit more irrationally rigid and inflexible behavior (Millon & Everly,
1985). These three versions of the paranoid disorder appear to be self-perpetuated by their own rigidity and suspiciousness. By ascribing slanderous
and malevolent motives to others, paranoid individuals remain in a defensive
and vindictive posture most of the time. Furthermore, keeping distance from
others fosters the maintenance of their illusion of superiority, which allows a
self-fulfilling pattern: as they expect others to be hostile and malevolent, others often become so.

Interpersonal Formulation

According to Benjamin (1996), persons diagnosed with paranoid personality
disorder were likely to have experienced sadistic, controlling, and degrading
parenting. Typically abused children themselves, parents of paranoid-
disordered individuals believe that children are basically evil or bad, require
containment, and deserve retribution. Family loyalty was a basic value, and
sharing family secrets with others was not tolerated. The adult consequence
of such harsh upbringing is that paranoid-disordered individuals expect attack and abuse even from those close to them. As children they were harshly
punished for dependency and even attacked when they were sick, hurt, or
cried. As a result, they learned not to cry, not to ask for help even if injured or
sick, and not to trust anyone. Subsequently, as adults they tend to avoid intimacy unless they can control their partner.

Often these individuals were subjected to covert as well as overt insidi-
ous comparisons within the family and later among peers. They learned that
mistakes and hurts were seldom forgotten and that grudges were long-last-
ing. Not surprisingly, paranoid individuals are exquisitely sensitive and angry
about exclusion, slights, and even whispering. They tend to be keenly aware
of any inequalities in punishments or privileges, and they are likely to sustain
grudges for long periods. Furthermore, as children they were rewarded for
competence in helping the family while staying out of the way. While they
were given permission and support to do well, they were degraded and humiliated for venturing out of an assigned area. They came to believe that being

a good and lovable person was outside their reach. Subsequently, as adults they can function competently and independently but are interpersonally withdrawn. Their expectations of not being acknowledged inspire fear, resentment, and alienation. Finally, they constantly fear that others will attack, blame, or hurt them, while they continue to wish that others will affirm and understand them. Not expecting to be affirmed, they angrily withdraw and tightly control themselves. If they perceive attack, they will reflexively counterattack.

Integrative Formulation

The following integrative formulations may be helpful in understanding how paranoid personality disorder is likely to be developed and maintained. Biologically, a low threshold for limbic system stimulation and deficiencies in inhibitory centers seem to influence the behavior of the paranoid personality. The underlying temperament can best be understood in terms of the subtypes of paranoid disorder. Each of three subtypes is briefly described in terms of underlying temperament and correlative parental and environmental factors. In the narcissistic type, a hyperresponsive temperament and precociousness, parental overevaluation and indulgence, as well as the individual's sense of grandiosity and self-behavior probably result in deficits in social interest and limited interpersonal skills. The antisocial type of the paranoid personality is likely to possess a hyperresponsive temperament. This, plus harsh parental treatment, probably contributes to the impulsive, hedonistic, and aggressive style. In the compulsive type, the underlying temperament may have been anhedonia. This, as well as parental rigidity and overcontrol, largely accounts for the compulsive behaviors. Finally, a less common variant is the paranoid passive-aggressive type. As infants, these individuals usually demonstrated the "difficult child" temperament and later affective irritability. This, plus parental inconsistency, probably accounts in large part for the passive-aggressiveness (Millon, 1981).

Psychologically, paranoid individuals view themselves, others, the world, and life's purpose in terms of the following themes. They tend to view themselves by some variant of the theme: "I'm special and different. I'm alone and no one likes me because I'm better than others." Life and the world are viewed by some variant of the theme: "Life is unfair, unpredictable, and demanding. It can and will sneak up and harm you when you are least expecting it." As such, they are likely to conclude, "Therefore, be wary, counterattack, trust no one, and excuse yourself from failure by blaming others." The most common defensive mechanism associated with paranoid disorder is projection.

Socially, predictable patterns of parenting and environmental factors can be noted for paranoid personality disorder. For all the subtypes the parental injunction appears to be "You're different. Don't make mistakes." Paranoid personality–disordered individuals tend to have perfectionistic parents who expose these children to specialness training. This, plus the parental style that has been articulated for the subtypes of the disorder and parental criticism, leads to an attitude of social isolation and hypervigilant behavior. To make sense of the apparent contradiction between being special and being ridiculed, the children creatively conclude that the reason they are special and that no one likes them is because they are better than other people. This explanation serves the purpose of reducing their anxiety and allows them to develop some sense of self and belonging.

This paranoid pattern is confirmed, reinforced, and perpetuated by the following individual and systems factors: A sense of specialness, rigidity, attributing malevolence to others, blaming others, and misinterpreting motives of others leads to social alienation and isolation, which further confirms the individual's persecutory stance (Sperry & Mosak, 1996).

ASSESSMENT OF PARANOID PERSONALITY DISORDER

Several sources of information are useful in establishing a diagnosis and treatment plan for personality disorders. Observation, collateral information, and psychological testing are important adjuncts to the patient's self-report in the clinical interview. This section briefly describes some characteristic observations that the clinician makes and the nature of the rapport likely to develop in initial encounters with specific personality-disordered individuals. Characteristic response patterns on various objective (i.e., MMPI-2 and MCMI-III) and projective tests (i.e., Rorschach and TAT) are also described.

Interview Behavior and Rapport

Interviewing paranoid personality–disordered individuals is a delicate challenge. Rapport with them is hampered by their pervasive belief that others will harm and exploit them. Therefore, they screen all questions for conspiratorial content and hidden meaning, and assume that any kindness shown by the clinician is a cleaver maneuver to take advantage of their weakness. Similarly, they cannot allow themselves to relax in the interview, fearful that easing up would make them too vulnerable, so they justify their suspiciousness and hypervigilance. They can easily confront others, but will not tolerate being

Table 9.3
Characteristics of Paranoid Personality Disorder

Triggering Event	Close interpersonal relationships and/or personal queries.
Behavioral Style	Guarded, defensive, and hypervigilant; resistant of external influence; chronically tense because constantly mobilized against perceived threats.
Interpersonal Style	Distrustful, secretive, isolated; blaming; provocative, counterattacking, hypersensitive.
Cognitive Style	Mistrusting, preconceptions; tendency to disregard evidence to the contrary; may become conspiratorial or delusional under stress.
Feeling Style	Aloof, humorless; restricted affect, jealous; easily provoked.
Temperament	*Narcissistic type*: active, hyperresponsive. *Compulsive type*: irritable. *Passive-aggressive type*: affective irritability.
Attachment Style	Fearful.
Parental Injunction	"You're different. Keep alert. Don't make mistakes."
Self-View	"I'm so special and different. I'm alone and no one likes me because I'm better than others."
Worldview	"Life is unfair, unpredictable, and demanding. It will sneak up and harm you. Therefore, be wary, counteract, trust no one, and excuse yourself from failure by blaming others."
Maladaptive Schemas	Abuse/mistrust; defectiveness.
Optimal DSM-IV-TR Criteria	Suspects, without sufficient basis, that others are exploiting, harming, or deceiving him or her.

confronted. Smooth transitions from topic to topic are essential. Any abruptness may be experienced as an unjustified attempt to trap them, which could lead to anger, counterattack, or termination of the interview (Othmer & Othmer, 2000).

Psychological Testing Data

The Minnesota Multiphase Personality Inventory (MMPI-2), the Millon Clinical Multiaxial Inventory (MCMI-III), the Rorschach Psychodiagnostic Test, and the Thematic Apperception Test (TAT) can be useful in diagnosing compulsive personality disorder as well as the obsessive-compulsive personality style or trait.

On the MMPI-2, an elevation on the 6 scale (paranoia) is common. Since these individuals tend to be hyperalert about being perceived as paranoid, this scale may be greatly elevated (Turkat, 1990). These individuals are easily irritated at the MMPI's forced-choice format as well as the self-disclosure required of many of the items (Meyer, 1995). Scales 3 (hysteria), 1 (hypochondriasis), and K (correction) tend to be high in these individuals, reflecting their use of denial and projection, their inclination to focus on somatic concerns, and their need to present a facade of adequacy (Graham, 2000).

On the MCMI-III, elevation on scale 6B (sadistic) and P (paranoid) are expected. Since this personality style often overlaps with the antisocial, the narcissistic, and the passive-aggressive, elevations are likely on scales 6A (antisocial), 5 (narcissistic), and 8A (passive-aggressive; Choca & Denburg, 1997).

On the Rorschach, these individuals produce records that are generally constricted but characterized by more P (popular) and A (animal) responses than C (pure color) and M (human movement) responses. These individuals typically resent ambiguous stimuli, so they respond to the test with condescending criticism and flipping of cards, and a focus on D (detail) responses. Occasionally they reject cards or refuse to continue with the examination (Meyer, 1995).

On the TAT, suspiciousness may characterize their stories. This is particularly likely to occur on cards 9, G, F, 11, and 16 (Bellak, 1997).

TREATMENT APPROACHES AND INTERVENTIONS

Treatment Considerations

Included in the differential diagnosis of paranoid personality disorder are the following Axis II personality disorders: antisocial personality disorder, narcissistic personality disorder, obsessive-compulsive personality disorder, and passive-aggressive personality disorder. The most common Axis I syndromes associated with paranoid personality disorder are generalized anxiety disorder, panic disorder, and delusional disorder. If a bipolar disorder is present, an irritable manic presentation is likely. Decompensation into schizophrenic reaction is likely. The paranoid and catatonic subtypes of schizophrenia are most commonly noted.

Until recently, the prognosis for treatment of paranoid personality disorder was considered guarded. Today more optimism prevails in achieving these goals of treatment: increasing the benignness of perception and interpretation of reality, and increasing trusting behavior. Several treatment strategies and modalities are useful in accomplishing these goals. To date, no controlled treatment outcome studies have been completed for paranoid personality disorder (Crits-Christoph & Barber, 2002).

Individual Psychotherapy

Psychodynamic Psychotherapy Approach

Patients with paranoid personalities tend to be individuals who lead reasonably adaptive and productive lives, and not surprisingly, are responsive to psychodynamic psychotherapy. Meissner (1978) contends, however, that their treatment is not easy but requires empathy, patience, and a great deal of sensitivity to their vulnerabilities. Meissner contends that the treatment process must be slowly paced with limited, long-term goals. Three treatment principles characterize such treatment (Meissner, 1978, 1986).

First, a meaningful therapeutic alliance must be established and maintained. The therapeutic alliance requires that the patient have a certain degree of trust in the clinician, which is considerable for paranoid patients. The clinician's empathic responsiveness and willingness to serve as a container for a range of negative affects is essential. The clinician must avoid responding defensively and challenging the patient's perception of events or the clinician. Instead, the clinician asks for more details and empathizes with the patient's perceptions and affects. Most importantly, the clinician must resist the countertransference tendency to be rid of undescribable projections by deflecting them back to the patient with premotive interpretations (Epstein, 1984). In short, the patient must come to view the clinician as a benign, disinterested but friendly helper (Salzman, 1980).

Second, the essential treatment strategy is to convert paranoid manifestations into depression and work through the underlying mourning. Gradual undermining of paranoid defenses and attitudes leads to the emergence of a depressive core in which the patient's inner sense of weakness, defectiveness, vulnerability, and powerlessness comes into focus. This is accomplished through the techniques of counterprojection and "creative doubt" (Meissner, 1986). Depressive elements are worked through in the transference, which allows individuals to begin the process of mourning their frustrated learning and disappointments with early objects.

Third, the clinician must respect the patient's fragile and threatened sense of autonomy and work toward building and reinforcing it in the therapeutic relationship. A commitment to openness, honesty, and confidentiality means that all decisions must be explored with the patient, and the ultimate choice must be the patient's. This even applies to decisions about medication, when and if it is indicated (Meissner, 1989).

Since these patients tend to be resistant, provocative, and contentious, countertransference issues cannot be underestimated. Behind their defensiveness and arrogance are narcissistic vulnerability, core feelings of shame and humiliation, and passive longing for dependence. Thus, these patients attempt to counter their anxieties by turning the tables and making the clinician feel vulnerable, humiliated, and helpless. Clinicians may react with annoyance, impatience, confrontative and argumentative behavior, or they may experience frustration, discouragement, and victimization. These reactions must be monitored, their impact on therapy analyzed, and efforts to rebalance the therapeutic alliance initiated (Meissner, 1989).

Brief Psychodynamic Psychotherapy. Long-term psychodynamically oriented psychotherapy involves two or more sessions per week for 3 or more years. However, since paranoid personality–disordered individuals do not easily engage in the therapeutic process, they may have reluctance to such intensive long-term work. On the other hand, receptivity to treatment increases during crisis periods, usually the experience of acute anxiety or depression. Shorter-term therapy that is more crisis oriented might be a preferable way of beginning treatment. This therapy could be a prelude to longer-term treatment.

Malan (1976) and Balint et al. (1972) describe short-term psychotherapy with acute paranoid difficulties. Although this treatment was effective for reactive paranoid presentations it may not be for the enduring presentations more typical of paranoid personality disorder. Currently, there are no published reports of completed successful treatments of paranoid personality disorder in the context of brief dynamic psychotherapy.

Cognitive-Behavioral Therapy Approach

Beck, Freeman, and Associates (1990) provide an extended discussion of the cognitive therapy approach with paranoid personality–disordered individuals. The initial phase of treatment can be exceedingly stressful for paranoid individuals in that participating in treatment requires self-disclosure, trusting another, and acknowledging weakness, all of which they experience as being quite dangerous. This stress can be reduced by focusing initially on less sensitive issues or by discussing issues directly—that is, talking about how "some individuals" experience and react to such situations, or by beginning with a more problem-solving approach and behaviorally focused interventions on presenting problems. Such strategies, as well as giving individuals more than the usual amount of control over scheduling appointments or the content of sessions, can facilitate development of a collaborative working relationship wherein they feel less distrustful, coerced, and vigilant. Trust can be engendered by explicitly acknowledging and accepting the individual's difficulty in trusting the therapist. As this becomes evident and gradually demonstrated through trustworthiness and actions, it provides the evidence on which trust can be based.

A guided discovery approach when working on treatment goals will reveal the manner in which their paranoid pattern contributes to their problems, facilitating collaborative work on their distrust of others, feelings, vulnerability, and desire for retribution, rather than the therapist insisting that these issues be directly addressed. As treatment progresses to working on specific goals, emphasis should shift to increasing the individual's sense of self-efficacy before attempting to modify interpersonal behaviors, automatic thoughts, or schemas. Developing an increased awareness of another's point of view and learning a more assertive approach to interpersonal conflict are other common treatment goals with these individuals. The use of traditional cognitive-behavioral techniques such as assertive communication training and behavioral rehearsal are commonly employed to reverse the provocation of hostile reactions from others that previously confirmed the paranoid individual's view of self and others. In instances where hypervigilance and ideas of reference are particularly resistant, the information-processing social skills intervention strategy described by Turkat and Maisto (1985) can be exceptionally useful.

The treatment goals are to decrease sensitivity to criticism and modify social behavior. Social skills training consists of instructional role-playing, behavioral rehearsal, and videotaped feedback. The patient is taught to attend to more appropriate social stimuli; to interpret that information more accurately; to attack, criticize, or single out himself or herself; and to receive others' feedback in a nondefensive way and utilize it constructively (Turkat, 1990). Turkat and Maisto (1985) present a detailed case report illustrating these treatment strategies.

Williams (1988) provides a detailed case report of time-limited cognitive therapy with a substance-abusing, depressed college student who also met criteria for paranoid personality disorder. The patient was distressed about poor interpersonal relations and drug use, and was quite intelligent and motivated for therapy. Noteworthy about Williams's treatment protocol is that only 11 sessions were available and needed to achieve three treatment goals: reduce depressive symptoms, lessen threatening perceptions of the world and other people, and increase skills in being more relaxed and comfortable with others. Cognitive restructuring and progressive muscle relaxation were the principal intervention strategies. Six-month follow-up showed that all gains had been maintained. Williams concludes that brief cognitive therapy may be particularly well suited for the paranoid personality disorder. In short, the cognitive therapy approach to working with paranoid individuals focuses considerable effort on carefully developing a working collaborative relationship and increasing self-efficacy early in treatment. It utilizes cognitive techniques and behavioral experiments to directly challenge the individual's remaining paranoid beliefs late in therapy.

Structured Skill Treatment Interventions. While research shows that medication can modulate or normalize dysregulated behaviors, a similar modulating effect has also been noted for social skills training (Lieberman, DeRisi, & Mueser, 1989). Thus, it appears that social skills training is a relatively potent bottom-up treatment strategy for normalizing limbic system–mediated behaviors that reflect specific skill deficits in personality-disordered individuals. When such skills deficits are present, Sperry (1999) contends that structured skill training intervention is a potent and effective strategy in treatment. Various structured intervention strategies for modifying a personality-disordered individual's affective, behavioral, and cognitive temperament styles are relevant to paranoid personality disorder (Sperry, 1999).

Schema Therapy. Schema therapy is an elaboration of cognitive therapy that has been developed by Young (1999) and Young et al. (2003) specifically for personality disorders and other difficult individual and couples problems. Schema therapy involves identifying maladaptive schemas and planning specific strategies and interventions. Four main strategies are cognitive, experiential, behavioral, and the therapeutic relationship itself. Cognitive restructuring—modification of maladaptive schemas—is an important cognitive strategy but is combined with imagery exercises, empathic confrontation, homework assignments, and "limited reparenting" (i.e., a form of corrective emotional experience; Young, 1999).

Maladaptive schemas typically associated with paranoid personality disorder include *mistrust/abuse*—that is, the belief that others will abuse, humiliate, cheat, lie, manipulate, or take advantage; and *defectiveness*—that is, the belief that one is defective, bad, unwanted, or inferior in important respects (Bernstein, 2002).

Interpersonal Approach

Benjamin (1996) explains that psychotherapeutic interventions with paranoid personality–disordered individuals can be planned and evaluated in terms of whether they enhance collaboration, facilitate learning about maladaptive patterns and their roots, block these patterns, enhance the will to change, and effectively encourage new patterns.

Benjamin notes that the major treatment problem with paranoid individuals is establishing a collaborative therapeutic relationship. To the extent that collaboration occurs, paranoia disappears. Accustomed to being abused and humiliated, paranoid individuals view therapists as critical and judgmental, look for "slip-ups," and want them to leave. Patience and kindness without hints of coercion, criticism, or appeasement are essential for a considerable period during the early stages of therapy.

As treatment proceeds, individuals must learn that their expectations of attack and abusive control stem from past experiences. As such, they can begin appreciating that these expectations are not always appropriate in the present and that hostility begets hostility. Furthermore, they must come to understand that their defenses of control, avoidance, and anticipatory relation will elicit attack and alienation in others. Benjamin advocates the use of "verbal holding" as an antidote to their original abuse. Accurate empathy, genuine affirmation of accomplishments, and understanding constitute verbal holding. At the same time, therapists need to gently but firmly confront provocations. Since confrontation is likely to be threatening to them, therapists must carefully balance affirmation with confrontation. The goal is for proactive criticism and for these individuals to learn the meaning of feedback, as well as that their feelings of vulnerability and fearfulness do not prove that others, including therapists, are attacking them.

Benjamin's discussion of blocking maladaptive patterns in paranoid individuals includes strategies for dealing with various crises such as aborting or redirecting rageful outbursts at therapists, or dealing with homicidal threats and abuse of their children. She believes that the therapist's honesty, caring, calmness, attentiveness, and clear commitment to resolving conflicts are extremely useful to paranoid individuals in crisis. Benjamin finds that the wish to relinquish patterns of alienation, hostile control, grudges, and fearfulness do not develop until these individuals feel safe to do otherwise. As therapy proceeds, they are helped to lessen their enmeshment with early controlling, attacking figures. As they can see that they are acting like a hated parent, they may become interested in becoming different.

Once safer bases are established with significant others and/or with their therapist, they can begin channeling their anger in a direction that encourages separation from earlier destructive patterns and beliefs. Finally, when therapeutic collaboration develops, considerably, new learning about trust, giving and receiving positive and negative feedback from and to others, and thinking more benignly about people and life circumstances have already taken place. As these are mastered, any residual learning that remains by the last stage of therapy is relatively easy to implement. For paranoid individuals at the last stage of treatment, excursions into the social world further the idea that friendly approaches elicit friendly reactions; these can be slightly frightening but also exhilarating.

Group Therapy

Because of their hypersensitivity, suspiciousness, and tendency to misinterpret comments of others, paranoid personality–disordered individuals tend to avoid group therapy and other forms of group treatment. Similarly, the paranoid tendency to be accusatory, self-righteous, obstinate, hostile, and evasive has been a contraindication to heterogeneous intensive group therapy (Yalom, 1995; Francis, Clarkin, & Perry, 1984; Vinogradov & Yalom, 1989).

On the other hand, higher-functioning paranoid patients who can maintain a degree of self-awareness and are able to tolerate a group confrontation of their paranoid distortion may derive considerable benefit from participation in an established group that is sufficiently cohesive and tolerant of divergent opinions (Messiner, 1989).

Marital and Family Therapy

There is relatively little published literature on therapy with the paranoid personality, per se. Nonetheless, either treatment modality can be used alone or concurrently with individual therapy. Meissner (1989) indicates that family therapy might be combined sometime during the course of long-term individual psychotherapy. Family therapy might be indicated for the paranoid adolescent whose family dynamics and interaction patterns interfere with or contribute to the patient's difficulties.

Harbir (1981) details some general principles for couples therapy for the paranoid personality. He notes that paranoid features often lead to severe marital dysfunction. The paranoid partner's hypersensitivity, joyless intensity, hypervigilance, extreme mistrust, and jealousy cause considerable suffering for his or her partner. Nevertheless, the nonparanoid partner also causes suffering because his or her actions often exacerbate the paranoid condition. Typically, nonparanoid spouses react passively and secretively when accused or criticized. The more they withdraw and are evasive, the more their paranoid partner becomes suspicious and mistrustful. Therefore, the clinician who is treating a married paranoid patient in individual therapy should consider concurrent couples therapy or, at least, a conjoint session with the nonparanoid partner to modify the marital interaction pattern that seems to be maintaining the psychopathology.

The goal of marital therapy is to enhance the positive growth of the couple by reducing the personality pathology of either or both partners. Harbir (1981) reports that paranoid patients can progress in couples therapy despite the inevitable issues of trust and confidentiality. The clinician needs to be con-

stantly aware of the paranoid partner's close monitoring of the clinician's behavior. These patients invariably become angry if they perceive the clinician
taking sides, or become jealous of the clinician's relationship with their partner, if the clinician is of the opposite sex. Thus, the clinician, just as in individual psychotherapy, must be open and forthright about the specific
therapeutic process and rationale. Once a therapeutic alliance has been established, the clinician can support the nonparanoid spouse to confront and challenge the constant mistrust of the paranoid partner. An angry response can
be expected at first, but the paranoia will start decreasing. Obviously, such
confrontation is only prescribed when the patient has adequate impulsive
control and has not been violent. Harbir describes a detailed case example of
conjoint couples therapy involving a paranoid spouse. The treatment involves
two stages and illustrates Harbir's therapy approach.

Medication

Until recently, there were few little data to support the use of psychotropics
with paranoid personality–disordered individuals. To date, paranoid personality disorder has not been subject to controlled pharmacological trials
(Koenigsberg, Woo-Ming, & Siever, 2002). However, an open clinical trial utilizing pimozide in an outpatient sample of personality-disordered individuals
showed that the neuroleptic greatly improved both the schizoid and paranoid
personality–disordered subgroups. Methodological problems aside, this study
was important in alerting clinicians to a medication whose approved indication is only for Tourette's syndrome (Munro, 1992).

Pimozide is a selective, postsynaptic antidopaminergic agent that is the
consensus drug of choice for delusional disorders (Munro, 1992). Because of
the boundaries between the paranoid spectrum disorders, these various disorders may have a common pathogenesis (Manschreck, 1992). While await-
ing controlled trials of pimozide with paranoid personality–disordered patients
and subsequent FDA approval, pimozide should be considered in paranoid
patients who exhibit blaming, a low frustration tolerance, and hypersensitivity to criticism.

Fieve (1994) reports that fluoxetine hydrochloride (Prozac) has been very
effective in reducing suspiciousness. Fluoxetine is one of several new serotonin reuptake inhibitors that has therapeutic potential in the treatment of paranoid personality when suspiciousness and irritability are prominent.

Medication Protocol. For individuals who are moderately symptomatic with
suspiciousness or paranoid thinking, the initial choice is an atypical antipsychotic, such as risperidone, at one-fourth to one-half the usual topic range

maintenance dose for psychosis. If there is no response, incrementally increase the dosage. If there is no response at the top dose, switch to another atypical. If there is a partial response, consider adding divalproex (Reich, 2002).

Combined and Integrated Treatment Approaches

There are sufficient data to suggest that paranoid personality disorder is no longer untreatable, as was previously believed, but can be successfully treated. Although treatment with psychodynamic and cognitive-behavioral approaches is considered long term, there has been at least one report of successful time-limited treatment (Williams, 1988). Currently, there is little published data on integrating and tailoring treatment with this disorder. Nevertheless, clinical experience shows that an integrative treatment approach probably can maximize therapeutic outcomes while decreasing the length of treatment.

Conceptualizing personality disorder as having temperament and characterological dimensions, it appears that the dynamic approaches are particularly effective with the characterological dimensions but less effective with the temperamental dimensions. It seems that cognitive restructuring and the behavioral information processing approach (Turkat & Maisto, 1985) are particularly effective with modifying the paranoid's cognitive style of hypervigilance. The cognitive-behavioral approach is also useful with difficulty relaxing and constricted affects. The interpersonal approach (Benjamin, 1993) seems particularly effective in reducing blame and hypersensitivity to criticism. Thus, integrating dynamic, cognitive-behavioral, and interpersonal approaches could have a synergistic effect at changing both temperamental and characterological dimensions of this disorder. It also appears that combining treatment modalities should increase treatment efficacy and cost-effectiveness, especially for the more severe presentations of this disorder. The most obvious combined treatment involves the concurrent or sequential use of family, marital, or group therapy with individual psychotherapy. Also quite promising is the combination of medications (i.e., pimozide or serotonergic reuptake inhibitors), when they are indicated, with individual psychotherapy.

CHAPTER 10

Schizoid Personality
Disorder

Schizoid personality disorder is a member of the "odd cluster" of personality disorders. Coined by Bleuler in 1924, schizoid described the tendency to turn inward and away from the external world, the absence of emotional expressiveness, the pursuit of vague interests, and simultaneous dullness and sensitivity. Despite its long clinical and theoretical tradition, schizoid personality was overly inclusive and poorly differentiated in DSM-I and DSM-II. DSM-III attempted to differentiate it by establishing the diagnoses of avoidant personality disorder and schizotypal personality disorder. The three criteria in DSM-III were sufficiently reflective of much of the descriptive literature. DSM-III-R expanded the criteria to seven, which increased its specificity (Kalus et al., 1993).

But there was dissatisfaction from dynamically oriented clinicians with DSM-III-R in that the withdrawal of interest in others that has characterized schizoid individuals is really an apparent retreat. Schizoid patients may secretly long for close relationships but assume a defensive posture of detachment because of their fears (Gabbard, 1994). DSM-IV has been somewhat modified to acknowledge these patients' difficulty in enjoying everyday activities.

Taking a broader view than DSM-IV-TR, Miller et al. (2001) describe some dimensional alternatives to diagnostic classification for schizoid personality disorder. For some time, researchers have considered schizoid personality disorder as a schizophrenic spectrum disorder. More recently, there has been speculation that schizoid personality disorder may also be related to autism, Asperger syndrome, and pervasive developmental disorder, not otherwise specified. Readers will find a useful comparison of similarities and differences in symptomatology and functioning among these disorders in Wolff (2000).

In epidemiological studies of prevalence, schizoid personality disorder is usually the least commonly diagnosed personality disorder in the general population. Even among the clinical population, the prevalence is only about 1 percent (Stone, 1993).

This chapter describes the characteristic features of schizoid personality disorder and its related personality style. Five different clinical formulations and several psychological assessment indicators are highlighted. And a variety of treatment approaches, modalities, and intervention strategies are described.

DESCRIPTION OF SCHIZOID PERSONALITY DISORDER

Schizoid personality disorder can be recognized by the following descriptors and characteristics: style vs. disorder, triggering event, behavioral style, interpersonal style, cognitive style, affective style, attachment style, and optimal criterion.

Style vs. Disorder. The schizoid personality can be thought of as spanning a continuum from healthy to pathological, with the dependent personality style at the healthy end and the schizoid personality disorder at the pathological end. Table 10.1 compares and contrasts differences between the dependent style and the disorder.

Triggering Event. The typical situation, circumstance, or event that most likely triggers or activates the characteristic maladaptive response of schizoid personality disorder (Othmer & Othmer, 2002), as noted in behavioral, interpersonal, cognitive, and feeling styles, is "close interpersonal relationships."

Behavioral Style. The behavioral pattern of schizoids can be described as lethargic, inattentive, and occasionally eccentric. They exhibit slow and monotonal speech and are generally nonspontaneous in both their behavior and speech.

Table 10.1
Comparison of Schizoid Personality Style and Disorder

Personality Style	*Personality Disorder*
Exhibit little need of companionship and are most comfortable alone	Neither desire nor enjoy close relationships including being part of a family; have no close friends or confidants (or only one) other than first-degree relatives
Tend to be self-contained, not requiring interaction with others in order to enjoy experiences or live their lives	Almost always choose solitary activities
Even-tempered, dispassionate, calm, unflappable, and rarely sentimental	Rarely if ever claim or appear to experience strong emotion, such as anger or joy
Little driven by sexual needs, and while they can enjoy sex, they do not suffer in its absence	Indirect battle if any desire to have sexual experiences with another person
Tend to be unswayed by either praise or criticism and can confidently come to terms with their own behavior	Indifferent to the praise and criticism of others; display constricted affects, e.g., they are aloof, cold, and rarely reciprocate gestures or facial expressions, such as smiles or nods

Interpersonal Style. Interpersonally, they appear to be content to remain socially aloof and alone. These individuals prefer to engage in solitary pursuits, they are reserved and seclusive, and they rarely respond to others' feelings and actions. They tend to fade into the social backdrop and appear to others as "cold fish." They do not involve themselves in group or team activity. In short, they appear inept and awkward in social situations.

Cognitive Style. Their style of perceiving, thinking, and information processing can be characterized as cognitively distracted. That is, their thinking and communication can easily become derailed through internal or external distraction. This is noted in clinical interviews when these patients have difficulty organizing their thoughts, are vague, or wander into irrelevance such as the shoes certain people prefer (Millon, 1981). They appear to have little ability for introspection or ability to articulate important aspects of interpersonal relationships. Their goals are vague and appear to be indecisive.

Affective Style. Their emotional or affective style is characterized as being humorless, cold, aloof, and unemotional. They appear to be indifferent to praise and criticism, and they lack spontaneity. Not surprisingly, their rapport and ability to empathize with others are poor. In short, they have a constricted range of affective response.

Attachment Style. Individuals with a dismissing attachment style are characterized by a sense of self that is worthy and positive as well as a low and negative evaluation of others that typically manifests as mistrust. Because they believe they are emotionally self-sufficient while others are emotionally unresponsive, they dismiss the need for friendship and contact with others. This dismissing attachment style is common in individuals with schizoid personality disorder (Lyddon & Sherry, 2001).

Optimal DSM-IV-TR Criterion. Of all the stated DSM-IV-TR criteria for schizoid personality disorder, one criterion has been found to be the most useful in diagnosing this disorder. The belief is that by beginning with this criterion, the clinician can test for the presence or absence of the criterion and quickly diagnose the personality disorder (Allnutt & Links, 1996). The "optimal criterion" for this disorder is "neither desires nor enjoys close relationships, including being part of a family." The following case examples further illustrate the differences between schizoid personality disorder (Mr. Y.) and schizoid personality style (Mr. P.)

Case Study: Schizoid Personality Disorder

Mr. Y. is a 20-year-old freshman who met with the director of the introductory psychology course program to arrange an individual assignment in lieu of participation in the small-group research project course requirement. He told the course director that because of a daily 2-hour commute each way, he "wouldn't be available for the research project," and that he "wasn't really interested in psychology and was only taking the course because it was required." Upon further inquiry, Mr. Y. disclosed that he preferred to commute and live at home with his mother, even though he had the financial resources to live on campus. He admitted he had no close friends or social contacts and preferred being a "loner." He had graduated from high school with a B average but did not date or participate in extracurricular activities, except the electronics club. He was a computer science major and "hacking" was his only hobby. Mr. Y.'s affect was somewhat flattened, he appeared to have no sense of humor, and he failed to respond to attempts by the course director to make contact through humor. There was no indication of a thought or perceptual disorder. The course director arranged for an individual project for the student.

Case Study: Schizoid Personality Style

Mr. P. is 28 years old and is a 6-year veteran of the U.S. Department of the Interior. He has been a forest ranger since graduating from college. While in school he excelled in the classroom but was considered a loner by others. Unlike most of his classmates, he did not pledge a fraternity, feeling he really needed to live in a place that was quiet and distraction-free. Mr. P. enjoys his work and has received commendations for it. A year ago, he was offered a promotion to field supervisor, which he turned down since it would have required him to have regular phone or face-to-face contact with up to ten forest rangers who would report to him. Mr. P. had a college friend who he roomed with for 3 years and he continues to have occasional contact with this friend. Mr. P. has never considered marriage or a family, so he has little interest in dating.

DSM-IV-TR Description and Criteria

The DSM-IV-TR description and criteria for schizoid personality disorder are in Table 10.2.

FORMULATIONS OF SCHIZOID PERSONALITY DISORDER

Psychodynamic Formulation

The inner world of schizoid individuals appears to be different than their outward appearance. Ahktar (1987) describes them as overtly detached, asexual, self-sufficient, and uninteresting, while covertly emotionally needy, exquisitely sensitive and vulnerable, creative, and acutely vigilant. These stark differences represent a splitting or fragmentation of different self-representations that remain integrated. The result is identity diffusion.

Balint (1968) and Nachmani (1984) believe that their difficulty relating to others stems from a deficit—inadequate mothering—rather than from an oedipal conflict. In short, these individuals base their decision to be isolative on the conviction that because they failed to receive maternal nurturance and support as infants, they cannot expect or attempt to receive any emotional

Table 10.2
DSM-IV-TR Criteria for Schizoid Personality Disorder (301.20)

A. A pervasive pattern of detachment from social relationships and a restricted range of expression of emotions in interpersonal settings, beginning by early adulthood and present in a variety of contexts, as indicated by at least four of the following:

(1) neither desires nor enjoys close relationships, including being part of a family
(2) almost always chooses solitary activities
(3) little, if any, interest in having sexual experiences with another person
(4) takes pleasure in few, if any, activities
(5) lacks close friends or confidants other than first-degree relatives
(6) appears indifferent to the praise or criticism of others
(7) emotional coldness, detachment, or flattened affectivity

B. Does not occur exclusively during the course of schizophrenia, a mood disorder with psychotic features, another psychotic disorder, or a pervasive developmental disorder, and is not due to the direct effects of a general medical condition.

Note: If criteria are met prior to the onset of schizophrenia, add "premorbid," e.g., "schizoid personality disorder (premorbid)."

Reprinted with permission from the *Diagnostic and Statistical Manual of Mental Disorders, Fourth Edition–Text Revision.* Copyright 2000. American Psychiatric Association.

supplies from subsequent significant figures. Fairburn (1954) views the isolation of schizoid individuals as a defense against a conflict between a wish to relate to others and a fear that their neediness will harm others. Thus, they vacillate between a fear of driving others away by their neediness and a fear that others will smother or consume them. Consequently, all relationships are experienced as dangerous and must be avoided.

Kellerman and Burry (1989) view this isolation and social distancing as a way of managing anxiety. Schizoid individuals are remote, cool, and aloof but not necessarily malicious toward others. Typically, schizoid individuals utilize the defenses of repression, suppression, isolation of fantasy affect, displacement, and compensation to ensure distance from others and to avoid anxiety.

Biosocial Formulation

Millon and Davis (1996) believe the schizoid personality is formed by an interaction of biogenic and environmental factors. Millon and Everly (1985) suggest that a proliferation of dopaminergic postsynaptic receptors in limbic and frontal cortical regions account for the unusual cognitive activity and inhibited emotional responses of schizoid individuals. Along with this excessive parasympathetic nervous system, dampening could account for their apathy, flattened affect, and underresponsiveness. Finally, Millon and Everly note that an ectomorphic—thin and frail—body type, which has been associated with shyness and introversion, is common among schizoid individuals.

Major environmental factors involve parental indifferences and fragmented communication patterns. Families of schizoid individuals are typically characterized by interpersonal reserve, formality, superficiality, and coldness. They tend to communicate in a fragmented, aborted, and circumstantial fashion. Not surprisingly, individuals raised in such environments are likely to be vague, abortive, and circumstantial in all their communications. These disjointed communication patterns tend to be confusing to others and foster misunderstanding, frustration, lack of tolerance, and hostility on the part of others. Schizoid individuals are prone to be isolative and come to believe that others do not understand them. Furthermore, these individuals are usually incapable of correcting the problem.

The schizoid disorder is perpetuated by social distancing, by having their social isolation reinforced, and by their cognitive and social insensitivity. Their infrequent social activities limit their ability to grow, and their social isolation is frequently reinforced by others who ostracize isolative individuals. Furthermore, their social and cognitive insensitivity tends to oversimplify and make boring a world that is so rich and diverse to others.

Cognitive-Behavioral Formulation

From the cognitive therapy perspective, the schizoid personality is characterized by a pattern of certain assumptions, automatic thoughts, and cognitive distortions. The basic assumptions of schizoid individuals involve their view of self and others. They tend to view themselves as loners and as self-sufficient of others, and they view the world and others as intrusive. Their core beliefs include: "I am basically alone"; "Relationships are messy and undesirable because they interfere with my freedom of action." Subsequently, their primary interpersonal strategy is to distance themselves from others.

Beck and Freeman (1990) note that schizoid individuals have difficulty identifying automatic beliefs. This is probably because emotions are related to thoughts and schizoids have limited emotions. Nonetheless, their automatic thoughts reflect their preference for solitude and perception of being detached observers of life: "I'd rather do it myself"; "I prefer to be alone"; and "Keep your distance." Finally, neither Freeman et al. (1990) nor Beck and Freeman (1990) describe cognitive distortions unique to the schizoid personality.

From the behavioral perspective, neither Turkat nor Maisto (Turkat & Maisto, 1985; Turkat, 1990) offer a formulation for this disorder. They admit interviewing individuals who met criteria for this disorder, but they were unable to offer a generic behavioral formulation.

Interpersonal Formulation

According to Benjamin (1996), persons diagnosed with schizoid personality disorders were likely to have been raised in a home that was orderly and formal. While these children's physical and educational needs were met, there was little warmth, play, or social and emotional interaction within the family or elsewhere. The schizoid individual would have modeled social isolation and colorless, unemotional functioning. Such identification with withdrawn parents leads schizoid individuals to expect little and give little. Though they may be socialized for work, they are not predisposed to intimate contact, and prefer fantasy and solitary advocating instead. In short, they have neither fears of nor desires about others. Underdeveloped in social awareness and skills, they can still meet social role expectations as employees or even as parents. They may be married but do not develop close, intimate relationships.

Integrative Formulation

The following integrative formulation may be helpful in understanding how the schizoid personality develops and is maintained. Biologically, the schizoid personality is likely to have had a passive and anhedonic infantile pattern and temperament. Millon (1981) suggested that this pattern results, in part, from increased dopaminergic postsynaptic limbic and frontal lobe receptor activity. Constitutionally, the schizoid is likely to be characterized by an ectomorphic body type (Sheldon & Stevens, 1942).

Psychologically, schizoids view themselves, others, the world, and life's purpose in terms of the following themes. They view themselves by some variant of the theme: "I'm a misfit from life, so I don't need anybody. I am indifferent to everything." For schizoid personalities, the world and others are viewed by some variant of the theme: "Life is a difficult place and relating to people can be harmful." As such, they are likely to conclude, "Therefore, trust nothing and keep a distance from others and you won't get hurt." Adler (1956) and Slavik, Sperry, and Carlson (1992) further describe these lifestyle dynamics. The most common defense mechanism utilized by them is intellectualization.

Socially, predictable patterns of parenting and environmental factors can be noted for schizoids. Parenting style is usually characterized by indifference and impoverishment. It is as if the parental injunction was: "You're a misfit," or, "Who are you? What do you want?" Their family pattern is characterized by fragmented communications and rigid, unemotional responsiveness. Because of these conditions, schizoids are grossly undersocialized and develop few if any interpersonal relating and coping skills. This schizoid pattern is confirmed, reinforced, and perpetuated by the following individual and systems factors: Believing themselves to be misfits, they shun social activity. This, plus social insensitivity, leads to reinforcement of social isolation and further confirmation of the schizoid style (Sperry & Mosak, 1996).

ASSESSMENT OF SCHIZOID PERSONALITY DISORDER

Several sources of information are useful in establishing a diagnosis and treatment plan for personality disorders. Observation, collateral information, and psychological testing are important adjuncts to the patient's self-report in the clinical interview.

Table 10.3
Characteristics of Schizoid Personality Disorder

Triggering Event	Close interpersonal relationships.
Behavioral Style	Slow and monotonous speech; lethargic, inattentive, nonspontaneous.
Interpersonal Style	Minimal "human" interests and friends; "cold fish"; fades into social background; rarely responsive to others' feelings or actions; isolative and content to remain aloof.
Cognitive Style	Cognitively distracted in thinking and communications; easily derailed and tangential; absent-minded; minimally introspective.
Feeling Style	Aloof, indifferent.
Temperament	Passive and anhedonic infantile pattern.
Attachment Style	Dismissing.
Parental Injunction	"Who are you? What do you want?"
Self-View	"I'm a misfit from life, so I don't need anybody." "I'm indifferent to everything."
Worldview	"Life is a difficult place and can be harmful. Therefore, trust nothing and keep a distance from others so that you won't get hurt."
Maladaptive Schemas	Social isolation; emotional deprivation; defectiveness; subjugation; undeveloped self.
Optimal DSM-IV-TR Criteria	Neither desires nor enjoys close relationships, including being part of a family.

This section briefly describes some characteristic observations that the clinician makes and the nature of the rapport likely to develop in initial encounters with specific personality-disordered individuals. Characteristic response patterns on various objective (i.e., MMPI-2 and MCMI-III) and projective tests (i.e., Rorschach and TAT) are also described.

Interview Behavior and Rapport

Interviewing schizoid personality–disordered individuals can seem like an exercise in futility given their pervasive emotional withdrawal. They express little or no emotionality even when talking about anxious or depressed feelings. More intelligent individuals with this disorder may complain about anhedonia and may even use the label "depression" but seldom report associated sadness or guilt. Since emotional warmth is absent, it is difficult to judge whether problems or concerns are central to them. Typically, they have one-word or short phrase answers to all questions. Neither open-ended questions, structured questions, nor other interview strategies will change the flow of information or expression of affect. Unlike paranoid individuals, this restricted verbal and emotional expression is not due to self-protectiveness but rather to emotional and mental emptiness. Rapport usually reflects a willingness to reveal symptoms, problems, and innermost feelings. Since these patients are so impoverished, rapport and engagement with them may seem impossible. Long periods of silence are not uncommon. If these patients return for sessions, it usually means they are "connecting" insofar as they know how. Thus, the clinician's persistence, patience, and tolerance for limited verbal interchange may have a therapeutic effect (Othmer & Othmer, 2002).

Psychological Testing Data

The Minnesota Multiphase Personality Inventory (MMPI-2), the Millon Clinical Multiaxial Inventory (MCMI-II), the Rorschach Psychodiagnostic Test, and the Thematic Apperception Test (TAT) can be useful in diagnosing schizoid personality disorder as well as the schizoid personality style or trait. On the MMPI-2, a normal profile is common for reasonably well-integrated schizoid individuals. In such instances, O (social introversion) may be elevated (Lachar, 1974). As these individuals become distressed, a rise in F (frequency), 2 (depression), and 8 (schizophrenia) is likely. Occasionally, a 1–8 (hypochondriasis-schizophrenia) "normadic" profile is noted wherein interpersonal attraction is limited (Graham, 2000).

On the MCMI-II, an elevation on scale 1 (schizoid) with low scores on 4 (histrionic), 5 (narcissistic), and N (bipolar-manic) are likely (Choca & Denburg, 1997).

On the Rorschach, a high percentage of A (animal) and few C (color) responses are likely. The overall record tends to be constricted and certain blots may be rejected. Reaction time to many of the cards may be slow. There may be a higher experience potential than experience actual, and M (human movement) production will be high relative to the overall quality of the protocol (Exner, 1986).

On the TAT, constricted response along with a blindness of theme is common. So also is an impoverished portrayal of story characters (Bellak, 1997).

TREATMENT APPROACHES AND INTERVENTIONS

Treatment Considerations

Included in the differential diagnosis of schizoid personality disorder are the following Axis II personality disorders: avoidant personality disorder, schizotypal personality disorder, and dependent personality disorder. The most common Axis I syndromes likely to be associated with schizoid personality disorder are depersonalization disorder, bipolar and unipolar disorders, obsessive-compulsive disorder, hypochondriasis, schizophreniform, and disorganized and catatonic schizophrenias.

Schizoid personalities rarely volunteer for treatment unless decompensation is present. However, they may accept treatment if someone, such as a family member, demands it. To date, no controlled treatment outcome studies have been completed for this personality disorder (Crits-Christoph & Barber, 2002).

Individual Psychotherapy

Some form of individual psychotherapy is indicated for the majority of schizoid patients. Whether the clinician chooses an active confrontative approach, or a cognitive restructuring and social skills training approach, or one that is more supportive depends on a number of factors including a patient's psychological mindedness, resilience, and treatment expectations, the clinician's therapeutic repertoire, and resources for treatment. This section briefly describes the psychodynamic, cognitive-behavioral, and interpersonal approaches to individual therapy.

Psychodynamic Psychotherapy Approach

Because the dynamic understanding of both the schizoid and schizotypal personality is inherently similar, Gabbard (1990, 1994) proposes that their treatment should be similar. Schizoid patients can be treated effectively with dynamically oriented psychotherapy, both expressive and supportive, depending on their level of functioning and treatment readiness (Gabbard, 1994). The basis for dynamic treatment is not interpretation of conflict but rather internalization of a therapeutic relationship (Stone, 1985).

Essentially, the clinician's task is to meet the patient's frozen internal object relations by providing a correct emotional experience. The schizoid's style of relatedness results from inadequacies in early relationships with parental figures. As a result, these patients distance themselves from others. Therapy must therefore provide a new relationship for internalization (Gabbard, 1994).

Supportive Therapy. Since their basic mode of functioning is nonrelational, they find the task of therapy very challenging and difficult. Not surprisingly, they respond to the challenge with silence and emotional distancing. Clinicians need to adopt a permissive, accepting attitude, and must be exceedingly patient with these individuals. It is more helpful to understand silence as a nonverbal form of relating rather than as treatment resistance. By listening with a third ear, the clinician can learn much about their patients. Through projective identification they will evoke certain responses in the clinician that contain valuable diagnostic information regarding their inner world (Gabbard, 1989). Dealing effectively with countertransference issues is critical in working with schizoid patients. Accepting silent nonrelatedness is foreign to the clinician's psychological predisposition and training. Thus, when silence is prolonged, the clinician must guard against acting out and projecting his or her own self- and object representations onto the patient. Accepting the silence and refraining from interpreting it legitimizes the patient's private, noncommunicative core self. And it may be the only viable technique for building a therapeutic alliance (Gabbard, 1989).

The proper pace and depth of therapy is controversial. Bonime (1959) advocates an active, confrontative approach, whereas Gabbard (1990) and others maintain that a more restrained approach is more respecting and less threatening for these patients.

Supportive techniques can be utilized to encourage the lower-functioning schizoid to become more active. For example, the patient is first urged to engage in activities where others are present, but where the patient's participation is minimal—for example, a sports event. If some level of comfort is achieved, further involvement may be encouraged. Involvement in a computer club, travel tour, or aerobics class is more risky than attending a sports event, but less risky than a social gathering or dance class. Kantor (1992) advocates the techniques of "productive substitution" and "modification total push" with these therapeutic tasks. In productive substitution, the clinician suggests gratifying replacements for what is missing from the patient's life. Thus, relationships with peers in a therapy group substitute for the unmarried patient. Using modified total push, the clinician urges the patient to become more socially active. Suggestions are presented tentatively to test the patient's limits. Problems encountered are brought back into therapy and discussed. Treatment goals and outcomes may be quite limited: the patient may eventually work, albeit in isolation (e.g., as a night watchperson), may have one or two social friends, and possibly even a long-term relationship with someone who is willing to remain a distant companion (Kantor, 1992).

Long-Term vs. Short-Term Dynamic Therapy. Decisions about the type and frequency of dynamic therapy should be based on the patient's level of functioning and motivation and readiness for treatment. Higher-functioning schizoid patients who exhibit some depressive symptoms or some capacity for empathy and emotional warmth tend to have better outcomes in dynamic psychotherapy (Stone, 1983).

Those patients who are highly motivated for exploratory psychotherapy can make dramatic gains in intense long-term treatment of two to three sessions per week over several years. On the other hand, long-term supportive psychotherapy is indicated for the majority of schizotypal patients who present with major ego deficits and personal eccentricities. The goal of such treatment is improved adaptive functioning in day-to-day living. The frequency of sessions is one to two times per week for the majority of patients (Stone, 1989).

Short-term dynamic therapy is indicated for crisis issues and situational difficulties related to job or personal life. It may also serve as follow-up for a previous course of long-term psychotherapy. Not surprisingly, there are no reports of short-term dynamic individual treatment as curative intervention.

Cognitive-Behavioral Therapy Approach

Beck, Freeman, and Associates (1990) describe the cognitive therapy approach to working with schizoid personality–disordered individuals. Since schizoid individuals tend to have limited motivation for social interaction, a principal treatment goal is to establish or increase positions of social interaction, as well as reduce social isolation. These individuals enter treatment largely because of symptomatic Axis I disorders rather than to alter their manner of relating to others. Thus, the initial goal of treatment is a collaborative focus on presenting problems. As this occurs, the therapist can be commenting on the individual's relational patterns, discussing their advantages and disadvantages, and how these patterns affect the presenting problem.

The collaborative therapeutic relationship can itself serve as a prototype for other interpersonal relationships, as well as a basis for increasing the individual's range and frequency of interactions outside sessions. After rapport has been established, the therapist can point out the characteristic interaction pattern as well as give feedback on how this impacts others. As these individuals develop a greater awareness and understanding of interpersonal relating, they are guided in learning social skills and practicing them both within and outside the sessions. Given their lack of expressiveness, routinely soliciting feedback on their level of anxiety should reduce the likelihood of premature termination. Unlike work with other personality disorders where considerable therapeutic leverage and motivation for change are available, relatively little of either is likely with schizoid individuals besides reason. Accordingly, Freeman et al. (1990) advise therapists to clearly present the rationale for therapy, reasons for acting differently, the advantages and disadvantages of changing behavior, and the concrete gains possible. Presumably this strategy can induce these individuals to change.

Beck et al. (1990) indicate that the following techniques are effective with schizoid individuals. The dysfunctional thought record is not only useful in challenging dysfunctional automatic thoughts but also in identifying a variety of affects and their subtle gradation in intensity, as well as indicating the reactions of others. Teaching social skills is best done directly through role-playing, in vivo exposure, and homework assignments. Helping these individuals become more attentive to positive emotions and experiencing them can be facilitated by guided discovery. For example, as these individuals are helped to recognize their overgeneralized view of others—"I don't like people"—they can learn to be specific about things they do not like, as well as things they do like about others.

As treatment needs termination, the matter of relapse prevention is discussed. Beck et al. (1990) report that schizoid individuals are very likely to relapse into an isolative lifestyle after termination. Thus, they suggest maintaining contact with these individuals through booster sessions. Finally, although treatment with these individuals can be difficult, with persistence it is possible to improve their social skills, increase their frequency of social interaction, and decrease their "strangeness." However, the therapist should anticipate that schizoid individuals are likely to retain some distance and passivity in interpersonal relations after planned termination.

Structured Skill Treatment Interventions.   While research shows that medication can modulate or normalize dysregulated behaviors, a similar modulating effect has also been noted for social skills training (Lieberman, DeRisi, & Mueser, 1989). Thus, it appears that social skills training is a relatively potent bottom-up treatment strategy for normalizing limbic–system mediated behaviors that reflect specific skill deficits in personality-disordered individuals. When such skills deficits are present, Sperry (1999) contends that structured skill training interventions is a potent and effective strategy in treatment. Various structured intervention strategies for modifying a personality-disordered individual's affective, behavioral, and cognitive temperament styles are relevant for treatment of schizoid personality disorder (Sperry, 1999).

Schema Therapy. Schema therapy is an elaboration of cognitive therapy that has been developed by Young (1999) and Young et al. (2003) specifically for personality disorders and other difficult individual and couples problems. Schema therapy involves identifying maladaptive schemas and planning specific strategies and interventions. Four main strategies are cognitive, experiential, behavioral, and the therapeutic relationship itself. Cognitive restructuring, particularly modification of maladaptive schemas, is an important cognitive strategy, but is typically combined with imagery exercises, empathic confrontation, homework assignments, and "limited reparenting" (i.e., a form of corrective emotional experience; Young, 1999).

Maladaptive schemas typically associated with schizoid personality disorder include *social isolation*—that is, the belief that one is alienated, different from others, or not part of any group; *defectiveness*—that is, the belief that one is defective, bad, unwanted, or inferior in important respects; *emotional deprivation*—that is, the belief that one's desire for emotional support will not be met by others; *subjugation*—that is, the belief that one's desires, needs, and feelings must be suppressed in order to meet the needs of others and avoid retaliation or criticism; and *undeveloped self*—that is, the belief that one must be emotionally close with others at the expense of full individuation or normal social development (Bernstein, 2002).

Interpersonal Approach

There is very little in the literature about treatment of this disorder from an interpersonal perspective. For example, Benjamin (1996) provides no discussion of treatment goals or strategies for schizoid personality disorder.

Group Therapy

Schizoid patients can profit from group therapy, particularly dynamic group therapy (Azima, 1983). Group therapy offers these patients a socialization experience involving exposure to and feedback from others in a safe, controlled environment. It is an environment in which new parenting can occur. Here group members can function as a reconstructed family and provide a corrective emotional experience that can counterbalance the schizoid's negative and frightening internal objects (Appel, 1974). As their worst fears are not realized and they feel accepted, these patients gradually become more comfortable with others.

From an object relations perspective, Leszcz (1989) contends the group's function is as a holding environment that provides an opportunity for these patients to be initially involved in a "nonrelated" way while slowly building trust. They do not have to leave their cocoon of self-sufficiency but can observe how others relate in the group, how feelings make a difference, and how to deal with negative affects. The wise group leader will permit this nonrelated position until the patient is better able to tolerate the ambiguities of the group.

From a systems perspective, Bogdanoff and Elbaum (1978) maintain that the schizoid's isolation is not simply due to a fragile ego but is also a function of the group's need to maintain that isolation. So, while the schizoid patient may provoke the group to make him or her talk, at other times the group effectively silences the schizoid by ragefulness or blaming that frightens him or her. Essentially, the schizoid is caught in an interpersonal trap called a "role lock." Successful group interaction can occur only when the role lock is broken. If the group is avoiding the schizoid, the therapeutic task is to focus the group's attention on the role lock. The aim is for group members to reveal their contribution to the lock and to relieve pressure on the locked member; and for the locked member to reveal how he or she sees the group process in isolating himself or herself.

From an interpersonal perspective, Yalom (1995) discusses other useful interventions for dealing with role lock. The schizoid is helped to differentiate responses to different group members, to take seriously feelings in the here-and-now, to become more aware of specific avoidance strategies, and to become more aware of bodily response. Yalom insists that these goals and strategies are preferable to cathartic methods, which can drive the schizoid from the group. He cautions that this process is slow and that patience is essential for the clinician.

Finally, there seems to be a consensus of sorts that heterogeneous groups are preferable to homogeneous groups (Leszcz, 1989; Bogdanoff & Elbaum, 1978; Slavik, Sperry, & Carlson, 1992). Spotnitz (1975) suggests that the schizoid patient should be referred to a group that is homogeneous in terms of global functioning but heterogeneous in terms of personality types.

Marital and Family Therapy

Schizoid patients, particularly males, usually do not marry and seldom become self-supporting. They may reside with and become dependent on their families. This can result in a vicious cycle in which limited motivation for so-cial contacts and a job or career leads to interferences and bitterness on the part of the family, which is followed by lowered self-esteem and an even greater reluctance to leave home (Stone, 1989).

Clinicians working with the schizoid patient still living at home often confront family tension, impatience, and discord arising from differences be-tween parental expectations and the patient's capacities and motivation. Family therapy can be quite effective in addressing these expectational differences, discord, and impatience (Anderson, 1983). Shapiro (1982) describes how the family therapist can function to contain such displaced and projected affects and impulses, and acknowledge, bear, work through, and redirect them. Fam-ily treatment can also help family members reestablish more functional com-munication patterns between themselves and the schizoid patients.

McCormack (1989) describes a common marital constellation in which schizoid individuals marry borderline individuals. In discussing the treatment of the schizoid spouse, McCormack indicates that the core of the schizoid's difficulty is an overwhelming fear of attachments. Insecurity arises from esca-lating aggression because their dependency needs lead to marital dissatisfac-tion and discord. Schizoid spouses experience their love as lethal, and then abort awareness of these feelings and dependency needs as a defense against them. Thus, they develop and maintain relationships in which they are never fully involved.

The treatment of the schizoid spouse emphasizes clarification and care-ful interpretation and deemphasizes confrontation. Exploration should involve the schizoid's narcissistic vulnerability, legitimization of needs, acknowledg-ment of the potential risks and gains attached to pursuing them, and the "schiz-oid compromise." McCormack describes the schizoid compromise as a means of maintaining relationships that require limited emotional involvement, at the cost of limiting personality development. The clinician needs to acknowl-edge to these patients that this compromise has been adaptive but is a stage through which they must pass before facing their fear of genuine, healthy relationships.

Schizoid spouses tend to treat others as they fear being treated, which is frustrating to those wanting an intimate relationship with them. In conjoint sessions, the clinician helps both spouses to see that each suffers from diffi-culties that are both similar to and different from each other's, and that al-though these difficulties are fostered in the marriage relationship, they also exist independent of it.

Couples therapy with the schizoid-borderline relationship may require referral of one spouse for individual therapy, the use of medication, or hospi-talization. Long-term couples treatment is usually necessary if the goal is to foster separation and autonomy, increased marital satisfaction, and harmony.

Medication

To date, there have been relatively few controlled pharmacological trials for schizoid personality disorder. This contrasts markedly with schizotypal personality disorder where some controlled trials have been reported (Koenigsberg, Woo-Ming, & Siever, 2002).

Stone (1989) notes that schizoid patients show the target symptoms like anxiety and depression for which common psychotropic agents are indicated. Their basic temperamental traits of aloofness and uncommunicativeness tend to be nonresponsive to current medications.

Because of its apparent overlap with avoidant personality disorder and schizotypal disorder, Liebowitz et al. (1986) suggested that the clinician consider two potential target symptoms for pharmacotherapy. Because hypersensitivity to rejection and criticism—a criterion for avoidant disorder—may be related to the schizoid patient's social isolation and aloofness, a trial of a monoamine oxidase inhibitor or a serotonin reuptake blocker has some efficacy with this target symptom. Fluoxetine (Coccaro, 1993) is another choice. Furthermore, because the schizoid and schizotypal personality disorders lie on the schizophrenic spectrum, and because low-dose neuroleptics have had some efficacy with mixed personality disorder groups that included schizoid patients (Reyntjens, 1972; Barnes, 1977), they may have some place in the treatment of the schizoid personality (Liebowitz et al., 1986).

Medication Protocol. For individuals with psychotic-like symptoms, consider starting with an atypical antipsychotic, such as risperidone, at one-fourth to one-half the usual topic range maintenance dose for psychosis. If there is no response, incrementally increase the dosage. If there is no response at the top dose, switch to another atypical. If there is a partial response, consider adding divalproex. Clozapine should be considered only in refractory individuals (Reich, 2002).

Combined and Integrated Treatment Approaches

Schizoid patients tend to avoid mental health professionals just as they avoid relationships in general. When they do present for help, often at the urging of their family, they have a tendency to prematurely terminate therapy (Stone, 1989). Thus, there is only a small window of opportunity to engage these patients in the therapeutic process. Combining treatment modalities and integrating treatment approaches can facilitate both commitment to treatment and positive treatment outcomes.

Gabbard (1994) advocates combining dynamic group therapy with dynamic individual psychotherapy as the treatment of choice for the majority of schizoid patients. However, he cautions that many of these patients will recoil at the recommendation for group therapy, even feeling betrayed by their clinician. Thus, Gabbard suggests that prior to making a group referral, fantasies about the group experience need to be explored and worked through. Stone (1989) also recommends combining individual and group modalities. However, he proposes a developmental approach in which the patient first forms a stable dyadic relationship with the clinician, then proceeds to group therapy with the same clinician. In both instances the combined treatment is concurrent.

As noted earlier, McCormack (1989) makes the case for combining marital therapy with individual therapy, particularly when there is considerable splitting and projective identification. Combining family therapy and individual therapy has advantages, particularly if the schizoid patient is financially dependent on the family and/or resides with the family. Family can greatly influence the patient's continuation in individual and/or group treatment.

Slavik, Sperry, and Carlson (1992) advocate both combining treatment modalities and integrating treatment approaches. They indicate the utility of concurrent individual and group treatment. And they describe how an Adlerian approach can be integrated with an object-relations theory approach, social skills training, hypnosis, and psychodrama depending on the patient's style, needs, and expectations. These authors believe that schizoid personality disorder is eminently treatable and that these patients are largely untreatable because clinicians have not found sufficient ways to engage and encourage them in the change process.

CHAPTER 11

Schizotypal Personality Disorder

Schizotypal personality disorder is part of the odd cluster of DSM-IV personality disorders. It is the first of the personality disorders to be defined because of its genetic relationship to schizophrenia. The genesis of this disorder came from concerns of a DSM-III committee that the definitions of borderline and schizoid personality disorders were too broad and diffuse. The borderline disorder originally was to include both affective instability and schizophrenic-like symptoms. Similarly, the schizoid personality was broadly defined to characterize individuals with enduring psychotic-like traits. As a result, schizotypal personality disorder was designated to be distinct from both borderline and schizoid personality disorders.

DSM-III designated eight criteria. Essentially, the only change in DSM-III-R was to add another criterion: odd and eccentric behavior or appearance. Considerable controversy about the overlap between schizotypal and avoidant personality disorder regarding interpersonal relations was lodged at both DSM-III and DSM-III-R criteria. Between DSM-III-R and DSM-IV, compelling evidence demonstrated a link between schizotypal personality disorder and schizophrenia in terms of phenomenological, genetic, biological, outcome, and treatment response characteristics. As a result, serious consideration was given to shifting the diagnosis from the Axis II to the Axis I category of

239

schizophrenia and other psychotic disorders (Siever et al., 1991). However, the disorder has remained in Axis II of DSM-IV but with some significant modification in criteria. Now, psychotic-like symptoms must be persistent rather than episodic as in borderline personality disorder. Furthermore, the qualification that severe social anxiety does not decrease with familiarity further distinguished it from avoidant personality. Despite change in DSM-IV criteria, many psychodynamically oriented clinicians are not convinced that schizoid and schizotypal personality disorders are really different and consider them inherently similar (Gabbard, 2000). Taking a broader view than DSM-IV-TR, Miller et al. (2001) describe some dimensional alternatives to diagnostic classification for schizotypal personality disorder.

Research suggests that like individuals with schizophrenia, individuals with schizotypal personality disorder have similar cognitive and neurobiological deficits (Cadenhead et al., 2002). Cognitive deficits in those meeting diagnostic criteria for schizotypal personality disorder are noted in working memory, verbal learning, and cognitive tasks with high context dependence (Siever et al., 2002). Furthermore, just as individuals with schizophrenia evidence longstanding social deficits, so too do individuals with schizotypal personality disorder. Waldeck and Miller (2000) found specific social skill deficits in labeling emotions, displaying socially competent behaviors, and selecting socially appropriate behaviors in those with this personality disorder; these deficits are also noted in those with schizophrenia.

Because of these deficits, these individuals tend to experience deterioration in social and occupational functioning. A study of occupational functioning among a nonclinical population of individuals experiencing mild schizotypal symptoms but not meeting criteria for the personality disorder revealed some surprising findings. The study found that otherwise healthy individuals with mild schizotypal symptoms showed severe difficulties with occupational functioning (Thaker, Adami, & Gold, 2001).

Prevalence data show that this disorder occurs in 3 percent of the general population. There are no current data on the prevalence of this disorder in the clinical population.

This chapter will describe the characteristic features of schizotypal personality disorder and its related style. Five clinical formulations of the disorder and psychological assessment indicators are highlighted. A variety of treatment approaches, modalities, and intervention strategies are also described.

DESCRIPTION OF SCHIZOTYPAL PERSONALITY DISORDER

Schizotypal personality disorder can be recognized by the following descriptors and characteristics: style vs. disorder, triggering event, behavioral style, interpersonal style, cognitive style, affective style, attachment style, and optimal criterion.

Style vs. Disorder. The schizotypal personality can be thought of as spanning a continuum from healthy to pathological, wherein the schizotypal personality style is closer to the healthy end and the schizotypal personality is on the pathological end. Table 11.1 compares and contrasts schizotypal personality style and disorder.

Triggering Event. The typical situation, circumstance, or event that most likely triggers or activates the characteristic maladaptive response of schizotypal

Table 11.1
Comparison of Schizotypal Personality Style and Disorder

Personality Style	Personality Disorder
Tend to be tuned into and sustained by their own feelings and belief	Ideas of reference; suspicious or paranoid ideation; inappropriate or constricted affect
Keen observation of others and are particularly sensitive to how others react to them	Excessive social anxiety, e.g., extreme discomfort in social situations involving unfamiliar people
Tend to be drawn to abstract and speculative thinking	Odd beliefs or magical thinking, influencing behavior and inconsistent with subculture with norms, e.g., superstitiousness, belief in clairvoyance, telepathy or "sixth sense"; "others can feel my feelings"
Receptive and interested in the occult, the extrasensory, and the supernatural	Unusual perceptual experiences, e.g., illusions, sensing the presence of a force or person not actually there (e.g., "I felt as if my dead mother were in the room with me")
Tend to be indifferent to social convention, and lead interesting and unusual lifestyles	Odd or eccentric behavior or appearance, e.g., unkempt, unusual mannerisms, talks to self; odd speech (without loosening of association or incoherently, e.g., speech that is impoverished, digressive, vague, or inappropriately abstract)
Usually are self-directed and independent, requiring few close relationships	No close friends or confidants (or only one) other than first-degree relatives

personality disorder (Othmer & Othmer, 2002), as noted in behavioral, interpersonal, cognitive, and feeling styles, is "close interpersonal relationships."

Behavioral Style. Behaviorally, schizotypals are noted for their eccentric, erratic, and bizarre mode of functioning. Their speech is markedly peculiar without being incoherent. Occupationally, they are inadequate, either quitting or being fired from jobs after short periods of time. Typically, they become drifters, moving from job to job and town to town. They tend to avoid enduring responsibilities and in the process lose touch with a sense of social propriety.

Interpersonal Style. Interpersonally, they are loners with few if any friends. Their solitary pursuits and social isolation may be the result of intense social anxiety that may be expressed with apprehensiveness. This apprehensiveness does not diminish with familiarity and is associated with paranoid features rather than negative self-appraisal. If married, their style of superficial and peripheral relating often leads to separation and divorce in a relatively short period of time. Their lives tend to be marginal, and they gravitate toward jobs that are below their capacity or demand little interaction with others.

Cognitive Style. The cognitive style of schizotypals is described as scattered and ruminative, and is characterized by cognitive slippage. Presentations of superstitiousness, telepathy, and bizarre fantasies are characteristic. They may describe vague ideas of reference and recurrent illusions of depersonalizing, derealizing experiences without the experience of delusions of reference, or auditory or visual hallucinations.

Affective Style. Their affective style is described as cold, aloof, and unemotional with constricted affect. They can be humorless and difficult individuals to engage in conversation probably because of their general suspicious and mistrustful nature. In addition, they are hypersensitive to real or imagined slights.

Attachment Style. Individuals with an other-view that is negative and a self-view that vacillates between positive and negative exhibit a composite fearful–dismissing style of attachment. They tend to view themselves as special and entitled but are also mindful of their need for others who can potentially hurt them. Accordingly, they use others to meet their needs while being wary and dismissive of them. This fearful–dismissing attachment style is common in individuals with schizotypal personality disorder.

Optimal DSM-IV-TR Criterion. Of all the stated DSM-IV-TR criteria for schizotypal personality disorder, one criterion has been found to be the most useful in diagnosing this disorder. The belief is that by beginning with this criterion, the clinician can test for the presence or absence of the criterion and quickly diagnose the personality disorder (Allnutt & Links, 1996). The optimal criterion for this disorder is "odd thinking and speech: behavior or appearance that is odd, eccentric, or peculiar." The following two case examples further illustrate the differences between schizotypal personality disorder (Ms. S) and schizotypal personality style (Belinda S.).

Case Study: Schizotypal Personality Disorder

Ms. S. is a 41-year-old single female who was referred to a community mental health clinic by her mother because she has no interests, friends, or outside activities and is considered by neighbors to be an "odd duck." Her father recently retired, and because of a limited pension, the parents are having difficulty in making ends meet. Ms. S. has been living with them for the past 8 years after having been laid off from an assembly line job she had held for about 10 years. The patient readily admits she prefers to be alone but denies that this is a problem for her. She believes that her mother is concerned about her because of what might happen to her after her parents die. Ms. S. is an only child who graduated from high school with average grades but was never involved in extracurricular activities. She has never dated and mentioned she had a female friend with whom she had not talked in 4 years. Since moving back with her parents, she stays in her room preoccupied with books about astrology and charting her astrological forecast. On examination, she is an alert, somewhat uncooperative female appearing older than her stated age, with moderately disheveled hair and clothing. Her speech is monotonal and deliberate. She makes poor eye contact with the examiner. Her thinking is vague and tangential, and she expresses a belief that her fate lay in "the stars." She denies specific delusions or perceptual abnormalities. Ms. S.'s affect is constricted except for one episode of anger when she thought the therapist was being critical.

Case Study: Schizotypal Personality Style

Belinda S. is a 37-year-old acquisitions editor for a large publisher. Her primary responsibility is to review proposals and manuscripts in science fiction and the occult to determine if her company should publish them. She finds her job fascinating and energizing, particularly since her boss has allowed her to work from home four days out of five. She has great difficulty in working a typical 9 to 5 workday as she prefers to sleep days and work at night. When reading a submitted manuscript she literally tries to put herself into the plot by imagining herself as the hero or heroine and enhances the effect by donning appropriate clothing, burning incense, and putting on suitable background music. Mark N. is her "soul mate" rather than a boyfriend. They don't actually date—he lives in another city—but spend long hours on the phone and "let their spirits commune" the rest of the time. They meet each other at various science fiction, UFO, and Star Trek conventions throughout the year.

DSM-IV-TR Description and Criteria

In addition to having features similar to those of schizoid personality disorder and avoidant personality disorder, the schizotypal disorder is characterized by odd, eccentric behavior and peculiar thought content. Table 11.2 specifies the DSM-IV-TR description and criteria.

Table 11.2
DSM-IV-TR Criteria for Schizotypal Personality Disorder (301.22)

A.   A pervasive pattern of social and interpersonal deficits marked by acute discomfort with, and reduced capacity for, close relationships as well as by cognitive or perceptual distortions and eccentricities of behavior, beginning by early adulthood and present in a variety of contexts, as indicated by at least five of the following:

(1)   ideas of reference (excluding delusions of reference)
(2)   odd beliefs or magical thinking that influence behavior and are inconsistent with subcultural norms (e.g., superstitiousness, belief in clairvoyance, telepathy, or "sixth sense"; in children and adolescents, bizarre fantasies or preoccupations)
(3)   unusual perceptual experiences, including bodily illusions
(4)   odd thinking and speech (e.g., vague, circumstantial, metaphorical, overelaborate, or stereotyped)
(5)   suspiciousness or paranoid ideation
(6)   inappropriate or constricted affect
(7)   behavior or appearance that is odd, eccentric, or peculiar
(8)   lacks close friends or confidants other than first-degree relatives
(9)   excessive social anxiety that does not diminish with familiarity and tends to be associated with paranoid fears rather than negative judgments about self

B.   Does not occur exclusively during the course of schizophrenia, a mood disorder with psychotic features, another psychotic disorder, or a pervasive developmental disorder.

Note: If criteria are met prior to the onset of schizophrenia, add "premorbid," e.g., "schizotypal personality disorder (premorbid)."

Reprinted with permission from the *Diagnostic and Statistical Manual of Mental Disorders, Fourth Edition–Text Revision.* Copyright 2000. American Psychiatric Association.

FORMULATIONS OF SCHIZOTYPAL PERSONALITY DISORDER

Psychodynamic Formulation

Gunderson (1988) admits that little is known about the dynamics of schizotypal personality disorder. Gabbard (1990), among other psychoanalytically oriented writers, believes that except for a few symptoms suggestive of an attenuated form of schizophrenia, the schizoid personality and the schizotypal personality are inherently similar.

On the other hand, Kellerman and Burry (1989) believe that the dynamics of the two disorders are quite different. They classify schizoid personality disorder as an emotionally controlled character type—along with paranoid and obsessive-compulsive personality disorders—while they classify schizotypal personality disorder as an emotionally avoidant character type—along with borderline and avoidant personality disorders.

Kellerman and Burry believe that schizotypal individuals probably experienced consistent object contact in early childhood. However, their parents failed to provide sufficient emotional closeness and warmth and were probably punitive and critical. These factors probably account for the social hypersensitivity that serves as a defense against intense social anxiety noted in these individuals. Emotion is generally restricted, but when expressed, it tends to be inappropriate. These individuals typically utilize a wide variety of defense mechanisms including projection to externalize fear and anger, preoccupation with magic thinking and intellectualization to reduce emotional overstimulation, and hysterical denial to screen out undesirable social interactions in order to rationalize them.

Biosocial Formulation

The schizotypal personality is viewed by Millon and Everly (1985) as a syndromal continuation of schizoid and avoidant personality disorders. Thus, the etiological and developmental determinants of the schizotypal disorder will be similar as in schizoid and avoidant disorders, but in greater intensity or chronicity. Biogenic factors in the schizotypal schizoid variant include a genetic predisposition at least as reported in one study (Torgerson, 1984). Millon and Everly suggest that schizotypal-schizoid individuals have shown a passive infantile reaction pattern that probably initiated a sequence of impoverished infantile stimulations and consequent parental indifference. Further, they point out that a dampening of the ascending reticular activity system of the limbic system may result in the autostimulation and fantasy of these individuals. Environmentally, a cold and formal family environment combined with fragmented parental communication probably interact with biogenic factors to produce this personality pattern and disorder.

The background of schizotypal-avoidant individuals is somewhat different. Biogenically, these individuals are more likely to exhibit a "slow-to-warm-up" temperament (Thomas & Chess, 1977). These individuals tend to be apprehensive, tense, and do not adapt quickly to new situations. Such behavior can precipitate parental tension and derogation, which further aggravates this temperament. Socially, the developmental histories of these individuals typically show parental deprecation as well as peer and sibling humiliation, which results in interpersonal mistrust and lowered self-esteem. Continuation of these derogating and humiliating attitudes eventually leads to self-criticism and self-deprecation.

The schizotypal personality is self-perpetuated by social isolation, overprotection, and self-insulation. While social isolation and overprotectiveness have immediate benefits, in the long run they are counterproductive as they deprive these individuals with opportunities to develop social skills and they foster dependency. Furthermore, the individual's tendency toward self-insulation further perpetuates the spiral of cognitive and social deterioration that typifies this disorder (Millon & Davis, 1996).

Cognitive-Behavioral Formulation

Of all the personality disorders, cognitive therapy has the least to say about schizotypal personality disorder. Nevertheless, a characteristic pattern of automatic thoughts and cognitive distortions can be discerned. Beck and Freeman (1990) note four types of automatic thoughts utilized by schizotypal individuals: suspicious or paranoid thoughts, ideas of reference, magical thinking, and illusions. For example: "Is that person watching me"? "I know they are not going to like me"; I know what she's thinking"; and "I feel like the devil in him." Beck and Freeman indicate that oddities in cognition are the most striking feature of this disorder, and that these cognitive processes are further reflected in odd speech—circumstantial, vague, or overelaborate—as well as constricted, unappropriated affect. Typically, schizotypal individuals utilize the cognitive distortions of emotional reasoning—the belief that because they feel a negative emotion there must be a corresponding negative external situation—and personalization—the belief that they are responsible for external situations when it is not the case.

From a behavioral perspective, Turkat and Maisto (1985; Turkat, 1990) describe schizotypal personality disorder. However, they are unable to provide a generic behavioral formulation. Rather, Turkat (1990) notes that these patients are quite diverse in terms of behavioral presentation. This, of course, is consistent with Millon's (1981) and Millon and Everly's (1985) notion that the schizotypal personality is a decompensation of either the avoidant or schizoid personality.

Interpersonal Formulation

According to Benjamin (1996), persons diagnosed with schizotypal personality disorder likely had parents who punished them for allegedly inappropriate customary talking, while their parents did the same. Thus, the father who was rarely home might severely reprimand the child for not staying home. Essentially, such a parent modeled "mind reading," suggesting that even though not present, he "knew" something vitally important about the child. The adult consequence of this schizotypal modeling is that the individual imitates this pattern of "knowing" through special means such as telepathy, mind reading, or a "sixth" sense.

Parents were also likely to inappropriately rely on children for performance of household duties with undue threat and duress. Thus, these children learned that proper behavior and obedience could avert bad outcomes. The adult consequence is the paradoxical tendency to submit to rituals that bring control. Severe abuse, often involving invasion of these children's personal boundaries, is common. Furthermore, it also is likely that strong injunctions against leaving the home for peer play or other reasons were levied by the parents. Such prohibitions interfered with the development of social feelings and skills, and reinforced social isolation as well as fantasy and autism. Finally, there is a fear of being attacked and controlled by humiliation. These individuals are prone to hostile withdrawal and self-neglect. They believe they can magically influence—from a distance—circumstances and individuals through telepathy or ritual. Although they may be aware of their aggressive feelings, they usually constrain them.

Integrative Formulation

The following integrative formulation may be helpful in understanding how the Schizotypal Personality Disorder is likely to develop and be maintained.

This personality disorder is described by Millon (1981) as a syndromal extension or deterioration of the schizoid or avoidant personality disorders. As such, a useful procedure is to describe the biological and temperamental features of both of these subtypes. The schizoid subtype of a schizotypal personality is characterized with a passive infantile pattern, probably resulting from low autonomic nervous system reactivity and parental indifference that led to impoverished infantile stimulation. On the other hand, the avoidant subtype is characterized by the fearful infantile temperamental pattern (Millon, 1981). This probably resulted from the child's high autonomic nervous system reactivity combined with parental criticalness and deprecation that was further reinforced by sibling and peer deprecation. Both subtypes of the schizotypal personality have been noted to have impaired eye tracking motions, which is a characteristic shared with schizophrenic individuals.

Psychologically, the schizotypals view themselves, others, the world, and life's purpose in terms of the following themes. They tend to view themselves by some variant of the theme: "I'm on a different wavelength than others." They commonly experience being selfless—that is, they experience feeling empathy, estranged, and disconnected or dissociated from the rest of life. Their worldview is some variant of the theme: "Life is strange and unusual, and others have special magical intentions." As such, they are likely to conclude, "Therefore, observe caution while being curious about these special magical intentions of others." The most common defense mechanism utilized by them is undoing—the effort to neutralize "evil" deeds and thoughts by their eccentric, peculiar beliefs and actions.

Socially, predictable patterns of parenting and environmental factors can be noted for schizotypal personality disorder. The parenting patterns noted previously of the cold indifference of the schizoid subtype or the deprecating and derogatory parenting style and family environment of the avoidant subtype are noted. In both cases, the level of functioning in the family of origin would then be noted in schizoid personality disorder or avoidant personality disorder. Fragmented parental communications are a feature common to both subtypes of schizotypal personality disorder. The parental injunction is likely to have been "You're a strange bird" (Sperry & Mosak, 1996). Table 11.3 lists characteristics of schizotypal personality disorder.

ASSESSMENT OF SCHIZOTYPAL PERSONALITY DISORDER

Several sources of information are useful in establishing a diagnosis and treatment plan for personality disorders. Observation, collateral information, and psychological testing are important adjuncts to the patient's self-report in the clinical interview. This section briefly describes some characteristic observations that the clinician makes and the nature of the rapport likely to develop in initial encounters with specific personality-disordered individuals. Characteristic response patterns on various objective (i.e., MMPI-2 and MCMI-III) and projective tests (i.e., Rorschach) are also described.

Table 11.3
Characteristics of Schizotypal Personality Disorder

Triggering Event	Close interpersonal relationships.
Behavioral Style	Eccentric, erratic, bizarre speech; markedly peculiar but not incoherent; tends to drift from job to job.
Interpersonal Style	Socially isolative, peripheral relationships; with apprehension or apathy; if married, relationship is utilitarian and superficial.
Cognitive Style	"Cognitive slippage," scattered, ruminative; engages in magical thinking, superstitious.
Feeling Style	Hypersensitive, hostile, and aloof; may experience intense social anxiety.
Temperament	*Schizoid type:* passive infantile pattern. *Avoidance type:* fearful infantile pattern.
Attachment Style	Fearful and dismissing.
Parental injunction	"You're a strange bird."
Self-View	"I'm on a different wavelength than others." Experience of being "selfless," empty, estranged, depersonalization, dissociation.
Worldview	"Life is strange and unusual and others have special magic intentions. Therefore, observe with caution while being curious."
Maladaptive Schemas	Alienation; abandonment; dependence; vulnerability to harm.
Optimal DSM-IV-TR Criteria	Odd thinking and speech: behavior or appearance that is odd, eccentric, or peculiar.

Interview Behavior and Rapport

Interviewing schizotypal personality–disordered individuals usually elicits surprising statements and peculiar ideas. Rapport is hampered as long as individuals feel the clinician cannot appreciate their experiences. To the extent that the clinician is empathic and indicates understanding, they will be more willing to share their secret and autistic world. Unlike the schizoid, these individuals establish rapport easily and are usually willing to respond to all types of questions. The clinician will frequently need to ask for clarification of the impressions and constructions. Empathic listening together with continuation techniques is usually sufficient in encouraging individuals to explain their experience. On the other hand, doubting questions or confronting their views will cause them to recoil. More intelligent individuals with this disorder may query the clinician, wanting to know whether the clinician has had experiences similar to theirs. Handling this situation is more a matter of rapport than an issue of formulating questions more effectively (Othmer & Othmer, 2002).

Psychological Testing Data

The Minnesota Multiphase Personality Inventory (MMPI-2), the Millon Clinical Multiaxial Inventory (MCMI-III), and the Rorschach Psychodiagnostic Test can be useful in diagnosing schizotypal personality disorder as well as the schizotypal personality style or trait.

On the MMPI-2 a 2-7-8 (depression-psychasthenia-schizophrenia) code is likely (Edell, 1987). Scales F (frequency) and O (social introversion) are also likely to be elevated (Graham, 2000).

On the MCMI-III, elevations on S (schizotypal), 2 (avoidant), 7 (obsessive-compulsive), and 8A (passive-aggressive) can be expected (Edell, 1987; Choca & Denburg, 1997). On the Rorschach, these individuals have records that are more similar to schizophrenics and borderline personality–disordered individuals than to schizoid individuals (Swiercinsky, 1985).

TREATMENT APPROACHES AND INTERVENTIONS

Treatment Considerations

Included in the differential diagnosis of schizotypal personality disorder are three other Axis II personality disorders: schizoid personality disorder, avoidant personality disorder, and borderline personality disorder. The most common Axis I syndromes associated with schizotypal personality disorder are the schizophrenias, particularly the disorganized, catatonic, and residual types. Other disorders noted are anxiety disorders, somatoform disorders, and dissociative disorders.

Schizotypal personality disorder makes it very difficult to engage and remain in a psychotherapeutic relationship. For the majority of schizotypal patients, the most realistic treatment goal is to increase their ability to function more consistently, although on the periphery of society, rather than major personality restructuring. To date, no controlled treatment outcome studies have been completed for the schizotypal personality disorder (Crits-Christoph & Barber, 2002).

Individual Psychotherapy

Psychodynamical Psychotherapy Approach

Schizotypal personality–disordered individuals tend to be treated in offices, clinics, and day treatment programs rather than in acute inpatient programs. They may profit from dynamically oriented psychotherapy, both expressive and supportive, depending on their level of functioning and treatment readiness. The basis for dynamic treatment is not interpretation of conflict but rather internalization of a therapeutic relationship (Stone, 1985).

Essentially, the clinician's task is to "melt" the patient's frozen internal object relations by providing a correct emotional experience. The schizotypal's style of relatedness results from inadequacies in early relationships with parental figures. As a result, these patients distance themselves from others. Therapy must therefore provide a new relationship for internalization (Gabbard, 2000).

Since their basic mode of functioning is nonrelational, they find the task of therapy very challenging and difficult. Not surprisingly, they respond to the challenge with silence and emotional distancing. Clinicians need to adopt a permissive, accepting attitude, and must be exceedingly patient with these individuals. It is more helpful to understand silence as a nonverbal form of relating rather than as treatment resistance. By listening with a third ear, the clinician can learn much about these patients. Through projective identification, they will evoke certain responses in the clinician that contain valuable diagnostic information regarding the patient's inner world (Gabbard, 1990). Dealing effectively with countertransference issues is critical in working with schizotypal patients. Accepting silent nonrelatedness is foreign to the clinician's psychological predisposition and training. Thus, when silence is prolonged, the clinician must guard against acting out and projecting his or her own self- and object representations onto the patient. Accepting the silence and refraining from interpreting it legitimizes the patient's private, noncommunicative core self. It may be the only viable technique for building a therapeutic alliance (Gabbard, 1990).

Long-Term vs. Short-Term Dynamic Therapy. Decisions about the type and frequency of dynamic therapy should be based on the patient's level of functioning and motivation and readiness for treatment. Higher-functioning schizotypal patients who exhibit some depressive symptoms, or some capacity for empathy and emotional warmth, tend to have better outcomes in dynamic psychotherapy (Stone, 1983). Similarly, patients with better ego functioning in terms of judgment, reality testing, and cognitive slippage tend to do better than those with poorer ego functioning.

Patients who are highly motivated for exploratory psychotherapy can make dramatic gains in intense, long-term treatment of two to three sessions per week over several years. On the other hand, long-term supportive psychotherapy is indicated for the majority of schizotypal patients who present with major ego deficits and personal eccentricities. The goal of such treatment is improved adaptive functioning in day-to-day living (Stone, 1989). Mehlum et al. (1991) described a long-term day treatment program for schizotypal personality–disordered individuals based on psychodynamic principles.

Short-term dynamic therapy is indicated for crisis issues and situational difficulties related to job or personal life. It may also serve as a follow-up for a previous course of long-term psychotherapy. Not surprisingly, there are few case reports of short-term dynamic individual treatment as a curative intervention.

Cognitive-Behavioral Therapy Approach

Stone (1989) indicates that for schizotypal patients who aspire to fit in better and feel less alienated corrective training or experiences may be necessary—for instance, referral to elocution lessons, or a Dale Carnegie course, or accompanying the patient to a clothing store to assist in selecting appropriate apparel for a job interview. Stone has also found videotape feedback useful in pointing out the patient's awkwardness of gait or gestures. Turkat (1990) recommends that anxiety management and modification of hypersensitivity and hypervigilance may be necessary, depending on the case formulation.

Cognitive Therapy. Beck, Freeman, and Associates (1990) briefly describe the cognitive therapy approach to working with schizotypal personality–disordered individuals. Developing a collaborative working relationship is the starting point for treatment with these individuals. Since they hold a number of irrational beliefs about others, the importance of the therapeutic relationship should not be underestimated. Since these individuals desire social relationships and experience distress with social isolation, assisting them in increasing their social support network is an initial treatment goal. Increasing social appropriateness is a related goal. Social skills training as well as the therapist modeling appropriate behavior and speech are effective strategies. In combination with these behavioral strategies, the clinician works collaboratively with the individual to identify automatic thoughts and underlying schemas about social interactions. Role-playing more appropriate behavior then becomes much more meaningful.

Perhaps the most critical aspect of treatment is helping schizotypal individuals seek out objective evidence in the environment to evaluate their thoughts, rather than relying on emotional responses. As they learn to disregard inappropriate thoughts, they are able to consider the consequences that responding emotionally or behaviorally to such thoughts would have, and they can respond more rationally. The individual's eccentric and magical thoughts are perceived as symptoms, and predesigned coping statements are practiced, such as "There I go again. Even though I have this thought, it doesn't mean it's true." In addition to guided discovery and direct disputation of maladaptive beliefs, indirect strategies such as encouraging schizotypal individuals to keep track of the predictions they make and the accuracy of these predictions are effective but less threatening interventions. In addition to focusing on automatic thoughts and schemas, efforts to change the schizotypal's cognitive style are helpful. Since the communication patterns of these individuals tends to be circumstantial and idiosyncratic, collaborative experiments can be set up to modify this style. Futhermore, Beck et al. (1990) note that provided the therapist has realistic treatment expectations, much can be accomplished, and the collaborative work can be a positive experience as these individuals are able to control portions of their inappropriate behaviors and thoughts.

Freeman et al. (1990) are not optimistic about the cognitive treatment of schizotypal individuals, indicating that behavioral interventions such as social skills training are initially useful. It is only after these individuals can be more socially appropriate—that is, they begin acting more like schizoid personalities—that their automatic thoughts and cognitive distortions are amenable to cognitive methods.

Schema Therapy. Schema therapy is an elaboration of cognitive therapy that has been developed by Young (1999) and Young et al. (2003) specifically for personality disorders and other difficult individual and couples problems. Schema therapy involves identifying maladaptive schemas and planning specific strategies and interventions. Four main strategies are cognitive, experiential, behavioral, and the therapeutic relationship itself. Cognitive restructuring—particularly modification of maladaptive schemas—is an important cognitive strategy, but is combined with imagery exercises, empathic confrontation, homework assignments, and "limited reparenting" (i.e., a form of corrective emotional experience; Young, 1999).

Maladaptive schemas typically associated with schizotypal personality disorder include *abandonment*—that is, the belief that significant others will not or cannot provide reliable and stable support; *alienation*—that is, the belief that one must meet the needs of others at the expense of one's own gratification; *vulnerability to harm*—that is, the exaggerated fear that imminent catastrophe will strike at any time and that one will be unable to prevent it; and *dependence*—that is, the belief that one is unable to competently fulfill everyday responsibilities without considerable help from others (Bernstein, 2002).

Structured Skill Treatment Interventions. While research shows that medication can modulate or normalize dysregulated behaviors, a similar modulating effect has also been noted for social skills training (Lieberman, DeRisi, & Mueser, 1989). Thus, it appears that social skills training is a relatively potent bottom-up treatment strategy for normalizing limbic system–mediated behaviors that reflect specific skill deficits in personality-disordered individuals. When such skill deficits are present, Sperry (1999) contends that structured skill training intervention is a potent and effective strategy in treatment. Various structured intervention strategies for modifying a personality-disordered individual's affective, behavioral, and cognitive temperament styles are relevant for treatment of schizotypal personality disorder (Sperry, 1999).

Interpersonal Approach

Benjamin (1996) writes that psychotherapeutic interventions with schizotypal personality–disordered individuals can be planned and evaluated in terms of whether they enhance collaboration, facilitate learning about maladaptive patterns and their roots, block these patterns, enhance the will to change, and effectively encourage new patterns.

The therapist facilitates collaboration by deferring to the schizotypal individual's sensitivities. For example, at the beginning of therapy, the therapist may need to be quite tolerant about canceled appointments and control over the course of sessions. If not allowed to maintain distance and control in this manner, these individuals will quickly terminate. Gradually the therapist should be able to engage these individuals through empathic listening, accurate mirroring, and constancy. As treatment progresses, they may develop sufficient trust and insight to relinquish control by magic and ritual. Unlike parents, clinicians require no caregiving themselves. And unlike the parents of schizotypals, therapists can be consistent in mainstreaming focus and supportive attention. Such an experience is therefore emotionally corrective.

During the course of treatment, schizotypal individuals need to learn that the unrealistic responsibilities placed upon them when they were helpless was an abusive situation and predisposed them to magical thinking. Such early experiences led these individuals to assume they had inordinate power and influence. Next, they are helped to recognize when and how they distort reality. At the same time, they are taught new self-talk that can keep them grounded in the here and now. Later, they are helped to understand the contribution of early experiences and learnings to their unrealistic thoughts. However, for reconstructive changes to occur, these individuals must change their wish to magically protect their self and others while maintaining loyalty to early abusers. For example, interpreting suicidal or other fantasies in relation to underlying wishes can lead to fuller awareness, allowing the individual an opportunity for a new choice. Accurate mirroring and empathy can assist these individuals in mobilizing their will to recover and visualize better ways of viewing self, the world, and others. Benjamin (1996) is doubtful that major changes in learning patterns will occur, believing that this disorder is genetically mediated.

Group Therapy

Clinical reports of group therapy with schizotypal patients have been limited. Nevertheless, there is sufficient indication these patients may profit from supportive group therapy (Stone, 1989; Mehlum et al., 1991).

A reasonable outcome or goal of group therapy is increased awareness that others harbor fantasies and self-criticisms similar to schizotypals and that others may find them likable despite their conviction of unlikability. Group therapy may impact such social alienating tendencies as standoffishness and peculiarities of speech. An ongoing heterogeneous group may be able to tolerate some degree of these tendencies. But beyond the limits of tolerability, these behaviors may so affect either the patient or other group members that therapeutic group process is mollified. Obviously, appropriate selection of which schizotypal patients will benefit from being in a group is an important task of the group leaders (Stone, 1989).

Marital and Family Therapy

Clinical reports of marital or family therapy with schizotypal patients have not yet appeared. In general, schizotypal individuals tend to remain single. Because of either their rejection sensitivity or insensitivity to others' feelings, these patients are likely to avoid committed relationships. Not surprisingly, schizotypals who do marry tend to have problems stemming either from insensitivity to the feelings of their partner or from oversensitivity to the partner's behavior. Therefore, in couples therapy the clinician's first task is to assess the degree of and balance between these two tendencies. Typically, it is easier to assist a hypersensitive partner to respond more appropriately than to help an insensitive partner become more empathic (Stone, 1989).

Medication

While there is relatively little clinical or research literature on the various psychosocial treatment modalities, there is a growing literature on psychopharmacology of schizotypal personality disorder. In fact, next to borderline personality disorder, no other personality disorder has as many open-trial, controlled, and placebo-controlled drug studies as schizotypal personality disorder. The fact that this disorder lies on schizophrenic spectrum accounts and has some overlap with the borderline personality disorder accounts for this interest among both clinicians and researchers (Stein, 1992; Coccaro, 1993). To date, there have been five controlled pharmacological trials on schizotypal personality disorder (Koenigsberg, Woo-Ming, & Siever, 2002).

Several drug groups have been utilized with schizotypal patients. Anxiolytics in small doses have shown favorable response in schizotypal patients presenting with moderate anxiety (Akiskal, 1981). Amoxapine, an antidepressant with antipsychotic properties, has shown to be effective in improving schizophrenic-like and depressive symptoms in schizotypal patients (Jensen & Andersen, 1989). And fluoxetine (Prozac) has been reported to reduce symptoms of interpersonal sensitivity, anxiety, paranoid ideation, and self-injury in both schizotypal and borderline patients (Markovitz et al., 1991).

However, the data on the effectiveness of neuroleptics for schizotypal personality disorder are most impressive. Open trials, controlled trials, and even placebo-controlled trials show consistently that low-dose neuroleptics are very beneficial for patients with moderately severe schizotypal symptoms. In addition, neuroleptics have shown better efficacy for depressive symptoms in schizotypals than tricyclic antidepressants (Stein, 1992; Coccaro, 1993).

Medication Protocol. Start with an atypical antipsychotic, such as risperidone, at one-fourth to one-half the usual topic range maintenance dose for psychosis. If there is no response, incrementally increase the dosage. If there is no response at the top dose, switch to another atypical. If there is a partial response, consider adding divalproex. Clozapine should be considered only in refractory individuals. When dissociative symptoms are prominent, naltrexone can be considered (Reich, 2002). Koenigsberg, Woo-Ming, and Siever (2002) reports similar suggestions.

Combined and Integrated Treatment Approach

Probably because of the impairing nature of this disorder, there is surprisingly little resistance to combining and tailoring treatment. Combining medication and psychotherapy is perhaps the most common strategy. Liebowitz et al. (1986), among others, suggest beginning individual therapy and medication, where indicated, concurrently. Stone (1992) advocates beginning with medication or a behavioral intervention and adding a dimensional psychotherapy: a blending of supportive, exploratory, cognitive, and behavioral elements to match the concurrent needs and circumstances of the patient. This, of course, represents the epitome of integrated, tailored treatment.

Others have advocated social skills training as an adjunct to supportive psychotherapy (Liebowitz et al., 1986) or combining group therapy with individual dynamic psychotherapy (Gabbard, 1994). Mehlum et al. (1991) report on the combining of several treatment modalities for schizotypal and borderline personality–disordered patients: individual psychodynamic psychotherapy, group therapy, community meetings, art therapy, awareness group therapy, and milieu therapy. This unique prospective study of a day treatment program showed that efficacy of this combined treatment approach held up an average of 3 years later. Major changes were noted in symptom reduction. However, social adjustments and employment were not as robust as with borderline patients.

References

Abramson, R. (1983). Lorazepam for narcissistic rage. *Journal of Operational Psychiatry*, 14: 52–55.

Adler, A. (1956). Problems in psychotherapy. *American Journal of Individual Psychology*, 12: 12–24.

Adler, G. (1985). *Borderline psychopathology and its treatment*. New York: Jason Aronson.

Ahktar, S. (1987). Schizoid personality disorder: A synthesis of developmental, dynamic, and descriptive features. *American Journal of Psychotherapy*, 41: 449–518.

Ahktar, S. (1990). Paranoid personality disorders: A synthesis of developmental, dynamic and descriptive features. *American Journal of Psychotherapy*, 44: 5–25.

Ainsworth, M., Blehar, M., Waters, E., & Wall, S. (1978). *Patterns of attatchment: A psychological study of the strange situation*. Hillsdale, NJ: Earlbaum.

Akiskal, H. (1981). Subaffective disorders: Dysthymic, cyclothymic, and bipolar, II: Disorders in the borderline realm. *Psychiatric Clinics of North America*, 4: 26–46.

Alden, L. (1989). Short-term structured treatment for avoidant personality disorder. *Journal of Consulting and Clinical Psychology*, 57: 756–764.

Alden, L. (1992). Cognitive-interpersonal treatment of avoidant personality disorder. In P. Keller & S. Heyman (Eds.). *Innovations in clinical practice: A source book*. Vol. 11. Sarasota, FL: Professional Resources Exchange.

Alden, L. (2002). Avoidant personality disorder: Current status and future directions. *Journal of Personality Disorders*, 16, 1: 1–29.

Alexander, J., & Parsons, B. (1973). Short-term behavioral intervention with delinquent families: Impact on family process and recidivism. *Journal of Abnormal Psychology*, 8: 219–225.

Allnutt, S., & Links, P. (1996). Diagnosing specific personality disorders and the optimal criteria. In P. Links (Ed.), *Clinical assessment and management of severe personality disorders* (pp. 21–48). Washington, DC: American Psychiatric Press.

Allport, G. (1937). *Personality: A psychological interpretation.* New York: Holt.

Alonso, A., & Ruton, J. (1984). The impact of object relations theory on psychodynamic group therapy. *American Journal of Psychiatry,* 141: 1376–1380.

Alonzo, A. (1992). The shattered mirror: Treatment of a group of narcissistic patients. *Group,* 16: 210–219.

Altamura, A., Piolo, R., Vitto, M., & Mannu, P. (1999). Venlafaxine in social phobia: A study in selective serotonin reuptake inhibitor non-responders. *International Clinical Psychopharmacology,* 14: 239–245.

American Psychiatric Association. (1994). *Diagnostic and Statistical Manual of Mental Disorders, Fourth Edition (DSM-IV).* Washington, DC: Author.

American Psychiatric Association. (2000). *Diagnostic and Statistical Manual of Mental Disorders, Fourth Edition Text Revision (DSM-IV-TR).* Washington, DC: Author.

Anderson, C. (1983). A psychoeducational program for families of patients with schizophrenia. In McFarlene, W. (Ed.), *Family therapy in schizophrenia.* New York: Guilford.

Appel, G. (1974). An approach to the treatment of schizoid phenomena. *Psychoanalytic Review,* 61: 99–113.

Azima, F. (1983). Group psychotherapy with personality disorders. In Kaplan, H., and Sadock, B. (Eds.), *Comprehensive group psychotherapy,* 2nd ed. (pp. 262–268). Baltimore: Wilkins & Wilkins.

Baer, L. & Jenike, M. (1992). Personality disorders in obsessive compulsive disorder. *Psychiatric Clinics of North America,* 15: 803–812.

Bailey, G. (1998). Cognitive-behavioral treatment of obsessive-compulsive personality disorder. *Journal of Psychological Practice,* 4, 1: 51–59.

Balint, M. (1968). *The basic fault: Therapeutic aspects of regression.* London: Tavistock.

Balint, M., Ornstein, P., & Balint, E. (1972). *Focal psychotherapy.* London: Tavistock.

Barber, J. Morse, J., Kakauer, I., et al. (2002). Change in obsessive-compulsive and avoidant personality disorder following time-limited supportive-expressive therapy. *Psychotherapy,* 34, 133–143.

Barlow, D., & Waddle, M. (1985). Agoraphobia. In D. Barlow (Ed.), *Clinical handbook of psychological disorders: A step-by-step manual.* New York: Guilford.

Barnes, R. (1977). Mesoridazine (Serentil) in personality disorders: A controlled trial in adolescent patients. *Disease of the Nervous System,* April, 258–264.

Bartholomew, K., & Horowitz, L. (1991). Attachment styles in young adults: A test for a four-category model. *Journal of Personality and Social Psychology,* 61, 226–244.

Bartholomew, K. (1990). Avoidance of intimacy: An attachment perspective. *Journal of Social and Personality Relationships,* 7, 147–178.

Bateman, A., & Fonagy, P. (1999). Effectiveness of partial hospitalization in the treatment of borderline personality disorder: A randomized controlled trial. *American Journal of Psychiatry,* 156: 1563–1569.

Bateman, A., & Fonagy, P. (2001). Treatment of borderline personality disorder with psychoanalytically oriented partial hospitalization: An 18-month follow up. *American Journal of Psychiatry,* 158: 36–42.

Beck, A. (1976). *Cognitive therapy and the emotional disorders*. New York: International Universities Press.

Beck, A., Freeman, A., & Associates (1990). *Cognitive therapy of the personality disorders*. New York: Guilford.

Beitman, B. (1993). Pharmacotherapy and the stages of psychotherapeutic change. In Oldham, J., Riba, M., & Tasman, A. (Eds.), *American Psychiatric Press Review of Psychiatry, Vol. 12* (pp. 521–540). Washington, DC: American Psychiatric Press.

Bellak, L. (1997). *The TAT, CAT and SAT in clinical use*, 6th ed. Boston: Allyn & Bacon.

Bender, D., Donan, R., Skodol, A., Sanislow, C. et al. (2001). Treatment utilization by patients with personality disorders. *American Journal of Psychiatry, 158*, 2: 295–302.

Benjamin, L. (1993). *Interpersonal diagnosis and treatment of personality disorders*. New York: Guilford.

Benjamin, L. (1996). *Interpersonal diagnosis and treatment of personality disorders*, 2nd ed. New York: Guilford.

Benjamin , L. (2003). *Interpersonal reconstructive therapy*. New York: Guilford.

Berger, P. (1987). Pharmacologic treatment for borderline personality disorder. *Bulletin of the Menninger Clinic, 51*: 277–284.

Berkowitz, D. (1985). Self-object needs and marital disharmony. *Psychoanalytic Review, 72*: 229-237.

Berkowitz, D., Shapiro, R., Sinner, M., et al. (1974). Concurrent family treatment of narcissistic disorders in adolescents. *International Journal of Psychoanalysis*, 3: 371–396.

Berman, E. (1983). The treatment of troubled couples. In Grinspoon, L. (Ed.), *Psychiatric Updates, Vol. 2*. Washington, DC: American Psychiatric Association.

Bernstein, D. (2002). Cognitive therapy of personality disorders in patients with histories of emotional abuse or neglect. *Psychiatric Annals, 32*, 10, 618–628.

Bernstein, D., Stein, J., & Handelsman, L. (1998). Predicting personality pathology among adult patients with substance disorders: Effects of childhood maltreatment. *Addictive Behavior, 23*: 855–868.

Bernstein, D., Useda, D., & Siever, L. (1993). Paranoid personality disorder. Review of the literature and recommendations for DSM-IV. *Journal of Personality Disorders, 7*: 53–62.

Binder, J. (1979). Treatment of narcissistic problems in time-limited psychotherapy. *Psychiatric Quarterly, 51*: 257–270.

Blocher, D. (1974). *Developmental counseling*. New York: Wiley.

Blocher, D. (2002). *Counseling: A developmental approach*, 4th ed. New York: Wiley.

Bogdanoff, M., & Elbaum, P. (1978). Role lock: Dealing with monopolizers, isolates, helpful hannahs, and other associated characters in group psychotherapy. *International Journal of Group Psychotherapy, 28*: 247–281.

Bonime, W. (1959). The pursuit of anxiety-laden areas in therapy of the schizoid patient. *Psychiatry, 22*: 239–244.

Bornstein, R. (1995). Sex differences in dependent personality disorder prevalence rates. *Clinical Psychology: Science and Practice, 3*, 1, 1–12.

Bornstein, R. (1997). Dependent personality disorder in the DSM-IV and beyond. *Clinical Psychology: Science and Practice, 4*, 2, 175–187.

Bowlby, J. (1973). *Attachment and loss: Vol. 2, Separation and anger.* New York: Basic Books.

Brennan, K., & Shaver, P. (1998). Attachment styles and personality disorders: Their connection to each other and to parental divorce, parental death, and perceptions of parental caregiving. *Journal of Personality,* 66, 835–878.

Brown, E., Heimberg, R., & Juster, H. (1997). Social phobia subtype and avoidant personality disorder: Effects of severity of social phobia impairment and outcome of cognitive behavioral treatment. *Behavior Therapy,* 32, 1: 179.

Buie, D., & Adler, G. (1982). The definitive treatment of the borderline personality. *International Journal of Psychoanalysis,* 9: 51–87.

Cadenhead, K., Light, G., Geyer, M., et al. (2002). Neurobiological measures of schizotypal personality disorder. *American Journal of Psychiatry,* 159, 5: 869–871.

Cass, D., Silvers, F., & Abrams, G. (1972). Behavioral group treatment of hysterics. *Archives of General Psychiatry,* 26: 42–50.

Cavedini, P. Erzegovesi, S., Ronchi, P., & Bellodi, L. (1997). Predictive value of obsessive-compulsive personality disorder in antiobsessional pharmacological treatment. *European Neuropsychopharmacology,* 7, 1: 45–49.

Chadoff, P. (1989). Histrionic personality disorder. In Karasu, T. (Ed.), *Treatment of psychiatric disorders* (pp. 2727–2735). Washington, DC: American Psychiatric Press.

Chessick, R. (1982). Intensive psychotherapy of a borderline patient. *Achives of General Psychiatry,* 39: 413–419.

Chessick, R. (1985). *Psychology of the self and the treatment of narcissism.* New York: Jason Aronson.

Choca, J., & Denburg, E. (1997). *Interpretative guide to the Millon Clinical Multiaxial Inventory,* 2nd ed. Washington, DC: American Psychological Association.

Clarkin, J., Foelsch, P., Levy, K., et al. (2001). The development of a psychodynamic treatment for patients with borderline personality disorder: A preliminary study of behavior change. *Journal of Personality Disorders,* 15, 6: 487–495.

Clarkin, J., Marzaliali, E., & Munroe-Blum, H. (1991). Group and family treatment of borderline personality disorder. *Hospital and Community Psychiatry,* 42: 1038–1043.

Cleckley, H. (1941). *The mask of sanity.* St. Louis: Mosby.

Clinical Psychiatry News. (1991, September). Better personality disorders therapies foreseen. *Clinical Psychiatry News,* 26.

Cloninger, C. (1987). A systematic method for clinical description and classification of personality variables: A proposal. *Archives of General Psychiatry,* 44: 573–588.

Cloninger C. R. (2000). A practical way to diagnosis of personality disorders: A proposal. *Journal of Personality Disorders,* 14: 99–108.

Cloninger, C. (Ed.). (1999). *Personality and psychopathology.* Washington, DC: American Psychiatric Press.

Cloninger, C., Svrakic, D., & Przybeck, R. (1993). A psychobiological model of temperament and character. *Archives of General Psychiatry,* 50: 975–990.

Coccaro, E. (1993). Psychopharmacologic studies in patients with personality disorders: Review and perspectives. *Journal of Personality Disorders,* 7 (supplement): 181–192.

Coccaro, E., & Kavoussi, R. (1991). Biological and pharmacological aspects of border-line personality disorder. *Hospital and Community Psychiatry*, 42: 1029–1033.

Cortright, B. (1997). *Psychotherapy and spirit*. Albany, NY: State University of New York Press.

Costa, P., & McCrae, R. (1990). Personality disorders and the five factor model of personality. *Journal of Personality Disorders*, 4: 362–371.

Costa, P., & McCrae, R. (1992). *The NEO personality inventory: Revised manual*. Odessa, FL: Psychological Assessment Resources.

Cramer, Azima, F. (1983). Group psychotherapy with personality disorders. In Kaplan, H., and Sadock, B. (Eds.), *Comprehensive group psychotherapy*. Baltimore: Williams & Wilkins.

Crits-Christoph, P., & Barber, J. (2002). Psychological treatment for personality disorders. In P. Nathan & J. Gorman (eds.), *A guide to treatments that work*, (pp. 611–624) 2nd ed. New York: Oxford University Press.

Day, M., & Semrad, E. (1971). Group therapy with neurotics and psychotics. In Kaplan, H., and Sadock, B. (Eds.), *Comprehensive group psychotherapy* (pp. 566–580). Baltimore: Williams & Wilkins.

Deltito, J., & Perugi, G. (1989). A case of social phobia with avoidant personality disorder. *Comprehensive Psychiatry*, 30: 498–504.

Deltito, J., & Stam, M. (1989). *Psychopharmacological treatment of avoidant personality disorder. Comprehensive Psychiatry*, 30: 498–504.

Dick, B., & Wooff, K. (1986). An evaluation of a time-limited program of dynamic group psychotherapy. *British Journal of Psychiatry*, 148: 159–164.

Dolan, M., & Park, I. (2002). The neuropsychology of antisocial personality disorder. *Psychological Medicine*, 32, 3: 417–427.

Edell, W. (1987). Relationship of borderline syndrome disorders to early schizophrenia on the MMPI. *Journal of Clinical Psychology*, 43: 163–174.

Epstein, L. (1984). An interpersonal-object relations perspective working with destructive aggression. *Contemporary Psychoanalysis*, 20: 651–662.

Erdman, P., & Caffery, T. (Eds.). (2003). *Attachment and family systems: Conceptual, empirical and therapeutic relatedness*. New York: Brunner/Routledge.

Evans, K., & Sullivan, J. (1990). *Dual diagnosis: Counseling the mentally ill substance abuser*. New York: Guilford.

Everett, S., Halperin, S., Volgy, S., & Wissler, A. (1989). *Treating the borderline family: A systematic approach*. Boston: Allyn & Bacon.

Exner, J. (1986). *The Rorschach: A comprehensive system*, 2nd ed. New York: John Wiley.

Fairburn, W. (1954). *An object-relations theory of the personality*. New York: Basic Books.

Fawcett, J. (2002). Schemas or traits and states: Top down or bottom up? *Psychiatric Annals*, 32, 10, 567.

Fay, A., & Lazarus, A. (1993). Cognitive-behavior group therapy. In A. Alonso & H. Willer (Eds.), *Group therapy in clinical practice*. Washington, DC: American Psychiatric Press.

Feldman, L. (1982). Dysfunctional marital conflict: An integrative interpersonal intrapsychic model. *Journal of Marital and Family Therapy*, 8: 417–428.

Fenichel, O. (1945). *The psychoanalytic theory of the neurosis.* New York: Norton.

Fernando, J. (1998). The etiology of the narcissistic personality disorder. *Psychoanalytic Study of the Child,* 53: 141–158.

Fernbach, B., Winstead, B., & Derlega, V. (1989). Sex differences in diagnosis and treatment recommendations for antisocial personality and somatization disorders. *Journal of Social and Clinical Psychology,* 8: 238–255.

Fieve, R. (1994). *Prozac.* New York: Avon Books.

Finn, B., & Shakir, S. (1990). Intensive group psychotherapy of borderline patients, *Group,* 14: 99–110.

First, M. (2002). A research agenda for DSM-V: Summary of the white papers. *Psychiatric Research Report,* 18, 2: 10–13.

Flegenheimer, W. (1982). *Techniques of brief therapy.* New York: Jason Aronson.

Fossatti, A., Madeddu, F., & Maffei, C. (1999). Borderline personality disorder and childhood sexual abuse: A meta-analytic study. *Journal of Personality Disorders,* 13: 268–280.

Fraiberg, S. (1969). Libidinal object constancy and mental representation. *Psychoanalytic Study of the Child,* 24: 9–47.

Francis, A., & Clarkin, J. (1981). Differential therapeutics: A guide to treatment selection. *Hospital and Community Psychiatry,* 32: 537–546.

Francis, A., Clarkin, J., & Perry, S. (1984). *Differential therapeutics in psychiatry: The art and science of treatment selection.* New York: Brunner/Mazel.

Freeman, A., Pretzer, J., Fleming, B., & Simon, K. (1990). *Clinical application of cognitive therapy.* New York: Plenum.

Freud, S. (1914/1976). On narcissism: An introduction. *Complete psychological works, Standard edition* (pp. 69–102). Vol. 14. London: Hogarth Press.

Frosch, J. (1983). *The psychotic process.* New York: International Universities Press.

Gabbard, G. (1989). On "doing nothing" in the psychoanalytic treatment of the refractory borderline patient. *International Journal of Psychoanalysis,* 70: 527–534.

Gabbard, G. (1990). *Psychodynamic psychiatry in clinical practice.* Washington, DC: American Psychiatric Press.

Gabbard, G. (1994). *Psychodynamic psychiatry in clinical practice: The DSM-IV edition.* Washington, DC: American Psychiatric Press.

Gabbard, G. (2000). *Psychodynamic psychiatry in clinical practice,* 3rd ed. Washington, DC: American Psychiatric Press.

Gertsley, L., McLellan, T., Atterman, A., et al. (1989). Ability to form an alliance with the therapist: A possible marker of progress for patients with antisocial personality disorder. *American Journal of Psychiatry,* 146: 508–512.

Glantz, K., & Goisman, R. (1990). Relaxation and merging in the treatment of personality disorders. *American Journal of Psychotherapy,* 44: 405–413.

Glueck, S., & Glueck, E. (1950). *Unraveling juvenile delinquency.* Cambridge: Harvard University Press.

Goldberg, A. (1973). Psychotherapy of narcissistic injuries. *Archives of General Psychiatry,* 28: 722–726.

Goldberg, A. (1989). Self psychology and the narcissistic personality disorders. *Psychiatric Clinics of North America,* 12: 731–739.

Graham, J. (2000). *MMPI-2: Assessing personality and psychopathology*. New York: Oxford University Press.

Graybar, S., & Boutilier, L. (2002). Nontraumatic pathways to borderline personality disorder. *Psychotherapy: Theory/Research/Practice/Training*, 39, 2: 152–162.

Greist, J., & Jefferson, J. (1992). *Panic disorder and agoraphobia: A guide*. Madison, WI: Anxiety Disorders Center and Information Centers.

Groth-Marnat, G. (1999). *Handbook of psychological assessment*, 3rd ed. New York: Wiley.

Grotjahn, M. (1984). The narcissistic person in analytic group psychotherapy. *International Journal of Group Psychotherapy*, 30: 299–318.

Guerney, B. (1977). *Relationship enhancement: Skill-training programs for therapy, problem prevention, and enrichment*. San Francisco: Jossey-Bass.

Guideno, V., & Liotti, G. (1983). *Cognitive processes and emotional disorders*. New York: Guilford Press.

Gunderson, J. (1983). DSM-III diagnosis of personality disorders. In J. Frosch (ed.), *Current Perspectives on Personality Disorders*. American Psychiatric Press, pp. 23–38.

Gunderson, J. (1986). Pharmacotherapy for patients with borderline personality disorders. *Archives of General Psychiatry*, 43: 698–700.

Gunderson, J. (1988). Personality disorders. In Nicholi, A. (Ed.), *The new Harvard guide to psychiatry* (pp. 337–357). Cambridge, MA: Harvard University Press.

Gunderson, J., (1989). Borderline personality disorder. In Karasu, T. (Ed.), *Treatments of psychiatric disorders* (pp. 2749–2758). Washington, DC: American Psychiatric Press.

Gunderson, J., Ronningstam, E., & Smith, L. (1991). Narcissistic personality disorders: A review of data on DSM-III-R descriptions. *Journal of Personality Disorders*, 5: 167–177.

Gurman, A., & Kniskern, D. (1991). Family therapy outcomes research: Known and unknown. In Gorman, A., and Kniskern, D. (Eds.), *Handbook of family therapy*. New York: Brunner/Mazel.

Haley, J. (1978). *Problem solving therapy*. San Francisco: Jossey-Bass.

Haley, J., & Hoffman, L. (1976). *Techniques of family therapy*. New York: Basic Books.

Halleck, S. (1978). *The treatment of emotional disorders*. New York: Jason Aronson.

Handler, L. (1989). Utilization approaches and psychodynamic psychotherapy in a case of hospital phobia: An integrated approach. *American Journal of Clinical Hypnosis*, 31: 257–263.

Harbir, H. (1981). Family therapy with personality disorders. In Lion, J. (Ed.), *Personality disorders: Diagnosis and management*, 2nd ed. Baltimore: Williams & Wilkins.

Harwood, I. (1992). Advances in group psychotherapy and self psychology: An interobjective approach with narcissistic and borderline patients. *Group*, 16: 220–232.

Havens, L. (1976). Discussion: How long the Tower of Babel? *Proceedings of American Psychopathological Association* 64: 62–73.

Hazen, C., & Shaver, P. (1990). Love and work: An attachment theoretical perspective. *Journal of Personality and Social Psychology*, 59, 270–280.

Heard, H., & Linehan, M. (1994). Dialectical behavior therapy: An integrative approach to the treatment of the borderline personality disorder. *Journal of Psychotherapy Integration*, 4: 55–82.

Heimberg, R., Holt, C. & Schneier, F., et al. (1943). The issue of subtypes in the diagnosis of social phobia. *Journal of Anxiety Disorders*, 7: 249–269.

Hend, S., Balker, J., & Williamson, D. (1991). Family environment characteristics and dependent personality disorder. *Journal of Personality Disorders*, 5: 256–263.

Herman, J., Perry, J., & Van der Kolk, B. (1989). Childhood trauma in borderline personality disorders. *American Journal of Psychiatry*, 146, 490–495.

Hill, D. (1970). Outpatient management of passive dependent women. *Hospital and Community Psychiatry*, 21, 402–405.

Hirschfield, R., Shea, M., & Weise, R. (1991). Dependent personality disorder: Perspectives for DSM-IV. *Journal of Personality Disorders*, 5, 135–149.

Holmes, S., Slaughter, J., & Kashani, J.(2001). Risk factors in childhood lead to the development of conduct disorder and antisocial personality disorder. *Child Psychiatry and Human Development*, 31, 3: 183–193.

Horowitz, L. (1977). Group psychotherapy of the borderline. In Harticollis, P. (Ed.), *Borderline personality disorder* (pp. 399–422). New York: International Universities Press.

Horowitz, L. (1980). Group psychotherapy for borderline and narcissistic patients. *Bulletin of the Menninger Clinic*, 4: 181–200.

Horowitz, L. (1987). Indications for group psychotherapy with borderline and narcissistic patients. *Bulletin of the Menninger Clinic*, 51: 248–318.

Horowitz, L. (1997). Psychotherapy of histrionic personality disorder. *Journal of Psychotherapy Practice and Research*, 6, 2: 93-107.

Horowitz, M. (1988). *Introduction to psychodynamics: A new synthesis*. New York: Basic Books.

Horowitz, M., Marmar, C., Krupnick, J., et al. (1984). *Personality styles and brief psychotherapy*. New York: Basic Books.

Hulse, W. (1958). Psychotherapy with ambulatory schizophrenic patients in mixed analytic groups. *Archives of Neurology and Psychiatry*, 79: 681–687.

Imbesi, E. (2000). On the etiology of narcissistic personality disorder. *Issues in Psychoanlytic Psychology*, 22, 2: 43–58.

Ivey, A., & Ivey, M. (1998). Reframing DSM-IV: Positive strategies from developmental counseling and therapy. *Journal of Counseling and Development*, 76: 334–350.

Jenike, M. (1990). Approaches to the patient with treatment refractory obsessive compulsive disorder. *Journal of Clinical Psychiatry*, 51: 2 (supplement): 15–21.

Jenike, M. (1991). Obsessive compulsive disorder. In Beitman, B., & Klerman, G. (Eds.), *Integrating pharmacotherapy and psychotherapy* (pp. 183-210). Washington, DC: American Psychiatric Press.

Jenike, M., Baer, L., & Minichiello, W. (1990). *Obsessive-compulsive disorders: Theory and management*, 2nd ed. Chicago: Yearbook Medical Publishing.

Jensen, H., & Andersen, J. (1989). An open, noncomparative study of amoxapine in borderline patients. *Acta Psychiatrica Scandinavica*, 79: 89–93.

Jones, S. (1987). Family therapy with borderline and narcissistic patients. *Bulletin of the Menninger Foundation*, 51: 285–295.

Kabat-Zinn, J., Massion, A., Kristeller, J., et al. (1992). Effectiveness of a meditation-based stress reduction intervention in the treatment of anxiety disorders. *American Journal of Psychiatry,* 149: 936–943.

Kagan, J., Reznick, J., & Snidman, N. (1988). Biological basis of childhood shyness. *Science,* 240: 167–171.

Kalojera, I., Jacobson, G., Hoffamn, G., et al. (1999). The narcissistic couple. In J. Carlson & L. Sperry (Eds.), *The disordered couple* (pp. 207–238). New York: Brunner/Mazel.

Kalus, O., Bernstein, D., & Siever, L. (1993). Schizoid personality disorder: A review of current status and implications for DSM-IV. *Journal of Personality Disorders,* 7: 43–52.

Kantor, M. (1992). *Diagnosis and treatment of the personality disorders.* St. Louis: Ishiyaku EuroAmerica.

Kavoussi, R., Liu, J., & Coccaro, E. (1994). An open trial of sertraline in personality disordered patients with impulsive aggression. *Journal of Clinical Psychiatry,* 55: 137–141.

Kellerman, H., & Burry, A. (1989). *Psychopathology and differential diagnosis: Volume II: Diagnostic primer.* New York: Columbia University Press.

Kellner, R. (1978). Drug treatment of personality disorders and delinquents. In Reid, W. (Ed.), *The psychopath: A comprehensive study of antisocial disorders and behaviors.* New York: Brunner/Mazel.

Kellner, R. (1986). Personality disorders. *Psychotherapy and Psychosomatics,* 46: 58–66.

Kernberg, O. (1975). *Borderline conditions and pathological narcissism.* New York: Jason Aronson.

Kernberg, O. (1984). *Severe personality disorders: Psychotherapeutic strategies.* New Haven, CT: Yale University Press.

Khan, M. (1975). Grudge and the hysteric. *International Journal of Psychoanalysis and Psychotherapy,* 4: 349–357.

Klein, D. (1975). Psychopharmacology and the borderline patient. In Mack, J. (Ed.), *Borderline States in Psychiatry.* New York: Grune & Stratton.

Klein, R. (1989a). Diagnosis and treatment of the lower-level borderline patient. In Masterson, J., & Klein, R. (Eds.), *Psychotherapy of disorders of the self.* New York: Brunner/Mazel.

Klein, R. (1989b). Shorter-term psychotherapy of the personality disorders. In Masterson, J., and Klein, R. (Eds.), *Psychotherapy of disorders of the self* (pp. 90–109). New York: Brunner/Mazel.

Koenigsberg, H. (1993). Combining psychotherapy and pharmacotherapy in the treatment of borderline patients. In Oldham, J., Riba, M., & Tassman, A. (Eds.), *American Psychiatric Press Review of Psychiatry,* Vol. 12. (pp. 541–564). Washington, DC: American Psychiatric Press.

Koenigsberg, H., Woo-Ming, A., & Siever, L. (2002). Pharmacological treatment for personality disorders. In P. Nathan & J. Gorman (Eds.), *A guide to treatments that work,* 2nd ed. (pp. 625–641) New York: Oxford University Press.

Koerner, K., & Linehan, M. (2000). Research on dialectical behavior therapy for borderline personality disorder. *The Psychiatric Clinics of North America,* 23(1): 151–167.

Kohut, H. (1971). *The analysis of the self.* New York: International Universities Press.

Kohut, H. (1977). *The restoration of the self.* New York: International Universities Press.

Kristeller, J. L., & Hallet, B. (1999). Effects of a meditation-based intervention for binge eating disorder. *Journal of Health Psychology,* 4, 3: 357–363.

Kyrios, M. (1999). A cognitive-behavioural approach to the understanding and management of obsessive-compulsive personality disorder. In Perris, C., & McGorry, P. (Eds.), *Cognitive psychotherapy of psychotic and personality disorders* (pp. 351–378). New York: Wiley.

Lachar, D. (1974). *The MMPI: Clinical assessment and automated interpretation.* Los Angeles: Western Psychological Services.

Lachkar, J. (1986). Narcissistic/borderline couples: Implications for medication. *Conciliation Courts Review,* 24: 31–38.

Lachkar, J. (1992). *The narcissistic/borderline couple: A psychoanalytic perspective on marital treatment.* New York: Brunner/Mazel.

Lachkar, J. (1999). Narcissistic/borderline couples: A psychodynamic approach to conjoint treatment. In Carlson, J., & Sperry, L. (Eds.), *The disordered couple* (pp. 259–284). New York: Brunner/Mazel.

Lazarus, A. (1981). *The practice of multimodal therapy.* New York: McGraw-Hill.

Lazarus, A. (Ed.). (1985). *Casebook of multimodal therapy.* New York: Guilford.

Lazarus, L. (1982). Brief psychotherapy of narcissistic disturbances. *Psychotherapy: Theory, Research and Practice,* 19: 228–236.

Leszcz, M. (1989). Group psychotherapy of the characterologically difficult patient. *International Journal of Group Psychotherapy,* 39: 311–335.

Lieberman, R., DeRisi, W., & Mueser, K. (1989). *Social skills training for psychiatric patients.* New York: Pergamon.

Liebowitz, M., & Klein, D. (1981). Interrelationship of hysteroid dysphoria and borderline personality disorder. *Psychiatric Clinics of North America,* 4: 67–87.

Liebowitz, M., Stone, M., & Turkat, I. (1986). Treatment of personality disorders. In Frances, A., & Hales, R. (Eds.), *Psychiatric Update, American Psychiatric Association, Annual Review,* Vol. 5 (pp. 356–393). Washington, DC: American Psychiatric Press.

Liebowtiz, M., Schneier, F., Hollander, E., et al. (1991). Treatment of social phobia with drugs other than benzodiazepines. *Journal of Clinical Psychiatry,* 52, 11 (suppl): 10–15.

Linehan, M. (1983). *Dialectical behavior therapy for treatment of parasuicidal women: Treatment manual.* Seattle: University of Washington.

Linehan, M. (1987). Dialectal behavior therapy for borderline personality disorder: Therapy and method. *Bulletin of the Menninger Clinic,* 51: 261–276.

Linehan, M. (1993a). *Cognitive-behavioral treatment for borderline personality disorder.* New York: Guilford.

Linehan, M. (1993b). *Skill training manual for treating borderline personality disorder.* New York: Guilford.

Linehan, M. (1994). Acceptance and change. The central dialectic in psychotherapy.

In Hayes, S., Jacobson, N., Follette, V., & Dougher, M. (Eds.), *Acceptance and change: Content and context in psychotherapy* (pp. 73–86). Reno, NV: Context Press.

Linehan, M., Armstrong, H., Suarez, A., et al. (1991). Cognitive-behavioral treatment of chronically parasuicidal borderline patients. *Archives of General Psychiatry*, 48: 1060–1064.

Linehan, M., Heard, H., & Armstrong, H. (1993). Naturalistic follow-up of a behavioral treatment for chronically suicidal borderline patients. Archives of General Psychiatry, 48: 1060–1064.

Luborsky, L. (1984). *Principles of psychoanalytic psychotherapy: A manual for supportive-expressive treatment.* New York: Basic Books.

Lyddon, W., & Sherry, A. (2001). Developmental personality styles: An attachment theory conceptualization of personality disorders. *Journal of Counseling and Development*, 79, 4: 405–414.

Mackinnon, R., & Michels, R. (1971). *The psychiatric interview in clinical practice.* Philadelphia: Saunders.

Main, M., & Goldwyn, R. (1998). *Adult attachment scoring and classification systems* (Version 6.3). Unpublished manuscript. University of California at Berkeley.

Main, M., & Soloman, J. (1990). Procedures for identifying infants as disorganized/disoriented during the Ainsworth Strange Situation. In M. Greenberg, D. Cicchetti, & E. Cummings (Eds.), *Attachment in the preschool years: Theory, research, and intervention* (pp. 121–160). Chicago: University of Chicago Press.

Malan, D. (1976). *The frontier of brief psychotherapy.* New York: Plenum.

Malinow, K. (1981a). Dependent personality. In Lion, J. (Ed.), *Personality disorders: Diagnosis and management,* 2nd ed. Baltimore: Williams & Wilkins.

Malinow, K. (1981b). Passive-aggressive personality. In Lion, J. (Ed.), Personality disorders: Diagnosis *and management,* 2nd ed. Baltimore: Williams & Wilkins.

Mann, J. (1973). *Time-limited psychotherapy.* Cambridge, MA: Harvard University Press.

Mann, J. (1984). Time-limited psychotherapy. In Grinspoon, L. (Ed.), *Psychiatry Update,* Vol. 3. Washington, DC: American Psychiatric Association.

Manschreck, T. (1992). Delusional disorders: Clinical concepts and diagnostic strategies. *Psychiatric Annals*, 22: 241–251.

Markowitz, P., Calabrese, J., & Schulz, C. (1991). Fluoxetine in the treatment of borderline and schizotypal personality disorders. *American Journal of Psychiatry*, 148: 1064–1067.

Marlatt, G. (1994). Addiction, mindfulness and acceptance. In Hayes, S., Jacobson, N., Follette, V., & Dougher, M. (eds.), *Acceptance and change: Content and context in psychotherapy* (pp. 175–197). Reno, NV: Context Press.

Marlatt, G., & Kristeller, J. (1999). Mindfulness and meditation. In Miller, W. (Ed.), *Integrating spirituality into treatment: Resources for practitioners* (pp.67–84). Washington, DC: American Psychological Association.

Marmar, C., & Freeman, M. (1988). Brief dynamic psychotherapy of post-traumatic stress disorders: Management of narcissistic regression. *Journal of Traumatic Stress*, 1, 323–337.

Martin, J. (1997). Mindfulness: A proposed common factor. *Journal of Psychotherapy Integration*, 7, 291–312.

Masterson, J. (1976). *Psychotherapy of the borderline adult: A developmental approach.* New York: Brunner/Mazel.

Masterson, J. (1981). *The narcissistic and borderline disorders.* New York: Brunner/Mazel.

Masterson, J., & Klein, R. (Eds.). (1990). *Psychotherapy of the disorders of the self.* New York: Brunner/Mazel.

Masterson, J., & Orcutt, C. (1989). Marital co-therapy of a narcissistic couple. In Masterson, J., & Klein, R. (Eds.), *Psychotherapy of Disorders of the Self.* New York: Brunner/Mazel.

Mavissakalian, M. (1993). Combined behavioral and pharmacological treatment of anxiety disorders. In J. Oldham, MiRiba, & A. Tasman (Eds.), *American Psychiatric Press review of psychiatry,* Vol. 12 (pp. 541–564). Washington, DC: American Psychiatric Press.

McCormack, C. (1989). The borderline/schizoid marriage: The holding environment as an essential treatment construct. *Journal of Marital and Family Therapy,* 15: 299–309.

Meares, R., Stevenson, J., & Comerford, A. (1999). Psychotherapy with borderline personality patients: 1. A comparison between treated and untreated cohorts. *Australian & New Zealand Journal of Psychiatry,* 33, 467–472.

Megargee, E., & Bohn, M. (1979). *Classifying criminal offenders.* Beverly Hills, CA: Sage.

Mehlum, L., Fris, S., Irion, T., et al. (1991). Personality disorders 2-5 years after treatment: A prospective follow up study. *Acta Psychiatrica Scandinavica,* 84: 72–77.

Meichenbaum, D. (1977). *Cognitive-behavioral modification: An integrated approach.* New York: Plenum.

Meissner, W. (1978). *The paranoid process.* New York: Jason Aronson.

Meissner, W. (1986). *Psychotherapy and the paranoid process.* Northale, NJ: Jason Aronson.

Meissner, W. (1988). *Treatment of patients in the borderline spectrum.* New York: Jason Aronson.

Meissner, W. (1989). Parnaoid personality disorder. In Karasu, T. (Ed.), *Treatments of psychiatric disorders* (pp. 2705–2711). Washington, DC: American Psychiatric Press.

Meloy, J. (1988). *The psychopathic mind: Origins, dynamics, and treatment.* Northvale, NJ: Jason Aronson.

Messina, N., Wish, E., Hoffman, J., & Nemes, S. (2002). Antisocial personality disorder and TC treatment outcomes. *American Journal of Drug and Alcohol Abuse,* 28, 2: 197–212.

Meyer, R. (1995). *The clinician's handbook: Integrated diagnostics, assessment, and intervention in adult and adolescent psychotherapy,* 4th ed. Boston: Allyn & Bacon.

Miller, M. B., Useda, J. D., Trull, T. J., Burr, R. M., Minks-Brown, C. (2001). Paranoid, schizoid and schizotypal personality disorder. In Sutker, P., and Adams, H. (Eds.). *Comprehensive handbook of psychopathology,* 3rd ed. (pp. 535–559). New York: Plenum.

Millon, T. (1981). *Disorders of personality: DSM-III Axis II.* New York: Wiley.

Millon, T. (1990). *Toward a new personology: An evolutionary model.* New York: Wiley.

Millon, T. (1994). Manual for the MCMI-III. Minneapolis, MN: National Computer Systems.

Millon, T. (1999). *Personality guided therapy*. New York: Wiley.

Millon, T., & Davis, R. (1996). *Disorders of personality: DSM-IV and Beyond*, 2nd ed. New York: Wiley.

Millon, T., & Davis, R. (2000). *Personality disorders in modern life*. New York: Wiley.

Millon, T., & Everly, G. (1985). *Personality and its disorders: A biosocial learning approach*. New York: Wiley .

Minuchin, S. (1974). *Families and family therapy*. Cambridge, MA: Harvard University Press.

Minuchin, S., & Montalva, B. (1976). *Families of the slums*. New York: Basic Books.

Montgomery, J. (1971). Treatment management of passive-dependent behavior. *International Journal of Social Psychiatry, 17*, 311–319.

Munich, R. (1986). Transitory symptom formation in the analysis of an obsessional character. *Psychoanalytic Study of the Child*, 41: 515–535.

Munro, A. (1992). Psychiatric disorders characterized by delusions: Treatment in relation to specific types. *Psychiatric Annals*, 22: 232–240.

Munroe-Blum, H. (1992). Group treatment of borderline personality disorder. In Clarkin, J. & E. Marziali (Eds.), *Borderline personality disorder: Clinical and empirical perspectives* (pp. 288–299). New York: Guilford Press.

Nachmani, G. (1984). Hesitation, perplexity, and annoyance at opportunity. *Contemporary Psychoanalysis*, 20: 448–457.

Nehls, N. (1991). Borderline personality disorder and group therapy. *Archives of Psychiatric Nursing*, 5: 137–146.

Nehls, N., & Diamond, R. (1993). Developing a systems approach to caring for persons with borderline personality disorder. *Community Mental Health Journal*, 29, 161–172.

Nemiah, J. (1980). Obsessive compulsive neurosis. In Freedman, A., Kaplan, H., & Sadock, B. (Eds.), *A comprehensive textbook of psychiatry*. Baltimore: Williams & Wilkins.

Nichols, W. (1996). Persons with antisocial and histrionic personality disorders in relationships. In Kaslow, F. (Ed.), *Handbook of relational diagnosis and dysfunctional family patterns* (pp. 287–299). New York: Wiley.

Nurse, A. (1998). The dependent/narcissistic couple. In Carlson, J., & Sperry, L. (Eds.), *The disordered couple* (pp. 315–332). New York: Brunner/Mazel.

Oldham, J., & Skodol, A. (2000). Charting the future of Axis II. *Journal of Personality Disorders*, 14: 17–29.

Oldham, J., Gabbard, G., Goin, M., et al. (2001). Practice guidelines for the treatment of patients with borderline personality disorder. *American Journal of Psychiatry*, 158, 1–52.

O'Leary, K., Turner, E., Gardner, D., et al. (1991). Homogeneous group therapy or borderline personality disorder. *Group*, 15: 56–64.

Osterbaan, D., van Balkom, A., Sinhoven, P., et al. (2002). The influence of treatment gain on comorbid avoidant personality disorder in patients with social phobia. *Journal of Nervous and Mental Disease*, 190, 1: 41–43.

Othmer, E., & Othmer, S. (2002). *The clinical interview using DSM-IV: Volume 1: Fundamentals*. Washington DC: American Psychiatric Press.

Paris, J. (2002). Commentary on the American Psychiatric Association clinical practice guidelines for borderline personality disorder: Evidence-based psychiatry and the quality of evidence. *Journal of Personality Disorders*, 16, 2: 130–134.

Parsons, B., & Alexander, J. (1973). Short-term family interventions: A therapy outcome study. *Journal of Abnormal Psychology*, 8: 219–225.

Perry, J., Francis, A., & Clarkin, J. (1990). *A DSM-III-R casebook of treatment selection*. New York: Brunner/Mazel.

Pfohl, B. (1991). Histrionic personality disorder: A review of available data and recommendations for DSM-IV. *Journal of Personality Disorders*, 5: 150–166.

Pfohl, B., & Blum, N. (1991). Obsessive-compulsive personality disorder: A review of available data and recommendations for DSM-IV. *Journal of Personality Disorders*. 5: 363–375.

Pies, R. (1992, February). The psychopharmacology of personality disorders. *Psychiatric Times*, 23–24.

Pines, M. (1975). Group psychotherapy with difficult patients. In Wolberg, L., & Aronson, M. (Eds.), *Group therapy 1975: An overview*. New York: Stratton Intercontinental Medical Books.

Pretzer, J. (1988). Paranoid personality disorder: A cognitive view. *International Cognitive Therapy Newsletter*, 4, 4: 10–12.

Pukrop, R. (2002). Dimensional personality profiles of borderline personality disorder in comparision with other personality disorders and healthy controls. *Journal of Personality Disorders*, 16, 2: 135–147.

Quality Assurance Project. (1991). Treatment outlines for borderline, narcissistic and histrionic personality disorders. *Australian, New Zealand Journal of Psychiatry*, 25: 392–403.

Ratey, J., Morrill, R., & Oxenkrug, G. (1989). Use of propranolol for provoked and unprovoked episodes of rage. *American Journal of Psychiatry*, 140: 1356–1357.

Regier, D., Boyd, J., Burke, J., et al. (1988). One-month prevalence in mental disorders in the United States. *Archives of General Psychiatry*, 45: 977–986.

Reich, J. (1988). DSM-III personality disorders and the outcome of treated panic disorder. *American Journal of Psychiatry*, 145: 1149–1152.

Reich, J. (2000). The relationship of social phobia to the personality disorders. *European Psychiatry*, 15: 151–159.

Reich, J. (2002). Drug treatment of personality disorder traits. *Psychiatric Annals*, 32, 10: 590–600.

Reid, W. (1989). *The treatment of psychiatric disorders. Revised for the DSM-III-R*. New York: Brunner/Mazel.

Reid, W., Balis, G., & Sutton, B. (1998). *The treatment of psychiatric disorders*, 3rd ed. New York: Brunner/Routeledge.

Reid, W., & Burke, W. (1989). Antisocial personality disorder. In Karasu, T. (Ed), *Treatments of psychiatric disorders*. Washington, DC: American Psychiatric Press.

Rennenberg, B., Goldstein, A., Phillips, D., et al. (1990). Intensive behavioral group treatment of avoidant personality disorder. *Behavior Therapy*, 21: 363–377.

Reyntjens, A. (1972). A series of multicentric pilot trials with pimozide in psychiatric practice, I: Pimozide in the treatment of personality disorders. *Acta Psychiatrica Belgeimum*, 72: 653–661.

Rinsley, D. (1982). *Borderline and other self disorders.* New York: Jason Aronson.

Roemer, L., & Orsillo, S. (2002). Expanding our conceptualization of and treatment for generalized anxiety disorder: Integrating mindfulness/acceptance-based approaches with existing cognitive-behavioral models. *Clinical Psychology: Science and Practice, 9,* 1: 54–68.

Rush, A., & Hollon, S. (1991). Depression. In Beitman, G., & Klerman, G. (Eds.), *Integrating pharmacotherapy and psychotherapy* (pp. 121–142). Washington, DC: American Psychiatric Press.

Sadoff, R., & Collins, D. (1968). Passive-dependency in sufferers. *American Journal of Psychiatry, 124,* 1136–1127.

Salkovskis, P., & Kirk, J. (1989). Obsessional disorders. In Hawton, K., Salkovskis, P., Kirk, J., & Clark, D. (Eds), *Cognitive behavior therapy for psychiatric problems* (pp. 129–168). Oxford: Oxford University Press.

Salzman, L. (1980). *Treatment of the obsessive personality.* New York: Jason Aronson.

Salzman, L. (1989) Compulsive personality disorder. In Karasu, T. (Ed), *Treatment of psychiatric disorders* (pp. 2771–2782). Washington, DC: American Psychiatric Press.

Sanislow, C., Grilo, C., Morey, L, Bender, D., et al. (2002). Confirmatory factor analysis of DSM-IV criteria for borderline personality disorder: Findings from the collaborative longitudinal personality disorders study. *American Journal of Psychiatry, 159,* 2: 284–290.

Satterfield, J., & Contwell, D. (1975). Psychopharmacology in the prevention of antisocial and delinquent behavior. *International Journal of Mental Health,* 4: 227–337.

Schane, M., & Kovel, V. (1988). Family therapy in severe borderline personality disorder. *International Journal of Family Psychiatry,* 9: 241–258.

Schwartz, J., & Begley, S. (2002). *The mind and the brain: Neuroplasticity and the power of mental force.* New York: HarperCollins.

Segal, Z., Williams, J., & Teasdale, J. (2002). *Mindfulness-based cognitive therapy of depression.* New York: Guilford.

Shafer, R. (1954). *Psychoanalytic interpretation in rorschach testing.* New York: Grune & Stratton.

Shapiro, D. (1965). *Neurotic styles.* New York: Basic Books.

Shapiro, E. (1982). The holding environment and family therapy for acting out adolescents. *International Journal of Psychoanalysis,* 9: 209–226.

Sharoff, K. (2002). *Cognitive coping therapy.* New York: Brunner/Routledge.

Sheard, M. (1976). The effects of lithium on impulsive aggressive behavior in man. *American Journal of Psychiatry,* 133: 1409–1413.

Sheidlinger, S., & Porter, K. (1980). Group therapy combined with individual psychotherapy. In Karasu, T., & Bellak, L. (Eds), *Specialized Techniques in Individual Psychotherapy.* New York: Brunner/Mazel.

Sheldon, W., & Stevens, S. (1942). *The varieties of temperament: A psychology of constitutional differences.* New York: Harper.

Shostrum, E. (1976). *Actualizing therapy: Foundations for a scientific ethic.* San Diego: EdITS Publishers.

Shulman, B. (1982). An Adlerian interpretation of the borderline personality. *Modern Psychoanalysis*, 7: 137–153.

Siegel, D. (1999). *The developing mind*. New York: Guilford.

Siever, L. (1993). The frontiers of psychopharmacology. *Psychology Today*, 27, 1: 40–44, 70–72.

Siever, L., Bernstein, D., & Silverman, J. (1991). Schizotypal personality disorder: A review of its current status. *Journal of Personality Disorders*, 5: 178–193.

Siever, L., & Davis, K. (1991). A psychological perspective on the personality disorders. *American Journal of Psychiatry*, 148: 37–48.

Siever, L. Koenigsberg, H. Harvey, P., et al. (2002). Cognitive and brain function in schizotypal personality disorder. *Schizophrenia Research*, 54: 157–167.

Sifneos, P. (1972). *Short-term psychotherapy and emotional crisis*. Cambridge, MA: Harvard University Press.

Sifneos, P. (1984). The current status of short-term dynamic psychotherapy and its future: An overview. *American Journal of Psychotherapy*, 38: 472–487.

Silk, K. (2002). Borderline personality disorder: The lability of psychaitric diagnosis. *Current Psychiatry*, 1, 11: 25–33.

Skodol, A., Gunderson, J., McGlashan, T., Dyck, I., Stout, R., Bender, D., et al. (2002). Functional impairment in patients with schizotypal, borderline, avoidant or obsessive-compulsive personality disorder. *American Journal of Psychiatry*, 159, 2: 276–282.

Slavik, S., Sperry, L., & Carlson, J. (1992). The schizoid personality disorder: A review and an Adlerian view and treatment. *Individual Psychotherapy*, 7: 137–154.

Slavson, S. (1939). *Dynamics of group psychotherapy*. New York: Jason Aronson.

Slavson, S. (1964). *A textbook in analytic group psychotherapy*. New York: International Universities Press.

Smucker, M. (1999). *Cognitive behavioral treatment for adult survivors of childhood trauma: Imagery rescripting and reprocessing*. New York: Jason Aronson.

Snyder, M. (1994). Couple therapy with narcissistically vulnerable clients: Using the relationship enhancement model. *The Family Journal: Counseling and Therapy for Couples and Families*, 2: 27–35.

Soloff, P., Lynch, K., & Kelly, T. (2002). Childhood abuse as a risk factor for suicidal behavior in borderline personality disorder. *Journal of Personality Disorders*, 16, 3: 201–214.

Solomon, M. (1989). *Narcissism and Intimacy: Love and Marriage in an Age of Confusion*. New York: Norton.

Solomon, M. (1999). Treating narcissistic and borderline couples. In Carlson, J., & Sperry, L. (Eds.), *The disordered couple* (pp. 239–258). New York: Brunner/Mazel.

Sperry, L. (1990). Personality disorders: Biopsychosocial descriptions and dynamics. *Individual Psychology*, 46: 193–202.

Sperry, L. (1991). The neurotic personalities of our time: The narcissistic personality. *NASAP Newsletter*, 24, 9: 3–6.

Sperry, L. (1995). *Handbook of the diagnosis and treatment of DSM-IV personality disorders*. New York: Brunner/Mazel.

Sperry, L. (1999). *Cognitive behavior therapy of DSM-IV personality disorders: Highly effective interventions for the most common personality disorders*. New York: Brunner/Mazel.

Sperry, L. (2002). From psychopathology to transformation: Retrieving the developmental focus in psychotherapy. *Journal of Individual Psychology*, 58: 398–421.

Sperry, L., Gudeman, J., Blackwell, B., & Faulkner, L. (1992). *Psychiatric case formulations*. Washington, DC: American Psychiatric Press.

Sperry, L., & Maniacci, M. (1996). The histrionic-obsessive couple. In Carlson, J., & Sperry, L. (Eds.), *The disordered couple* (pp. 187–205). New York: Brunner/Mazel.

Sperry, L., & Mosak, H. (1993). Personality disorders. In Sperry, L., & Carlson, J. (Eds.), *Psychopathology and psychotherapy: From diagnosis to treatment*. Muncie, IN: Accelerated Development.

Sperry, L., & Mosak, H. (1996). Personality disorders. In Sperry, L., & Carlson, J. (Eds.), *Psychopathology and psychotherapy: From diagnosis to treatment*, rev. ed. Washington, DC: Accelerated Development/Taylor & Francis.

Spotnitz, H. (1975). The borderline schizophrenic in group psychotherapy. *International Journal of Group Psychotherapy*, 7: 155–174.

Stein, G. (1992). Drug treatment of the personality disorders. *British Journal of Psychiatry*, 161: 167–184.

Stevenson, J., & Meares, R. (1992). An outcome study of psychotherapy for patients with borderline personality disorder. *American Journal of Psychiatry*, 149: 144–150.

Stone, M. (1983). Psychotherapy with schizotypal borderline patients. *Journal of the American Academy of Psychoanalysis*, 11: 87–111.

Stone, M. (1985). Schizotypal personality: Psychotherapeutic aspects. *Schizophrenia Bulletin*, 11: 576–589.

Stone, M. (1989). Schizotypal personality disorder. In Karasu, T. (Ed.), *Treatment of psychiatric disorders* (pp. 2719–2726). Washington, DC: American Psychiatric Press.

Stone, M. (1992). Treatment of severe personality disorders. In Tasman, A. & Riba, M. (Eds). *American Psychiatric Press review of psychiatry*, Vol. II (pp. 98–115). Washington, DC: American Psychiatric Press.

Stone, M. (1993). *Abnormalities of personality: Within and beyond the realm of treatment*. New York: Norton.

Stone, M., & Weissman, R. (1984). Group therapy with borderline patients. In Slavinska, H. (Ed.), *Contemporary perspectives in group psychotherapy*. London: Routledge & Kegan Paul.

Stone, W., & Whiteman, R. (1980). Observation and empathy in group psychotherapy. In Wolberg, L., & Aronson, M. (Eds.), *Group and family therapy*. New York: Brunner/Mazel.

Stravynski, A., Grey, S., & Elie, R. (1987). Outline of the therapeutic process in social skills training with socially dysfunctional patients. *Journal of Consulting and Clinical Psychology*, 55: 224–228.

Stravynski, A., Marks, I., & Yule, W. (1982). Social skills problems in neurotic outpatients. *Archives of General Psychology*, 39: 1378-1383.

Strupp, H., & Binder, J. (1984). *Psychotherapy in a new key: A guide to time-limited dynamic psychotherapy*. New York: Basic Books.

Swiercinsky, D. (Ed.). (1985). *Testing adults*. Kansas City: Test Corporation of America.

Symington, N. (1980). The response aroused by the psychopath. *International Review of Psychoanalysis*, 7: 291–298.

Tacbacnik, N. (1965). Isolation, transference, splitting and combined treatment. *Comprehensive Psychiatry*, 6: 336–346.

Teasdale, J., Segal, Z., Williams, J., et al. (2000). Prevention of relapse/recurrence in depression by mindfulness-based cognitive therapy. *Journal of Consulting and Clinical Psychology*, 68: 615–623.

Tercet, I. (1990). *The personality disorders: A psychological approach to clinical management*. New York: Pergamon.

Thaker, G., Adami, H., & Gold, J. (2001). Functional deterioration in individuals with schizophrenia spectrum personality symptoms. *Journal of Personality Disorders*, 15: 229–234.

Thomas, A., & Chess, S. (1977). *Temperament and development*. New York: Brunner/Mazel.

Toman, W. (1961). *Family constellation: Theory and practice of a psychological game*. New York: Springer.

Torgerson, S. (1984). Genetic and nosological aspects of schizotypal and borderline personality disorders. *Achieves of General Psychiatry*, 41: 546–554.

Turkat, I. (1985). Formulations of paranoid personality disorders. In Turkat, I. (Ed.), *Behavioral case formulations* (pp. 161–198). New York: Plenum.

Turkat, I. (1986). The behavioral interview. In Ciminero, R., Calhoun, K., & Adams, H. (Eds.), *Handbook of behavioral assessment*, 2nd ed. (pp. 109–149). New York: Wiley-Interscience.

Turkat, I. (1990). *The personality disorders: A psychological approach to clinical management*. New York: Pergamon Press.

Turkat, I., & Banks, D. (1987). Paranoid personality and its disorder. *Journal of Psychopathology and Behavioral Assessment*, 9: 295–304.

Turkat, I., & Maisto, S. (1985). Application of the experimental method to the formulation and modification of personality disorders. In D. Barlow (Ed.), *Clinical handbook of psychological disorders* (pp. 503–570). New York: Guilford.

Turner, S., Beidel, D., & Burden, J. (1991). Social phobia: Axis I and II correlates. *Journal of Abnormal Psychology*, 100: 102–106.

Turner, S., Beidel, D., Dancu, C., et al. (1986). Psychopharmacology of social phobia and comparison to avoidant personality disorder. *Journal of Abnormal Psychology*, 95: 389–394.

Vaccani, J. (1989). Borderline personality and alcohol abuse. *Archives of Psychiatric Nursing*, 3: 113–119.

Vaillant, G., & Perry, J. (1985). Personality disorders. In Kaplan, H., & Sadock, B. (Eds.), *Comprehensive textbook of psychiatry*, 4th ed. Baltimore: Williams & Wilkins.

Vaughn, B., & Bost, K.(1999). Attachment and temperament: Redundant, independent, or interacting influences on interpersonal adaptation and personality development? In Cassidy, P., & Shaver, P. (Eds.), *Handbook of attachment: Theory, research and clinical applications* (pp 198–225). New York: Guilford.

Veith, I. (1977). Four thousand years of hysteria. In Horowitz, M. (Ed), *Hysterical personality* (pp. 7–23). New York: Jason Aronson.

Vinogradov, S., & Yalom, I. (1989). *Concise guide to group psychotherapy*. Washington, DC: American Psychiatric Press.

Wagner, E., & Wagner, C. (1981). *The interpretation of psychological test data*. Springfield, IL: Charles Thomas.

Waldeck, T., & Miller, L. (2000). Social skill deficits in schizotypal personality disorder. *Psychiatry Research*, 93, 3: 237–246.

Waldinger, R. (1986). Intensive psychodynamic psychotherapy with borderline patients: An overview. *American Journal of Psychiatry*, 144: 267–274.

Waldo, M., & Harman, M. (1993). Relationship enhancement therapy with borderline personality. *Family Journal*, 1: 25–30.

Waldo, M., & Harman, M. (1998). Borderline personality disorder and relationship enhancement marital therapy. In Carlson, J., & Sperry, L. (Eds.), *The disordered couple* (pp. 285–298). New York: Brunner/Mazel.

Walker, R. (1992). Substance abuse and B-cluster disorders: Treatment recommendations. *Journal of Psychoactive Drugs*, 24: 233–241.

Wallerstein, R. (1986). *Forty-two lives in treatment: A study of psychoanalysis and psychotherapy*. New York: Guilford.

Weeks, G., & L'Abate, L. (1982). *Paradoxical psychotherapy: Theory and practice with individuals, couples, and families*. New York: Brunner/Mazel.

Wells, M., Glickhauf-Hughes, C., & Buzzel, V. (1990). Treating obsessive-compulsive personalities in psychoanalytic/interpersonal group therapy, *Psychotherapy*, 27: 366–379.

Westin, D., & Shedler, J.(2000). A prototype matching approach to personality disorders. *Journal of Personality Disorders*, 14: 109–126.

Widiger, T., & Bornstein, R. (2001). Histrionic, dependent and narcissistic personality disorders. In Sutker, P., & Adams, H. (Eds.), *Comprehensive handbook of psychopathology*, 3rd ed. (pp. 509–531). New York: Plenum.

Widiger, T., & Corbitt, E. (1993). Antisocial personality disorder: Proposals for DSM-IV. *Journal of Personality Disorders*, 7: 63–77.

Widiger, T., Costa, P., & McCrae, R. (2002). A proposal for Axis II: Diagnosing personality disorders using the five factor model. In Costa, P., & Widiger, T. (Eds.), *Personality disorders and the five factor model of personality*, 2nd ed. (pp. 431–456). Washington, DC: American Psychological Association.

Williams, J. (1988). Cognitive intervention for a paranoid personality disorder. *Psychotherapy*, 25: 570–575.

Winer, J. A., & Pollock, G. H. (1989). Psychoanalysis and dynamic therapy. In Karasu, T. (Ed), *Treatments of psychiatric disorders* (pp. 2639–2648). Washington, DC: American Psychiatric Press.

Winston, A., & Pollack, J. (1991). Brief adaptive psychotherapy. *Psychiatric Annals*, 21: 415–418.

Wolff, S. (2000). Schizoid pesonality in childhood and Asperger syndrome. In Klin, A., Volkmar, M., & Sparrow, S. (Eds.), *Asperger syndrome* (pp. 278–305). New York: Guilford.

Woody, G., McLellan, T., Luborsky, L., & O'Brien, C. (1985). Sociopathy and psychotherapy outcome. *Archives of General Psychiatyr*, 42, 1081–1086.

Wurmser, L. (1981). *The mask of shame*. Baltimore: Johns Hopkins University Press.

Yalom, I. (1995). *The theory and practice of group psychotherapy. Fourth edition*. New York: Basic Books.

Young, J. (1999). *Cognitive therapy for personality disorders: A schema-focused approach*, 3rd ed. Sarasota, FL: Professional Resource Press.

Young, J., Klosko, J., & Weishaar, M. (2003). *Schema Therapy: A practitioner's guide*. New York: Guilford.

Young, J. (1990). *Cognitive therapy for personality disorders: A schema-focused approach*. Sarasota, FL: Professional Resource Exchange.

Young, J., Weishaar, M., & Klosko, J. (2003). *Schema therapy: A practitioner's guide*. New York: Guilford.

Yudofsky, S., William, D., & Gorman, J. (1981). Propranolol in treatment of rage and violent behavior in patients with chronic brain syndrome. *American Journal of Psychiatry*, 38: 218–220.

Zanarini, M. (1997). Evolving perspectives on the etiology of borderline personality disorder. In Zanarini, M. (Ed.), *Role of sexual abuse in the etiology of borderline personality disorder*. Progress in Psychiatry 49 (pp. 1–14). Washington, DC: American Psychiatric Press.

Zanarini, M., Frankenburg, F., Reich, B., et al. (2000). Biparental failure in the childhood experience of borderline patients. *Journal of Personality Disorders*, 14, 3: 264–273.

Zimbardo, P. (1977). *Shyness*. New York: Jove/Berkeley Publishing Group.

Zimmerman, M. (1994). Diagnosing personality disorders. *Archives of General Psychiatry*, 51: 225–245.

Name Index

Subject Index

285